D1129579

Restorative Justice for Domestic Violence Victims

Restorative Justice for Domestic Violence Victims

An Integrated Approach to Their Hunger for Healing

MARILYN FERNANDEZ

LEXINGTON BOOKS

A division of
ROWMAN & LITTLEFIELD PUBLISHERS, INC.
Lanham • Boulder • New York • Toronto • Plymouth, UK

Published by Lexington Books
A division of Rowman & Littlefield Publishers, Inc.
A wholly owned subsidary of The Rowman & Littlefield Publishing Group, Inc.
4501 Forbes Boulevard, Suite 200, Lanham, Maryland 20706
www.lexingtonbooks.com

Estover Road, Plymouth PL6 7PY, United Kingdom

British Library Cataloguing in Publication Information Available

Library of Congress Cataloging-in-Publication Data

Fernandez, Marilyn.
   Restorative justice for domestic violence victims : an integrated approach to their hunger for healing / Marilyn Fernandez.
      p. cm.
   Includes bibliographical references.
   ISBN 978-0-7391-1553-4 (cloth : alk. paper) — ISBN 978-0-7391-4806-8 (electronic)
   1. Family violence—United States. 2. Abused women—United States. 3. Wife abuse—United States. 4. Restorative justice—United States. I. Title.
HV6626.2.F467 20106/8
362.82'92—dc22   2010007074

∞ ™ The paper used in this publication meets the minimum requirements of American National Standard for Information Sciences—Permanence of Paper for Printed Library Materials, ANSI/NISO Z39.48-1992.

Printed in the United States of America

Contents

Tables

Acknowledgments

This is a manuscript that has been long in the making. A variety of factors have contributed to the long gestation period. The victim-survivors, with whom I had the privilege of talking, graciously shared their experiences with me. However, my difficulties in revisiting their painful experiences partly contributed to my resistance.

"Restorative justice" is not a term that long-time domestic violence service providers and victim advocates take to very kindly. On behalf of the women whose stories you will read in this monograph, I kindly request that you withhold judgment until you have read the case we have made.

I was first introduced to the field of domestic violence when I was invited to serve on the board of a domestic violence shelter in Chicago. My interest in the field continued even after I moved to Northern California and started my teaching career at Santa Clara University. Credit for rekindling my interest in family violence goes particularly to Dr. Bernadette Muscat and Dr. Kichiro Iwamoto. Two sets of former students, many of whom have moved on to their adult careers, deserve special gratitude: Satomi Takahashi and Dr. Demetra Kalogrides, for painstakingly transcribing the lengthy interviews and preparing the data for analysis; and the undergraduates who helped with conducting the telephone surveys. Special appreciation also goes to the community service providers, Mary Pat Panighetti (retired probation officer), Pam Butler, and other staff at the local battered women's agencies for facilitating contact with victim-survivors of domestic violence. Comments from the anonymous review of the manuscript were critical in strengthening the integration of restorative justice and domestic violence literatures. Thanks to Lexington Books for coordinating the review and for shepherding the manuscript through the publication process.

Dr. Kichiro Iwamoto, coauthor on chapters 5 and 6, was also a key collaborator in collecting and analyzing the survey data. This project would not have been possible without the support of Santa Clara University, through their internal grants and other research support. Dr. Charles Powers, my colleague in the sociology department, is a true intellectual and theoretical mentor. And special gratitude goes to my husband, Peter D'Souza, and my sister, Sr. Crystal Fernandez FMA, who honored the silent space within which I could explore these difficult relational issues.

This book is dedicated to all victim-survivors of intimate partner violence and particularly to the women whose courageous voices you hear in these pages. Thank you.

CHAPTER 1

Hunger For Healing

IS THERE A ROLE FOR INTRODUCING RESTORATIVE JUSTICE PRINCIPLES IN DOMESTIC VIOLENCE SERVICES?

The Research Problem

Academicians and practitioners have increasingly recognized domestic violence, particularly the battering of women by their intimate partners, as a social and public health risk to women (Cherlin, Burton, Hurt, and Purvin 2004; Holtz and Furniss 1993; Johnson 2006, 2008; Mills 2008; Roberts 1996; Rosenbaum and O'Leary 1981). Despite the difficulty in estimating accurately the prevalence and incidence of intimate violence, the American Bar Association's Commission on Domestic Violence (2005) reported the following: 28 percent of all annual violence against women is perpetrated by intimates; by the most conservative estimate, each year one million women suffer nonfatal violence by an intimate and that four million American women experience a serious assault by an intimate partner during an average twelve-month period; nearly one in three adult women experience at least one physical assault by a partner during adulthood; and that domestic violence crosses ethnic, racial, age, national origin, sexual orientation, religious, and socioeconomic lines. More locally, the California Partnership to End Domestic Violence (2007) reported that, in the year 2006, Californians placed about twenty thousand calls to the National Domestic Violence Hotline; in the same year, California law enforcement received 176,299 domestic violence–related calls.

There has been a rich history of theorizing about why violence in family relationships occurs as well as about the process and resolution of violence. Implicitly or explicitly associated with such theorizing about family violence are programs and services to address the problem. The earlier theoretical thinking, guided by feminist perspectives of gendered violence, focused primarily on the legal problematics in the relationship between the victim and batterer

1

(for example, Dobash and Dobash 1979, 1992; Dobash, Dobash, Wilson, and Daly 1992; Ferraro 1993; Yllo and Bograd 1988). The resulting programs were retributive in nature (Zehr 2002, 2005), centered on legally addressing the crime of family violence. More recently, there have been cautious attempts to introduce restorative justice principles into programs that address family violence, with an emphasis on repairing the harm caused by the violence and reintegrating the victim and batterer into their communities of care (see Curtis-Fawley and Daly 2005; Ptacek 2010; Umbreit, Vos, Coates, and Brown 2003; Van Ness and Strong 2006; Zehr 2001, 2002, 2005). In this monograph, we will examine women's voices as they describe the violence they experienced in intimate partner relationships and make an evidence-based case for the imperative need to introduce restorative justice principles into the existing menu of domestic violence services. In the process, the linkages between the two research traditions, of domestic violence and restorative justice, will also be explored.

An Overview of Domestic Violence and Restorative Justice Theories and Praxis: Theoretical Perspectives on Domestic Violence

SEXUAL SYMMETRY IN VIOLENCE

In the 1990s, there was a growing body of survey evidence that documented that it was not only men who perpetrated violence but that women were as likely to do so (Gelles 1980, 1989; McNeely and Mann 1990; Shupe, Stacey, and Hazelwood 1987; Straus 1973; Straus, Gelles, and Steinmetz 1980; Steinmetz 1977/1978). More recent data from the National Violence Against Women Survey suggest that approximately 835,000 men (aside from 1.3 million women) are physically assaulted by an intimate partner annually in the United States (Tjaden and Thoennes 2000). In this line of thinking, domestic violence was conceptualized as an outcome of the violent environment that occurs and is reinforced at the individual, family, and societal levels in the social system. Thus, the problem becomes not wife-beating by violent men, but "violent couples" and "violent people."

GENDERED VIOLENCE

This narrative of "sexual symmetry" in violence has been criticized by those who subscribe to the feminist perspective of gendered violence (some key examples are Dobash and Dobash 1979; Dobash, Dobash, Wilson, and Daly 1992; Ferraro

1993; Murphy 1992; Pagelow 1992; Yllo and Bograd 1988). Feminist researchers countered the sexual symmetry thesis by arguing that even though women too are known to engage in violence, the unique nature of the violence experienced by women sets it apart from male experiences of violence. Women are more likely to suffer injury and serious injury in the violent encounters than men, even when women use weapons. When women engage in acts of violence, it is often out of self-defense or retaliation. Women, on average, engage in one-time violent behavior while men engage in more repetitive or cumulative battering types of violence. It is because of this gendered nature of domestic violence that much of the research and program attention to date have focused on women.

MAKING SENSE OF THE CONTRADICTIONS

How do we explain these seemingly contradictory findings from the over thirty years of research? Michael Johnson, in his recent summative work *A Typology of Domestic Violence* (2008), attempts to clarify these empirical contradictions in intimate couple violence. He attributes the contradictions to the fact that different researchers have been using different types of samples. And the resulting evidence points to different types of violence. According to Johnson, family violence researchers derive their sexual symmetry thesis from examining information from large-scale, often national, survey data while the feminist, gendered researchers who focus on male violence have often used "agency samples" (which include women from shelters and records from police, courts, and emergency rooms). As Johnson goes on to ask, why are these methodological differences important?

National surveys, such as the National Family Violence Surveys or National Violence Against Women Survey, even if not truly representative of the broader population, survey large numbers of husbands and wives. Family violence researchers who have typically used such surveys have found that family stress and conflict sometimes lead family members, whether spouses, parents, children, or other relatives, to resort to violent behavior in the home. In other words, Johnson claims that the violence described in the family violence narrative was often the product of situationally provoked conflict, an expression of anger or frustration, or may even be a bid for attention. He appropriately refers to such violence as "situational couple violence."

On the other hand, agency samples typically have included women (most domestic violence agencies provide services to women and their children) who have come to the agencies seeking help. Violence, seen from these women victims' perspectives, was qualitatively different from the violence described by the sexual symmetry proponents. The agency sample women described a gender asymmetric pattern of abuse that was more frequent, more severe, and more likely to escalate over a period of time and be a product of violence used in the service of power and control (Pence and Paymar 1993) over the woman. Johnson terms this type of systematic violence "intimate terrorism." Johnson further argues that couples involved in intimate terrorism are most likely not to participate in surveys because of fear of reprisal (for the woman) or of being exposed to the police or domestic violence agencies (for the men and women). On the other hand, situational violence couples, particularly when the violence is not frequent and/or severe, often do not end up in agency samples. Thus, Johnson concluded that the two groups of researchers have been focused on two separate types of violence; the family violence scholars have studied situational couple violence while the feminist scholars focused on "intimate terrorism," or systematic battering.

In his comparison of the types of violence reported in three different samples from Pittsburgh in the 1970s—a general sample survey (thirty-seven), a court sample (thirty-five cases), and a shelter sample (n=50)—Johnson also identified an additional type of intimate couple violence, namely violent resistance. In the violent resistance situations, the woman's violence is in reaction to her partner's attempt to exert control. Drawing on research with women who have fought back their batterers' assault (Bachman and Carmody 1994; Burke et al. 2001; Miller 2005; Ferraro 1997; Pagelow 1981; Walker 1984), Johnson described violent resistance as violence that occurs as a reaction (immediate or even some time later) to an assault and is shortlived. Even though the woman's resistance might or might not result in fatal injury to the abuser, it does not do much to change the power imbalance in the relationship.

RISK MARKERS FOR GENDERED INTIMATE COUPLE VIOLENCE

There is also an extensive and growing body of empirical research on the factors—particularly, status characteristics and relational dynamics—associated with incidents of intimate couple violence and the consequences of such violence. Some of the status characteristics or axes of social differentiation that correlate with intimate partner violence are marital status, socioeconomic factors such as education and income, presence of children, and race/ethnicity. Relational risk factors include family concerns about economic security and other forms of stress; spousal disagreements over children; violence in family of origin; young marriages (less than ten years) and young spouses (under thirty years); verbally aggressive spouses; frequent alcohol use; and family not being part of an organized religion (Stith, Hosen, Middleton, Busch, Lundeberg, and Carlton 2000; Straus 1980; Strauss, Gelles, and Steinmetz 1980; Johnson 2008).

Scholars like Johnson (2008), Johnson and Ferraro (2000), and Stith et al. (2000) have clarified the impact of these risk markers by specifying whether these factors are predictive of systematic battering or situational couple violence. For example, while Stets and Straus's "marriage license is a hitting license" (1989) idea is valid in the case of systematic battering, the rates of situational couple violence are higher when the couple is not married (Macmillan and Gartner 1999). The abusive man's education is negatively related more clearly with battering types of violence than to situational violence (Johnson 2008). On the other hand, income per se is not related to battering but it is the stresses of economic difficulties that are associated with situational couple violence (Johnson and Ferraro 2000; Kantor and Jasinski 1998; Straus, Gelles, and Steinmetz 1980). Similarly, racial differences in partner violence, particularly situational couple violence, are more due to socioeconomic differences among race groups (Johnson and Ferraro 2000).

As for relational dynamics, it is the challenges in the relationship that arise from the status characteristics which act as risk markers. Disagreements about raising children and other household labor (indicating traditional sex role attitudes of the male spouse), and not necessarily just the presence of children, are positively associated with battering (but not with situational couple violence) even after controlling for socioeconomic status (Hotaling and Sugarman 1986; Straus, Gelles, and Steinmetz 1980; Johnson 2008). Similarly, growing up with violent experiences in the family is a better predictor of battering violence and less so of situational couple violence (Johnson and Ferraro 2000; Straus, Gelles, and Steinmetz 1980; Johnson 2008). On the other hand, it is arguments over the partner's heavy drinking, and not just alcohol and drug use, that precipitate situational couple violence (Kantor and Jasinski 1998; Kantor and Straus 1989). The husband's status inconsistency (say, between his education and occupation) or status inconsistency between the husband and wife as when the wife earns more than the husband (Gelles 1974) and the presence of other forms of violence, such as child or elder abuse (Finkelhor 1983), are additional risk markers of systematic battering.

Researchers (see Wodarski 1987) have also developed personality profiles of the batterer and the battered woman. For example, the batterer tends to blame the victim, to view the victim as a possession, to displace anger meant for authority figures, and to have unrealistic expectations of the woman. The abused woman was found to be socially isolated, to internalize blame for the abuse, to comply with the violence as a survival mechanism, and to be loyal to the abuser in the hope that he would change. More recently, Feldman and Ridley (2000) and Holtzworth-Munroe and her colleagues (1994; 2003) have identified skill deficits rather than just personality traits that are associated with systematic battering but not with situational couple violence.

How about the human and financial consequences of violence? As might be expected, the severity of the consequences varies by the type of violence. While physical injuries and psychological trauma (posttraumatic stress, fear, anxiety, depression, lowered self-esteem) are substantially more pronounced in systematic battering relationships, these negative consequences do occur in situational couple violence, particularly when it is severe and/or chronic (Johnson and Ferraro 2000; Stets and Straus 1989). Nonetheless, battering relationships often involved injuries or severe injuries requiring emergency room treatment (Johnson 2006; Johnson and Leone 2005; Leone, Johnson, Cohan, and Lloyd 2004; Rosenbaum and O'Leary 1981), high rates of suicide and homicide for women (Holtz and Furniss 1993), and related economic challenges, such as economic dependency, lack of economic resources, and worker absenteeism (Lloyd and Taluc 1999; New York Victims Services Agency 1987; Riger, Ahrens, and Blickenstaff 2001).

Researchers have also looked at the impact of violence on the relationships between the victim and the batterer. Many women who experience situational couple violence are typically the ones who continue to stay in the relationship and even report relatively happy marriages. Johnson (2008) and his colleagues suggest this is the case because in situational violence, violence is not a central feature of the relationship, and both partners might be violent. As for systematic battering, many women do escape such relationships, albeit over a prolonged period of time, either by leaving their partners or by changing their partners' behavior (Burke et al. 2001; Campbell et al. 1998; Ferraro 1997).

Overview of Domestic Violence Service Models

Much of this theorizing and research have guided the development and provision of domestic violence services (Browning 2002; Dobash, Dobash, Wilson, and Daly 1992; Dutton 1992, 1996; Dutton and Goodman 2005; Edleson and Eisikovits 1996; Fox and Benson 2000; Roberts 1996). Over time, the focus of this tradition has moved from blaming the woman victim to focusing on the family, on the batterer, on the relationship between the two, and, in recent years, on the community context of intimate violence.

BATTERED WOMAN: VICTIM OR SURVIVOR?

The early domestic violence research attempted to understand why women are battered and how they respond to the battery. These perspectives framed the thinking about what types of services the women needed, what would constitute effective service utilization, and even why many women failed to use the services or to use them ineffectively. Some examples of the conceptual models that framed these debates include battered women's syndrome, learned helplessness, dependency (Walker 1979, 1984), and family violence or sexual symmetry in violence where wife abuse was seen as a part of a pattern of violence that occurs among all family members (McNeely and Mann 1990; Shupe, Stacey, and Hazelwood 1987; Straus, Gelles, and Steinmetz 1980; Steinmetz 1977/1978). In contrast, Gondolf and Fisher's (1988) survivor model was presented as an alternative to the passive woman victim. In this model, battered women logically attempt to protect and ensure their own survival and that of their children by increasing their help-seeking in the face of increased violence, rather than decreasing help-seeking as learned helplessness would suggest. Despite these differences in foci, in the final analysis, these lines of thinking made the battered person responsible for her fate.

SHIFTING THE FOCUS TO THE BATTERER

Feminist approaches have taken such victim blaming or victim focused approaches to task and provided a set of alternative explanations for the why and the how of intimate partner violence. Researchers in this tradition focus on the sociocultural context in which domestic violence occurs—societal norms of male dominance and male entitlement, and the resulting inequalities in the structure of husband-wife roles. They contend that not recognizing these structured inequalities has unfortunate theoretical and practical implications. Not considering gendered inequalities has the potential for locating the source of the problem in the individual's characteristics and prior history and results in solely blaming the aggressor and the abused woman (Dutton 1992; Dutton and Goodman 2005; Fine 1989; Hart 1993). Women's coping strategies are considered pathological (Herbert, Silver, and Ellard 1991). For example, police officers, who often do not have an appreciation for women's subordinate status in the family, are generally unsympathetic toward women, particularly when the women are ambivalent about pressing criminal charges against their partners (Ferraro 1993). Or as Warshaw (1989) discovered, physicians and nurses medicalize the violence and treat the physical injuries as decontextualized events, which results in the true causes of the injury going unaddressed. In contrast, the gendered violence perspective would focus on the structural constraints that trap women in abusive relationships. It is the perceived sense of entrapment and dependency that sets women's experience with violence apart from the male experience.

POWER AND CONTROL MODEL

Another perspective that has in recent years gained much attention in the domestic violence service world is the "power and control" model (Pence and Paymar 1993; Santa Clara County Probation Department n.d.; Shepard and Pence 1999). In this model, abusive relationships are based on the belief that one person has the right to control the other and when nonphysical tactics (such as intimidation or other emotional abuse) do not work, the person in power moves on to physical and sexual violence to exercise control. The alternative to power and control that service programs aim for is an equality model of nonviolence, also known as the Duluth model (Pence and Paymar 1993). This shift in focus from the battered to the batterer has its corollaries in shifts in service models (such as programs for batterers in addition to and separate from the services for battered women and their children).

A BROADER CONTEXTUAL LENS

In a more recent article, Benson, Wooldredge, Thislethwaite, and Fox (2004) identified concentrated disadvantage in neighborhoods (measured by percent single parents, nonwhite, unemployed, families on public assistance and below the poverty line) as a critical factor in the differential rates of domestic violence between blacks and whites. But what roles do the service systems play in the efficacy of services, even if it is perceptual efficacy? Many battered women interviewed in this research talk about being doubly victimized, first by the batterer and then by the system. Thus, a contextual lens that includes the service delivery system is critical to develop a more holistic picture of service effectiveness in resolving and healing the wounds caused by the violent relationship. Bronfenbrenner's ecological perspective (1979), with its nested systems approach and the role of human agency in shaping the interactions between and among the systems, is an untapped theoretical resource. Translated to the context of intimate partner violence, the victim and the batterer are nested within the micro-system of their family and friends, which in turn are located within the meso-system of direct service providers, the exo-system of agencies and organizations that indirectly impact the victim/batterer, and the larger macro-system of the community, the sociocultural context, and other structures. Even though the victim and/or batterer are embedded in these nested concentric circles of systems, they have the *power* or *agency* to enact changes, even in systems as far removed as the exo- and macro-systems. Dutton (1996) has made a theoretical case for this type of analysis. But the needed empirical evidence has been lacking.

Introducing Restorative Justice Principles in Domestic Violence Praxis

RESTORATIVE JUSTICE THEORY AND PRINCIPLES

Conceptually, an innovative application of Bronfenbrenner's ecological model and, to some extent, the feminist family violence perspective with its focus on the gendered context of intimate partner relationships, is the restorative justice (referred to as RJ in the remaining pages) approach. Restorative justice is a holistic and systematic response to wrongdoing that emphasizes repairing the harms and healing the wounds of stakeholders (victims, offenders, and their communities) that were caused by the criminal behavior, and ultimately reintegrating the stakeholders involved. Central to the restorative justice approach is the principle that those—victims, offenders, their families (micro-system), and their communities, which includes the government (the meso-, exo-, and macro-level ecologies)—involved in a crime are the ones who should have the agency (be involved) in responding to the harm caused by the crime (Van Ness and Strong 2006; Umbreit et al. 2003; Zehr 2001, 2002, 2005). According to Zehr (2002), the three pillars or elements of restorative justice are "*harms* and related *needs* (of victims, first of all, but also of the communities and the offenders); *obligations* that have resulted from (and given rise to) this harm (the offenders', but also the communities'); and *engagement* of those who have a legitimate interest or stake in the offense and its resolution (victims, offenders, and community members)" (emphasis in original, 24) so that victims and/or offenders can be reintegrated into the community. Restorative justice is also preventive in its orientation to crime by building on and strengthening the community and the state. In short, the restorative justice approach is holistic both in its understanding of the causes and processes of the crime of family violence as well as in its approaches to dealing with the crime. A theoretical synthesis of the feminist and restorative justice perspectives is revisited in chapter 7.

How does the restorative approach differ from traditional criminal justice? As Zehr (2002, 2005) continues to elaborate, the collaborative, inclusive, and holistic nature of restorative processes as well as the mutually agreed upon (rather than imposed) outcomes is in direct contrast to the retributive criminal justice models. Criminal justice policy is focused on balancing offenders' rights and government power in the interest of maintaining public order and security (Van Ness and Strong 2006). As such, these policies address primarily the legal dimensions of the crime with limited role for the voices of the victim and/or the offender.[1] In contrast, restorative justice focuses on victim's needs (as opposed to needs of the state in the criminal justice model): Victims' needs for real *information* about what happened and what has happened since; *truth-telling* as an important element of healing; *empowerment* to regain lost control; and *restitution*, either real or symbolic, as a means to vindication (Zehr 2002). Restorative justice theory and practice have been shaped around efforts to genuinely acknowledge and seriously address victim needs. In the process, restorative justice also redefines the notion of community. Unlike in the traditional criminal justice parlance where the state/government represents the victims and their communities, restorative justice theory and praxis re-lenses the sense of community to include not only the victim and the offender, but also their communities of care, and other stakeholders such as the state.[2]

LIMITS AND PROMISE OF RESTORATIVE JUSTICE

The restorative justice model (with elements such as community reparation boards, family group conferencing, circle sentencing, and victim-offender mediation) has been used, with varying degrees of success, with juvenile justice issues, adult crimes, and community peacemaking (for specific examples, see Umbreit and Coates 2000; Umbreit et al. 2003; Van Ness and Strong 2006). However, criminal justice practitioners have been hesitant to include family violence as an offense appropriate for restorative justice intervention (see authors in Strang and Braithwaite 2002). Feminist critics (see Coker 1999; Curtis-Fawley and Daly 2005; Ptacek 2010) find the restorative justice process inappropriate to deal with domestic violence because the process and outcomes are not formal, the punishment not stringent enough for the batterer, the appearance that it is a "soft option"—perhaps even "cheap justice"—and concerns of reprivatizing gendered violence in ways that revictimize and are harmful to victims.

On the other hand, proponents argue that the restorative justice process might be better for victims than the court process because the former (the restorative justice process) holds batterers accountable and gives victims a greater voice (agency). In recent years, in Australia, Canada, and New Zealand, scholars and family violence practitioners have begun to explore restorative justice possibilities in dealing with family violence (Coward 2002; Curtis-Fawley and Daly 2005; Strang and Braithwite 2002; Umbreit and Coates 2000; Van Ness and Strong 2006). The empirical evidence from Australian victim advocates that Curtis-Fawley and Daly (2005) report suggest that while the advocates have reservations, many also saw positive aspects to the restorative justice process. For example, like the critics of restorative justice, victim advocates were concerned about the possibilities of victim revictimization (in face-to-face encounters), the appearance of leniency of the responses to a grievous harm, and the potential for victim retaliation against the offender. These reservations notwithstanding, several victim advocates affirmed the importance of the forum that restorative justice offers victims to express their voices and concerns. They also appreciated the informality of the process as being beneficial to the victims, particularly those who wished to continue their relationship with the offender. To the advocates, another attractive feature was the opportunity that restorative justice offered offenders to acknowledge responsibility and to assume accountability for the crime in a low stakes setting. On balance, the victim advocates felt that restorative justice could be an effective parallel and intersecting process to existing court proceedings, combining the sanctioning clout of the court with a forum for victims' voices.

Similarly, Canadian researchers found the restorative justice process empowering for women (Cameron 2005). Also, victim opposition is not necessarily to the restorative justice philosophy per se but rather to the initiatives as they have been presently developed (Coward 2002; Curtis-Fawley and Daly 2005; Van Ness and Strong 2006). Many of the feminist critics of restorative justice in the Ptacek (2010) volume, while finding the restorative principles of empowerment laudable, are critical of existing implementation of RJ programs and vehemently opposed to restorative practices replacing criminal prosecution. On balance, the much needed explorations of the theoretical intersectionalities between the feminist antiviolence and restorative justice movements and the recent development and implementation of programs combining feminist and restorative praxis are hopeful signs for victims of intimate partner violence.[3]

REVIEW OF EXISTING RESTORATIVE JUSTICE PRINCIPLED PROGRAMS

More specifically, what do restorative justice–based programs look like when they have been tried, particularly in the domain of family violence? Several general as well as specific examples are available from Mills (2008); Pranis, Stuart, and Wedge (2003); Strang and Braithwaite (2002); Van Ness and Strong (2006); and Zehr (2002).[4] Below we draw from these sources.

But first, a brief history of restorative justice praxis. The contemporary field of restorative justice theory and practice, with some kind of "encounter" between the victim and the offender as its centerpiece, originated in the 1970s in Mennonite communities in Canada and later in the United States as they experimented with ways to apply their faith-based peace perspective to criminal justice issues. However, as is widely acknowledged in the restorative justice circles, the roots of the restorative justice movement can be traced back to the indigenous communities in North America and New Zealand. In its modern incarnation, programs based on restorative justice principles were originally developed and implemented to deal with property crimes and juvenile crimes, and later expanded in some communities to deal with other severe forms of criminal violence such as assault, murder, rape, and family violence.

RJ Principles and Praxis

Zehr (2002) has succinctly summarized what restorative justice is NOT and what it IS. Restorative justice is NOT primarily about forgiveness or reconciliation; it is NOT mediation (where the outcomes might be mandated by the mediator rather than by the victim and/or the batterer); its primary intent is NOT to reduce recidivism; and it is NOT a replacement for the legal system or prisons. So, what is restorative justice? As Zehr eloquently states, restorative justice is done because "[v]ictims' needs *should* be addressed, offenders *should* be encouraged to take responsibility, those affected by an offense *should* be involved in the process, regardless of whether offenders catch on and reduce their offending" (emphasis in original, 10). As for restorative justice goals, addressing the harms that have been done as well as the causes of the harms is primary. Even if the initial focus of restorative justice programs is on victims, these programs are also concerned with restoring and reintegrating the offender and their communities.

Restorative justice, with its focus on working through, resolving, and transforming conflicts, is based on the following fundamental principles: taking seriously the victims' needs (that result from the harms caused to them); holding offenders responsible for the harms and accountable for righting the harms; and involving victims, offenders, and their community in the process. A typical RJ program involves a process with, at its core, some of form of "encounter" or "engagement" of all legitimate stakeholders (victim, offender, and the community).[5] Even though the praxis of "engagement" can take many forms, the common goal is to facilitate maximum exchange of information between and involvement of relevant stakeholders. The process of engagement might take any, or a combination, of following forms of conferencing. Direct, facilitated, face-to-face encounters among relevant stakeholders, with adequate screening, preparation, and safeguards (as in the mediated victim-offender conferences, family group conferences, peacemaking circle process, or a combination), are one option. When direct encounters have not been possible or deemed inappropriate, indirect exchanges between the victim and batterer, using surrogates or other forms of communication, such as video exchanges or letters, have been used. Or some form of victim-oriented batterer program that might include victim-impact panels where a victim or a group of victims is given the opportunity to tell their stories to batterers other than their own (with the hope that the batterers understand the consequences of their actions for victims, including their own) and/or the batterers hear from victims other than their own. Restorative justice theorists and practitioners are mindful of the legitimate concerns of victim advocates for victim safety in an "encounter" situation, particularly for domestic violence victims, and advocate using such encounters only in the right situations and with appropriate safeguards.

RJ programs have typically been used along side the traditional justice system. But, as of 1989, New Zealand's juvenile justice system has been reconfigured with a restorative justice principled family group conference at its center. In most other cases, the restorative justice programs are used on a discretionary basis with referrals of program participants from the justice system. Some are even completely separate from the formal justice system and program participation is most often initiated by the victims.

Challenges and Evidence for Success of RJ Programs?

Because of its unique context, many feminist scholars and practitioners have been rightfully skeptical of the uncritical applicability of restorative justice processes to family violence. Unlike many crimes, family violence victims are often likely to be revictimized (cycle of violence), are not chosen as victims at random (in intimate partner relationships), and are dependent on their abusers, economically and through their children (Busch 2000, 2002; Stubbs 1995, 2002). The authors in Strang and Braithwaite's (2002) and Ptacek's (2010) edited volumes raise questions about the potential efficacy of restorative processes when applied to family violence. For example, they ask whether a one-time apology is sufficient to break the longstanding cycles of violence. Others worry that victims might be revictimized in a conference situation. They also wonder how well community involvement will work in the very communities that might sanction, even if tacitly, such violence. Others advise that restorative justice programs not ignore the state but rather engage and transform state-sanctioned inequalities. On the other hand, yet others (particularly in indigenous communities) worry whether RJ might facilitate more state control for poor and indigenous women. These critiques and cautions, notwithstanding, there is a tentative openness to exploring the viability restorative justice approaches to family violence, provided the programs are contextualized and tailored to address the nuances of domestic violence crimes.

Such openness to restorative justice praxis in the family violence arena stems from the growing body of preliminary evidence of outcomes in restorative justice conferencing programs for juvenile and even adult offenders (although not always in family violence cases). On the one hand, victims, offenders, and other participants have been found to perceive the restorative process to be fairer and more satisfying than their experiences with the traditional legal system

(Braithwaite 2001; Ptacek 2010; Strang and Braithwaite 2002; Umbreit et al. 2003; Van Ness and Strong 2006). While there was also evidence for reducing recidivism rates, such evidence was more tentative. These data, which came from Canberra (Australia), Indianapolis (Indiana), Maori communities (New Zealand), Newfoundland and Labrador (Canada), and Winnipeg (Canada), suggest that the model can work across quite different cultures and regions. On the other hand, many of these evaluations did not include family violence cases and were also not methodologically rigorous enough (not using experimental or quasi-experimental designs) to isolate the effects of the restorative conferencing intervention.

However, a more rigorous longitudinal evaluation of the impact of family group conferencing on family violence in Newfoundland and Labrador (Pennell and Burford 2002) found a reduction in child maltreatment and domestic violence, positive child development, and expanded social support for conference participants. These optimistic results, posit Strang and Braithwaite (2002) and many of their collaborators, have led to a new openness to thinking about the applicability of restorative justice principles to family violence. In fact, they go even further to say that given the successes of these programs, even if preliminary, the domestic violence community is obligated to its victim clients to rise up to the challenge of strategically incorporating restorative justice principled programs into the menu of existing services.

As will become clear in later chapters, even after women (as in the case of the women interviewed and surveyed for this monograph) have sought available legal services, and done so successfully, they often express a "hunger for closure" and "healing." The traditional legal framework is frequently experienced by women victims as adversarial. Besides, many women are not satisfied with the way the legal system currently works. Recently, Mills (2008) has made a case for restorative justice programs as an alternative to batterer intervention–type services. But the case made in this book is for services based on the principles of restorative justice *NOT AS AN ALTERNATIVE BUT AS A SUPPLEMENTAL OPTION* in the menu of traditional legal and community services.

This monograph will follow in the tradition of focusing on the battered woman–battering man dynamics and will examine the interactions of the battered woman with her batterer(s) and the community of domestic violence service providers. A battered woman, if she becomes known to the service delivery system, may have had contact with a whole host of agencies the mission of which is to help with the battering situation. Domestic violence services are offered by agencies, ranging from shelters and battered women's agencies to the police, the probation department, and family and criminal courts. As a battered woman negotiates a resolution to the abusive relationship, this service delivery system, in addition to her family and neighborhood, becomes her community, and even community of care. A critical component in the effective and successful "closure" to the violence is the nature and quality of the interactions between the battered woman and the service system. In the chapters to follow, an evidence-based case is made for supplemental (to the extant legal and other service) programs based on the principles of restorative justice that might offer the abused woman hope for "healing" and "closure."

Brief Review of Chapters to Follow

A brief road map to the content of the following chapters is provided below.

CHAPTER 2—FROM DOMESTIC VIOLENCE TO RESTORATIVE JUSTICE IN DOMESTIC VIOLENCE SERVICES: METHODOLOGIES AND ANALYSES PLANS

This chapter outlines the methodological and analytical journey that the author undertook in the process of completing this manuscript. Restorative justice was not the primary focus at the outset of the study. The study, which started as a review and deductive understanding of existing domestic violence services and victims' perceptions of their effectiveness in addressing violence in intimate partner relationships, soon turned also into an inductive exploration of the possibility of introducing restorative justice principles in domestic violence service programs. During the analyses of the qualitative interviews and survey data, it became amply clear that the victim-survivors of intimate partner violence longed for much more than a retributive legal conclusion of their domestic violence experiences. There was a palpable hunger for healing and closure that restorative justice principles could address.

CHAPTER 3—PORTRAIT OF THE BATTERED WOMEN: POTENTIAL FOR RESTORATIVE JUSTICE INTERVENTION

In this chapter, a profile of the battered women is developed using their demographic (age, family life-cycle) and socioeconomic (education, employment history, economic) background characteristics, and the social and personal resources to which they report having access. Do the victims have a unique profile that has been associated in past research with the probability of women experiencing intimate partner violence and/or seeking available services? Is she a dependent victim or is she a survivor who has access to resources that she could tap into in dealing with her violence experiences? In ecological terms, how much "agency" might she have in resolving her violent relationship? From a restorative justice perspective, who would be her community of care and what types of social and personal resources does she have that might be mobilized as she finds ways to heal and prevent future violence in her intimate relationships? And what do these survivors' narratives tell us about the stakeholders that might be involved in a restorative justice setting?

CHAPTER 4—POWER AND CONTROL DYNAMICS IN THE BATTERER-BATTERED RELATIONSHIPS

Using data from the survey (Service Utilization Survey) and interview samples in an iterative fashion, the systematic violent relationships between the batterer and the woman victim, who comprise the micro-system, are outlined to illustrate the power and control dynamics in the battering relationships. The goal of domestic violence interventions, particularly of the restorative justice type, is to help the victim-survivors transform the power and control dynamics in their violent intimate relationships into an "equality model." A review of the survivors' violence histories is imperative in order to identify the harms to be addressed and the causes of the harms so that the batterer can be held accountable (primary restorative justice goals). It is in this personal historical context that the specifics of any programmatic intervention, including identifying the relevant stakeholders, need to be located.

CHAPTER 5—HELP-SEEKING PATTERNS: ARE WOMEN VICTIMS OR SURVIVORS?

In this chapter, the impacts of women's domestic violence histories on their probability of seeking interventions—law enforcement/legal services and services provided by battered women's agencies—to deal with their violent relationships are addressed. The analysis of service utilization is guided by the dependency and survivor theoretical perspectives which offer contradictory predictions about help-seeking. If the prediction of the survivor theory is supported in the data, it is a hopeful signal that if restorative justice principled services (with their emphasis on holding the batterer accountable, repairing harms, and reintegration into the community) are available to the survivors, they will have the personal agency to use them. However, restorative programs will need to be supplemental to the legal and other community services because intimate partner violence is too serious a crime to not have the stick of the legal system behind any nonlegal interventions.

CHAPTER 6—HOW WELL DO EXTANT DOMESTIC VIOLENCE SERVICES SERVE SURVIVORS? SOME RESTORATIVE JUSTICE IMPLICATIONS

The battered woman's experiences with the extant domestic violence service systems are explored in this chapter. The service systems typically activated in a domestic violence case are the police, the criminal and family courts, probation, batterers' treatment programs, and those provided by battered women's agencies. The following questions are addressed: (1) Which services did the victims use when they encountered their most severe violence? (2) What happened when they encountered a service? (3) How satisfied were they with the services? From an ecological theoretical perspective, the analysis in this chapter broadens the focus beyond the dyadic relationship between the batterer and victim in the micro-system. The relationship between the victim-survivors and the service systems external to the micro-system and how well the victims think the services met or did not meet their needs are analyzed. Even though there were no restorative justice programs for domestic violence victims at the time of the study, comments will be made about elements of the current system that might be restorative although they are not titled as such or explicitly intended to be. Besides, the survivors' responses provide clues to the need for supplemental restorative programs which set the dyadic relationship in the context of relevant stakeholders and communities of care.

CHAPTER 7—A HUNGER FOR HEALING AND CLOSURE: A CASE FOR RESTORATIVE JUSTICE APPROACHES IN DOMESTIC VIOLENCE SERVICES

This chapter includes concluding remarks about the theoretical and practical need for supplementing extant legal/community services with restorative justice approaches in resolving intimate partner violence. Ten guiding principles for restorative justice–principled programs are offered. Restorative justice programs signal a new partnership between the criminal law and restorative justice processes and provide a forum for community involvement. However, one can never underscore enough the need to approach these new initiatives with the appropriate degree of caution. As proponents and detractors of restorative justice in the domestic violence arena reviewed in this manuscript have exhorted, the safety of the victim and her loved ones has to be paramount.

Notes

1. See Zehr (2002) and Van Ness and Strong (2006) for excellent elaborations of the differences between the traditional criminal justice and restorative justice systems.

2. For an example of the shortfalls in the operationalization and idealization of community in RJ theory and practice, see chapters by Rubin and Stubbs in Ptacek (2010).

3. See chapters by Frederick and Lizdas, Pennell, Kim, and Julich, among others, in Ptacek (2010) for specific examples.

4. For a more detailed exposition of restorative justice principles, practice, and programs refer to these sources and the following chapters in Strang and Braithwaite's 2002 edited volume by Pranis, Daly, Morris, Pennell and Burford, Coker, and Bazemore and Earle.

5. In RJ practice, communities refer to communities of care (micro- or meso-system in ecological parlance) either in a geographic or place sense and/or networks of relationships, as well as the justice community (Zehr 2002).

CHAPTER 2

From Domestic Violence To Restorative Justice In Domestic Violence Services

METHODOLOGIES AND ANALYSES PLANS

The initial goals and design of this project were to understand women's experiences of intimate partner violence and their encounters with the service delivery system in their county of residence as they dealt with the violence. Competing theoretical perspectives on domestic violence (outlined in chapter 1) provided the deductive frameworks for the hypotheses about service utilization to be tested. As of the date of writing this monograph, the existing menus of service programs in the county do not include restorative justice programs; hence the women were not asked specific questions about restorative justice. However, as the analysis of the survivors' experiences progressed, a hunger for healing became very palpable and clear in their voices. Restated in Zehr's (2002) victim needs language, the hunger for healing arose out of unmet victim needs: for clear information (information); to tell their side of the story (truth-telling); to reclaim the control they lost with the violence (empowerment); and to have their losses restituted and vindicated, either in real terms or symbolically (restitution and vindication). That this hunger might be satisfied with supplemental programs based on restorative justice principles also became very clear. It is through this inductive process that the restorative justice focus of this monograph evolved.

Research Questions

This book will examine the experiences of women who had encountered intimate partner violence and received services from the domestic violence service delivery system. The project follows an ecological analytical mode that places the micro-system of the survivor and her batterer in the larger nested context of the meso-system (direct service providers), the exo-system (the service agencies), and the macro-system (the culture and larger structures). The focus will be on the women's efforts (human agency) in making the systems work (or not) for them and the challenges they faced in the process. Using the experiential lessons the women learned from the service delivery system, a case for supplemental programs using restorative justice approaches to family violence will be explored.

Data Sources and Analyses Plans

This project uses multiple methodologies that include qualitative and quantitative data. Two primary sources of data, qualitative interviews and a survey, as well as a secondary national survey are examined in *an iterative fashion*. The author conducted qualitative, narrative interviews in 1997–1998 with thirty-five women who had experienced intimate partner violence and had used different domestic violence services provided in a Northern California county. The potential outcomes, in terms of help-seeking behavior or service utilization, of violence patterns that are identified in these qualitative interviews will be deductively tested with data from a telephone survey, also conducted around the same time frame in the same county, of perceptions of domestic violence services. Roughly 120 battered women (the author was the primary investigator) were included in the survey. In late 1999, the survey findings were shared with and discussed by the local Domestic Violence Council, which included service providers ranging from criminal and family court judges, district attorney's office staff, a probation officer, and the director of a domestic violence shelter. Finally, national data from the National Violence Against Women (NVAW) Survey will be used to contextualize the local data.

QUALITATIVE INTERVIEW DATA

The qualitative interview sample (referred to as "interview sample" in the rest of the book) uses what Johnson (2008) calls an "agency sample"—that is, women who have used services from local community agencies. In the summers of 1997 and 1998, the author completed thirty-five in-depth interviews. Each interview lasted between an hour and a half to two hours (see appendix 1 for the interview schedule). All respondents were victims of intimate partner violence and lived in the Northern California county mentioned above.

Because of the difficulties in generating a sampling frame of women at risk for domestic violence, purposive sampling techniques were used to select the respondents. All respondents for the study were identified through the local domestic violence service providers. Staff members from a victim advocacy group, a transitional housing program, and shelters agreed to inform the women who were receiving services at their agencies about the study. Women who were interested in participating in the study were given the researcher's telephone number. When the women called the researcher, they were given a brief description of the study and of the interview procedures over the phone (that the interview will be audiotape-recorded and that there is an honorarium of $25 for completion of the interview). They were then asked whether they were interested in participating in the study. If they were, a meeting time and place were set for the interview.

The first step of the interview process was the reading and signing of the consent form (see appendix 1). Prior to starting the interview, the researcher briefly described to the respondent the kind of questions that she would be asked and also informed her that she could refuse to answer any question that she was not comfortable discussing. At the completion of the interview, she was given the honorarium and asked to sign or initial a receipt for the same.

The interview process was kept as free-flowing and nonintrusive as possible, allowing the woman to tell her story in the order in which she felt most comfortable. Appropriate probes were used to make sure that all the study questions were covered.

Although fifty interviews were originally planned, the interviewing process was stopped at thirty-five. This was because the author was beginning to hear similar themes in the domestic violence experiences and help-seeking behavior after the thirtieth interview. This process is referred to by qualitative researchers as saturating the study phenomenon (Byrne 2001). A sample size of thirty-five was, therefore, deemed appropriate for this specific population of women. No doubt, the purposive sampling methodology used imposes limits on the generalizability of the findings to a national or even a countywide population of women. Large-scale community studies are necessary to provide a fully developed portrayal of the help-seeking experiences of battered women. But the rich and extensive data collected in these in-depth case studies not only provide valuable insights into the problem of domestic violence but also clues to the feasibility of restorative justice–type interventions, the main purpose of this monograph. The tape-recorded interviews were transcribed by university student research assistants during the following years.

DOMESTIC VIOLENCE SERVICE UTILIZATION SURVEY

During 1995–1997, 120 survey interviews were completed with women who had sought domestic violence services in the same Northern California county (referred to as the "survey sample" or "service utilization sample"). The data were collected as part of a study titled "Evaluating the Effectiveness of Domestic

Violence Services in S. C. County." The study was funded through a grant received by the Domestic Violence Council of the County from the Bureau of Justice Assistance.

Because of the difficulties in generating a sampling frame of women at risk for domestic violence, once again, purposive sampling techniques were used to select the survey respondents. The battered women were selected from the shelters and the county probation department's records on batterers and victims. Interviewers were trained to conduct telephone interviews using the survey instrument that was developed by the researchers. The instrument started out with demographic questions. Questions were then asked about the women's experiences with domestic violence with a focus on the most severe incident of violence, and the use of the following services for the most severe incident—police, criminal court, probation, diversion (the court-ordered batterer's treatment program), family court, counseling, battered women's agencies (BWAs), and victim witness services. If the police were not called in the most severe incident and/or if BWA services were not used, the respondents were asked about another recent incident in which the police were called and BWA services were used (see appendix 2 for the survey instrument).

Almost all of the women in this study currently lived in the two major cities of the county; city 1 was represented by 35 percent of the survey women, and city 2 by 25 percent. The rest were from surrounding communities in the county. Similar to the "interview sample," this group also represents an agency sample.[1]

Some Relevant Analytical Caveats

Before we proceed, five caveats that have bearing on the analyses and how they will be addressed are in order. The caveats relate to sampling issues, changes in domestic violence services since the data were collected, the relevance of decade old data, terminology used, and matters of recall.

SAMPLING ISSUES

As was noted earlier, given the difficulty of identifying women at risk for or who have experienced domestic violence, the two primary data sources used a sample of convenience. That is, women were selected due to their availability in the formal or informal records of local community agencies (such as shelters and the county probation department records) rather than through a systematic sampling procedure. This methodology, even if the phenomena are saturated, prevents generalizations to a larger group of abuse victims in the county or in the nation. Also, difficulties in following battered women or persons for follow-up studies because of the need to protect their confidentiality and because of their geographical mobility rendered a longitudinal study difficult, making this a one-shot study. These limitations notwithstanding, the types of domestic violence experiences that the sample women had, the range of services they utilized, and their satisfaction and/or dissatisfaction with the services provide a first glimpse into the women's experience with the extant service system and make a case for restorative justice interventions.

ADDITIONAL METHODOLOGICAL ISSUES

Possible Changes in Service Programs?

As the data collection for the primary data sources were being completed, some changes were made in the domestic violence services offered in the county in focus. The California State Legislature passed Assembly Bill 226 in which the county probation departments were given the sole authority to oversee the certification and renewal of the batterers' program. In March 1997, Santa Clara County's probation department revised the standards for batterers' programs to better reflect the law's intent and purpose—namely, that of advancing the safety of the victims and their children, and holding batterers personally accountable for all acts of abusive behavior (Santa Clara County Probation Department, *Standards for Batterers Programs and Certification* adopted in March 1997). Some specific procedures and policies, such as victim/partner notification of the requirements and completion of the batterer's participation in the intervention program and panic buttons, were put in place to better help abused women. Other changes include the elimination of the diversion program in 1996. Thus, this study covers the set of domestic violence programs that existed in 1997, all but one of which continue today (Santa Clara County Probation Department, n.d.).

Are Data from the Late 1990s Still Relevant?

The answer, unfortunately, is YES. National survey data summarized in chapter 3 indicate that rates of intimate partner violence have not declined and the violence patterns captured by the power and control model have not altered substantially. Besides, the purpose of this monograph is not to update prevalence data on domestic violence. Rather, as has been noted before, the goal is to use the women's experiences to think about how to help women reach closure in their battering relationships, possibly through the addition of restorative justice programs.

BRIEF NOTE ON TERMINOLOGY

Gendered Terms

Domestic violence or family violence covers a wide range of violent relationships between intimate partners, between parents and children, adult children and their parents, and among other household members. But the shifts in conceptual and program frameworks outlined above have resulted in the evaluation of service effectiveness and satisfaction to be conducted primarily from the perspective of the women in intimate partner relationships (Roberts 2002). Besides, as was noted earlier, some reasons for this gendered perspective include the reliance on agency samples to tap into experience-based perceptions. In this research, the focus is on the battering types of violence or coercive control violence (what Johnson calls intimate terrorism) in intimate heterosexual relationships. Therefore, a gendered pronoun—"women"—will be used; research reviewed above has shown that battered victims in heterosexual relationships are typically women.

Victim or Survivor?

There is much debate in the theoretical and practitioners' discourses on domestic violence on the appropriate terminology to denote those who have experienced domestic violence. Do we call them victims or survivors or targets (of violence) or even simply study respondents? Those who are against the victim terminology argue that the (victim) term connotes the victim blaming discourse, as described in Walker's (1979, 1984) concepts of battered women's syndrome, learned helplessness, and dependency. The academic and service fields have moved beyond these terms. Many in this camp prefer that we refer to the woman by the more empowering term "survivor" (Gondolf and Fisher 1988). On the other hand, there are those, including many women in this study, who prefer the use of the term "victim" because it better captures their experiences, particularly when they were in the midst of the violence and even after. Even if they have survived the experience, to tell the tale in a manner of speaking, the term "survivor" minimizes the trauma they have experienced. Therefore, in order to capture the full range of women's experiences, as victims and survivors, both terms will be used in this book. More generally, the women will be referred to as "victims" when their violence experiences are described and analyzed. They will be referred to as "survivors" when their help-seeking behavior is the focus. Terms such as "targets" and "study respondents" will generally not be used because, in the context of the kinds of traumatic violence analyzed in this study, the neutrality of these terms are more likely to depersonalize the woman, even revictimize her.

RECALL ISSUES

In order to account for recall issues (because of the time that might have elapsed between the timing of the interview versus the violent incidences and service utilization), the analyses of service experiences will be disaggregated by the amount of time elapsed between the interview and the violent incidents, when relevant data are available. Three groups of battered women are identified for the analyses. Group 1, the "abated violence" group (an adaptation of Cherlin et al.'s 2004 "abated unions"), will depict cases where domestic violence had occurred three or more years prior to the interview; group 2 is the "intermediate" group (violence occurred between one and two years prior to the interview); and group 3 is the "fragile" group (less than one year with some in a shelter at the time of the interview and others outside shelters).

From Doing Domestic Violence Research to Suggesting Restorative Approaches

To sum up, the methodological journey in this project, from doing research on domestic violence to suggesting restorative approaches, was very inductive. In the pages that follow, existing theories of domestic violence and service utilization are deductively tested. At the same time, the inductive analytical process that was followed led to the strong case that is being made for introducing restorative justice principled programs into the existing menu of services and programs.

In the next chapter, both the survey and interview data are examined to develop a portrait of the victim-survivor and to identify her personal and social resources that she might tap into as she attempts to resolve the violence in her intimate relationships. Ecological concepts such as "ecologies" and "agency" and restorative justice concepts such as "stakeholders" and "communities of care" provide the orienting frameworks (Van Ness and Strong 2006; Umbreit et al. 2003; Zehr 2001, 2002, 2005). That is, who is in the victim-survivor's communities of care that might help her reclaim her personal "agency" or ability to make decisions and guide outcomes? Who are the relevant stakeholders? Which ecological systems do they belong to? These are some of the questions that will be explored next.

Note

1. See chapter 3 for demographic and socioeconomic comparisons of the women in the interview and survey samples with relevant county characteristics.

CHAPTER 3

Portrait of the Battered Women

POTENTIAL FOR RESTORATIVE JUSTICE INTERVENTION

Before we proceed further in exploring the research topics of inquiry that have been outlined for this project—namely, the violence experienced by the women covered in this study, the services they used, their challenges in service utilization, and the role that restorative justice principles might play in domestic violence services—it is useful to get a sense of who the victims are, their demographic (age, family life-cycle) and socioeconomic (education, employment history, economic) background characteristics, and the social and personal resources to which they have access. As was noted in chapter 1, many of these characteristics are associated with the probability of women experiencing intimate partner violence and/or seeking services. The following questions will be explored in this chapter: Does the victim have a unique profile? Is she a "dependent" victim (in domestic violence parlance)? Is she a "survivor" who has access to resources that she could tap into in dealing with her violence experiences? In ecological terms, how much "agency" might the survivor or the dependent victim have in resolving her violent relationship? From a restorative justice perspective, might her social and personal resources be useful to reclaim her personal agency as she finds ways to heal and prevent future violence in her intimate relationships? Who would be her social support or communities of care (micro- or meso-system, in ecological parlance) either in a geographic or place sense and/or networks of relationships, and/or in the justice community (see Zehr 2002)? Who could be the relevant stakeholders who need to be taken into consideration in a restorative justice framework?

This chapter will attempt to draw a portrait of these women using data primarily from the interview and service utilization samples (see chapter 2 for a description of both data sets). In order to contextualize these localized samples, relevant data will be used from the National Violence Against Women (NVAW) Survey that was conducted around the same time period, November 1995–May 1996 (Tjaden and Thoennes 2000). This national survey included both men and women; however, because the two agency samples used in this study include only women, data about women, and, more specifically, a subset of women who had experienced intimate partner violence (IP), in the national sample will be used.

Demographic Characteristics

AGE AND ETHNICITY

Data on the victims' ages at the time of the data collection presented below in table 3.1 indicate that the two agency samples are quite comparable to the national sample. On average, the women in both agency samples were approximately thirty-seven years old at the time of the data collection. Most of the survey women were in the twenty to forty-nine age range (41 percent were between thirty and thirty-nine years old; 25 percent were between twenty and twenty-nine years old; and another 24 percent between forty and forty-nine years). Only 9.6 percent of the women were over fifty years old and less than 1 percent of the survey women were under the age of twenty. We notice a similar age profile in the interview sample (n=35), with the typical woman being in the thirty to thirty-nine age range. Also, the age profile of the national sample, particularly the Intimate Partner Violence (IPV) subsample, was roughly similar to

Table 3.1.   Age and Ethnic Distribution

| | | | NVAW | |
| | Survey | Interview | (Full Sample) | (IPV) |
Age of the women respondents	(n=114)	(n=35)	(n=8000)	(n=1613)
50 years and older	9.6%	6.3%	34.7%	26.4%
40 to 49 years	23.7	18.8	22.1	27.8
30 to 39 years	41.2	53.1	24.2	29.4
20 to 29 years	24.6	21.9	16.3	15.6
Less than 20 years	0.9	0.0	2.7	0.7

| | | | NVAW | |
| | Survey | Interview | (Full Sample) | (IPV) |
Ethnicity of the women	(n=119)	(n=35)	(n=7939)	(n=1601)
African American	6.7%	12.5%	9.4%	10.6%
Asian American	7.6	3.1	1.5	0.9
Hispanic/Mex. American	36.9	25.0	7.9	7.6
White	34.5	50.0	78.3	76.3
American Indian	0.8	0.0	0.9	1.4
Other	10.1	9.4	1.9	3.1

*Note: Percentages may not total 100 because of rounding.

the two local agency samples. The national sample had a higher proportion (26.4 percent) of women who were fifty or older when they were surveyed.

The ethnic composition of the two agency samples (that were drawn from Northern California) and national samples broadly reflect the overall ethnic composition of the populations from which these samples were drawn. The two most common ethnic groups represented in the two agency samples were Hispanic/Mexican American (37 percent of the survey sample and 25 percent interview sample) and white (34.5 percent survey sample and 50 percent interview sample).[1] As might be expected, white women comprised three-quarters of the national sample. The proportions of African American women in the interview (12.5 percent) and national IPV (10.6 percent) samples were a little over 10 percent. The survey sample captured a higher percentage (7.6 percent) of Asian American victims than the other three samples. And less than 1 percent of all four samples were American Indians. Also, in the survey sample, 65 percent of the women indicated that English was their primary language, while 28 percent indicated that Spanish was their primary language.

Family Life-Cycle Characteristics

Given that the women studied in this project have all experienced violence in intimate relationships, it is instructive to describe their marital and family characteristics (see table 3.2). The women in the survey, and to a lesser extent in the interview samples, were as likely to be married as not to be married at the time of the data collection. For example, 54.2 percent of the survey sample and 36.4 percent of the interview samples were married. The corresponding proportions married in the national and IP samples were 62.1 percent and 50.4 percent. As to how long they have been married, three-quarters of the survey sample women had been married less than eleven years. The IPV sample was fairly evenly distributed across the spectrum (from less than five years to twenty-one or more) in terms of the length of time they had been married. The women in all four samples had between one to five children.

Socioeconomic Resources

As was outlined in chapter 1, social and economic resources available to victims are critical factors in their ability to deal with the aftermath of intimate partner violence, even if these resources may often not fully protect them from the experience of intimate partner violence. Data presented in table 3.3 provide a glimpse into the potential economic resources, an indicator of their "agency," available to the women victims.

Table 3.2. Family Life-Cycle Characteristics

| | | | NVAW | |
Are you currently married?	Survey (n=118)	Interview (n=35)	(Full Sample) (n=7999)	(IPV) (n=1613)
No	45.8%	63.6%	37.9%	49.6%
Yes	54.2	36.4	62.1	50.4

| | | | NVAW | |
Number of years married (in current marriage)	Survey (n=64)	Interview NA	(Full Sample) (n=4967)	(IPV) (n=813)
Up to 5 years	39.1%	NA	19.3%	32.2%
6 to 10 years	37.5	NA	14.9	21.1
11 to 20 years	15.6	NA	24.9	25.5
21 or more years	7.8	NA	40.9	21.2

| | | | NVAW | |
Number of children	Survey (n=116)	Interview (n=35)	(Full Sample) (n=7902)	(IPV) (n=1598)
0 children	8.6%	9.4%	0.0%	0.0%
1–2 children	56.0	71.9	46.2	43.2
3–5 children	31.9	18.8	47.9	50.5
6 or more children	3.3	0.0	5.9	6.3

*Note: Percentages may not total 100 because of rounding.

EDUCATIONAL BACKGROUND

More than half the women in all four samples reported having some college experience (thirteen or more years of education). In fact, more than a quarter (with the slight exception of the IPV national sample [19 percent]) had at least a college degree. In the two agency samples, a fifth of the women had finished high school while another fifth had not completed high school. Victims in the two national samples were more likely to be high school graduates than not (for example, 35.1 percent in the IPV sample).

WORK EXPERIENCE

Except for the women in the survey sample, women in the other three samples were more likely (between 59 and 65 percent) to be working (either full- or part-time) than not working at the time of the interview. Forty-one percent of the respondents in the survey sample were working full-time at the time of the

Table 3.3.   Social and Economic Characteristics

			NVAW	
Educational experience	Survey (n=117)	Interview (n=35)	(Full Sample) (n=7963)	(IPV) (n=1609)
Less than 12 years	22.7%	21.2%	10.7%	11.2%
12 years	24.4	18.2	34.6	35.1
13–15 years	27.7	33.3	29.3	34.3
16–20 years	25.2	27.3	25.4	19.3

			NVAW	
Are you currently employed (full or part-time)?	Survey (n=112)	Interview (n=35)	(Full Sample) (n=7981)	(IPV) (n=1611)
No	58.9%	39.4%	41.0%	34.9%
Yes	41.1	60.6	59.0	65.1

What type of work do you do?	Survey (n=76)	Interview (n=35)	NVAW
Employee in private/for profit	93.4%	60.0%	NA
Local gov't employee	1.3	30.0	NA
Self-employed	5.3	10.0	NA

How long have you been working at this current job?	Survey (n=61)	Interview NA	NVAW NA
Less than one year	13.2%	NA	NA
1–3 years	42.6	NA	NA
4–9 years	16.3	NA	NA
10 years	13.1	NA	NA
11 or more years	14.8	NA	NA

*Note: Percentages may not total 100 because of rounding.

survey. In the two agency samples (similar data are not available for the national sample), the majority (93 percent in the survey and 60 percent in the interview samples) worked for a private or for-profit company or business. A third (30 percent) of the interview sample worked for a local government organization. Among the women in the survey sample who were working at the time of the interview, 43 percent indicated they had been working one to three years. An additional 16 percent said that they had been working in their current job for four to nine years, with another 28 percent who had been employed for ten or more years; only 13 percent had been working less than a year.

Taken together, these data on the educational and work experience of the women in the samples support prior research that indicate that abuse happens to women of all educational backgrounds, and that advanced education does not protect women from being a victim of an abusive relationship. The two samples also broadly represent the socioeconomic diversity of the county in which they reside.[2]

Social Support Resources for Women's "Agency"

Domestic violence, particularly in intimate partner relationships, is often an isolating experience. Nevertheless, many "survivors" of domestic violence have access to social support from their "communities of care" that include family, friends, and even coworkers that could be tapped into if the appropriate structure and facilitating mechanisms are available. It is logical that a person experiencing violence will need support from loved ones or close friends to deal with the aftermath of the violent incidents. These communities of care might also be critical "stakeholders" in a restorative justice process.

In both the interview and the national samples (NVAW), women were asked whether they had received help from anyone in dealing with a domestic violence incident and who they were (table 3.4). Natal or biological family members, such as parents and siblings, were the most likely to have assisted women in both the interview (65.5 percent) and national IP (55.5 percent) samples. Friends were almost as frequently supportive (48.3 percent interview sample and 58.0 percent IP national sample). As will be discussed later (in chapter 7), it is these supportive persons in the women's lives who represent their communities

Table 3.4.   Social Support Resources

Social Support Available	Interview (n=29)[1]	NVAW (IPV) (n=897)[1]
Natal family (parents, siblings)	65.5%	55.5%
Extended family (aunts, cousins)	17.2%	0.0%
Friends	48.3%	58.0%
Children	10.3%	3.7%
Batterer's family	13.8%	5.0%
Legal officials (DA, police, employer)[2]	10.3%	9.4%
DV support Services[3]	NA	10.7%
Partners	NA	5.7%

Notes:
[1] Percentage of cases; percentages add up to more than 100 percent because women have received support from more than one source.
[2] District attorney, police, lawyers, social services, employer, coworker.
[3] Battered women's agencies, crisis hotlines, shelters, health professionals, religious, therapists, counselors.

of care that could be called upon in the event that the woman is offered a restorative justice service option and she chooses to avail of it.

The women in the interview sample were also asked about and provided more details on the type of support that family and friends provided them. Many were close to their natal family members (parents, siblings). And even if they were estranged from the natal family, they had friends who were supportive in need.

SUPPORT FROM FAMILY

Some survivors had parents and siblings who lived in the geographic area on whom they could rely. The survivors often turned to these family members in the immediate aftermath of the violent incidents. Some examples of the specific types of assistance provided by mothers, sisters, brothers, and other family members are provided below.

Survivor 19, a Hispanic woman, whose violent incident by her boyfriend was recent ("fragile" group),[3] when asked where she went to escape the violence (even if temporary), replied:

> I went to my sister's house. . . . She took me in. She knew about what was happening. . . . I'd left him a few times already.

In the context of talking about her first marriage, her children, and family, Survivor 21, an African American woman, shared the following. She had two children from her first marriage (eight years), a third from a second relationship, and a fourth with her current boyfriend, who is the most recent abuser ("fragile"). She talked about how she dealt with the abuse with her first husband ("abated violence"):

> Well, one day I told him that I wasn't, I wouldn't put up with him. And I'd given him a day, said I was gonna move out. No, I had to leave them. [When he turned physically violent, she] was on foot when I left. And I walked from . . . well, we were staying at my mother's house. . . . So I walked all the way there. And I moved in with my mother.

When probed about help in the most recent violent ("fragile") experiences, she said:

> So what I ended up doing is I called my sister, and told her to call the police. And my, uh, my sister showed up with the police.

Survivor 28, a Caucasian woman, who had experienced violence in her marriage more than a year before the interview ("intermediate" group), was in the process of getting a divorce at the time of the interview. Her marriage had lasted six years (separated for a year) and she had a sixteen-month-old child. She had a BS degree in elementary education from a prominent university. After the last violent incident, she said:

> [T]hen there was nothing else after that. The next day, I called my brother to let him know, I called a friend to let her know, and . . . then called here, and started seeing the therapist. [When asked how she knew to call the shelter, she said,] I looked in the telephone book. And saw Battered Women's Shelter, and called them.

Similarly, Survivor 8 ("fragile"), a Hispanic woman, described how her parents and friends helped her take pictures so that she could document the bruises from the abuse and helped with transportation.

> [Y]ou know, I have a very good support system. . . . And I think that makes every bit of difference. . . . My mother, my sister . . . my brother-in-law . . . my first husband . . . and be supportive through all this stuff.

Another Hispanic survivor (Survivor 27, "intermediate"), when asked about a support network (community of care) that she can turn to, said:

> [M]y father's remarried. He lives in . . . [out of state in the south]. And my mama lives right down the street from me. . . . She lives very close. She stayed with me for a while until I got my restraining order and went back home. She stayed with me for about one week.

Survivor 27 was married to her abuser for three years and had been separated for one year. She has two girls, both under seven years of age.

Many of the women's struggles often continue for several years. For example, an African American survivor (Survivor 20) who at the time of the interview was fighting a custody and visitation battle (they have a fourteen-year-old son) with her former husband (the abuser from more than three years since the interview, "abated" group) talked about how the relatives in her community of care assisted her in the legal struggle.

> And I have lots of relatives who're educators so they, you know, sent letters and things like that.

If their family did not live in the geographic area, some of the women had plans to move closer to family as soon as possible. Survivor 6 ("fragile"), a Caucasian woman, spoke about wanting to move out of state, once the custody case over her daughter was completed. She felt that she has many loving members in her new location. Besides, she wanted to get away as far as possible from the abuser and his mother.

> [W]hen we do move to . . . [out of state], my brother is there. He's a very loving and kind person . . . my uncle's there, and he was a guar . . . my guardian, and he's very loving and then B. and P. and C. have also been in her life since she was . . . [a toddler]. So that she can see how functioning males can be.

CLOSE FRIENDSHIPS, EVEN IF ESTRANGED FAMILY RELATIONSHIPS

Some of the survivors were estranged from their natal family, but had friends that they turned to in their crisis. For example, when asked about the support she had received, Survivor 3, a Caucasian woman whose violent incidents had occurred one to two years before the interview ("intermediate"), responded that she was not close to her parents.

> [M]y parents, I just can't call them and say send me money. I wish I could. They're in . . . [out of state], but my dad is very tight, very tight. Very, very, tight. And he thinks, you know, I made it on my own and you kids should be able to do it too.

But she vividly described how her friend helped her get through the violent incidents. Her abuser was a lawyer who, she said, always claimed "he knows the system" and that she was powerless. When asked whether she had any support to deal with the abuse, she said:

> Yeah, I had a couple of friends and I had a friend who had been through this like twenty years ago when they didn't do anything. And she goes just stay on the phone with me till the police get in here. And so then finally they came in and the officer came in and said, "are you okay?"

Similarly, Survivor 10 ("intermediate"), a Caucasian, was estranged from her parents. However,

> then my friend . . . she lent me the . . . dollars to bond, to bail out. They reduced my bond by $ . . . The judge did. 'Cuz my face. . . . She made me; she's just an angel. . . . I could not put her on a higher pedestal. She saved me in on so many ways.

This survivor had been arrested because she had resisted her abuser.

NEITHER FAMILY NOR FRIENDS

Needless to say, some of the women had neither family nor friends in their community of care that they could turn to. In fact, they talked about how in the process of the violent relationship with the abuser, they became isolated from family and friends. Survivor 12 (a Caucasian woman whose experience with violence was in the "intermediate" time frame and who dreams of going swimming with large fish) went back to the abuser because, she said,

> [T]hat's the only place I had to go. I don't really have much of a support system. . . . When you go through that with somebody, you kind of like start cutting off all your friends.

Survivor 14, a Caucasian woman, who, like many of the interviewees, had made lots of moves, geographically and in relationships, described her life this way. Her most recent abuser was her current husband; there was abuse in her first marriage also. She and her current husband (her current abuser) moved

> from the trailer, from friends to friends to friends. . . . 'Til I ran out of friends. . . . 'Cuz I've been married for so long, I only know so many friends and so many people. . . . 'Cuz all my relatives are in . . . [the East Coast] Both my parents are dead. They died when I was really young. . . . And I have a sister but what aunts and uncles and cousins I do have, I mean we're only good in speaking terms and . . . I haven't spoke to a lot of them in a lot of years, 'cuz I've been out here almost seventeen years. . . . But my sister, she's got problems of her own and she got her daughter and husband and . . . And I can't keep doing this to my children, I've got school starting soon, I gotta find a permanent residence.

Even when they do not have family or friends to turn to, the survivors find ways to continue going on. An African American survivor (Survivor 11), whose violent experience was recent ("fragile"), spoke about coping with the absence of family support thusly:

> I wasn't raised by my mother and father. I was raised by my grandmother . . . she died when I was fifteen. . . . And I've pretty much been on my own since then. [And she added,] I've, I've really gotten back into my Bible, because of this.

For these women, estranged from family and friends, the formal service delivery system (the battered women's agencies, the police, and the legal system, all examples of meso-systems) is often the only recourse or communities of care available. However, as will become clear in chapter 6, as important as these extant services are, they do not fully address the needs of victims of domestic violence.

Survivors: Personal Strength as a Resource for Agency

Equally important in dealing with the aftermath of the violence or even preventing future violence, and particularly intimate partner violence, are the personal or inner resources or strengths that some of the women articulated and demonstrated. Personal resources in this context are defined in terms of the woman's life perspectives on life and on her future. For example, the woman's responses to questions about the potential she sees for future battering experiences in her life might indicate a sense of personal control she feels. That she is able to be self-reflective about her past experiences, to see the irony in her experience, and even laugh as she recounts the violent relationship, indicates the personal resiliency of these women. In the scholarly literature, these resources are loosely captured by concepts such as "self-efficacy" (Bandura 2003). No doubt, self-reports of personal resources might be a reaction to the immediacy of the violent incidents. In order to discern the reliability (for example, do they feel this way a few years after the incident?) and validity (for example, will they act on how they feel?) of these responses, it is instructive to set them in the context of how much time had elapsed between the interview and the incidence of violence.

The survey sample victims' responses to questions about their future, particularly about future violence, might give some clues about the personal or inner resources that they self report. Such data are available from the women in the survey sample. For example, when asked if they anticipated being battered in the future, two-thirds (66 percent) of the 116 women who responded, including the "fragile" group, said "no." And, if they were ever to be in a domestic violence situation, very few (in fact, 4 out of 112) said they would not know what to do or do nothing. The remaining, particularly the "abated violence," women said that they would use a combination of calling or reporting the incident to the police, seeking counseling, getting out of the situation, or even making sure that they were never battered again. It is interesting that the most common single strategy suggested by a third of the "fragile" women was to call the police, perhaps reflecting their more recent experience with violence and the legal service system.

The women in the interview sample provide a more detailed and vivid glimpse into the variety of personal (inner) resources that the women self-report. As the following quotes demonstrate, personal strength and resources are manifested in diverse ways. The portrait that emerges is a combination of strength (even if self-reported) and fragility.

RESOURCEFUL, DETERMINED, RESILIENT, INITIATIVE

More generally, a young Caucasian college student (Survivor 1, "fragile") exemplifies the personal strength many of these survivors demonstrate. When asked what she plans to do, she said, "Not search on the outside, search within myself for the strength to end it and reasons." Or another, Survivor 9, a Hispanic woman, said, "I knew how to get help. . . . But I didn't know what my rights were."

Survivor 33, who had been out of the violent relationship more than three years ("abated violence"), demonstrates more fully the resolve and resourcefulness that captures the "survivor" model. She is a Caucasian woman, fifty-eight, not married at the time of the interview, but was married for thirty years to a medical professional, and had five adult children. She had no formal degree but considered herself educated. In talking about life after her abuser husband was arrested, she went "from a big income, a husband with an . . . and down to, uh, below the poverty level." Yet she considers herself to be a strong woman. She says, "[W]ell, I'm not so freshly out of it [violence]. . . . And so, um, I'm really strong. . . . And so I have no problems with anything you ask me." Describing the last violent incident, this survivor recalled:

> Instead of going to the hospital and getting treated, I spent that time searching for the guns until I found all the guns and we put 'em in one of the cars, drove the car far away and parked it some place with the guns in the trunk. And then we rented . . . and then the next thing I did, let's see, the next day, I found the lawyer, I went down and got as many of my credit cards changed. [When asked how she found the lawyer to bring charges against her husband, she responded] Ah, Yellow Pages . . . Called them up, small town. [Later her therapist, through role play and other techniques, helped her get over her fear of bringing charges against her abuser. She said,] Uh, we practiced going to court . . . mentally, you know. . . . I, I went to the court room and took a look at it . . . and saw that it was not threatening. We practiced what it was gonna be like and what they would possibly say. This role play. Went into court, piece of cake . . . I had him arrested March. [Later, talking about the aftermath of her divorce, she said,] The first year was really, really hard, various government agencies are really a pain [but she was successful].

Two additional examples of resolve and determination in ending the violent relationship are demonstrated by the following cases. Survivor 5 ("fragile") is a Caucasian professional who owns her home and business. She was engaged to be married to her abuser. This was to be her second marriage. While she is grateful for the assistance she received from a local battered women's agency in securing a restraining order and other services, she describes her last contact with her abuser fiancé thusly.

> [I]n the morning I was dressing to go to work and I left him a message and there was a phone call and I had been screening my phone calls. And I thought that this was a message return and it was him. And he was requesting some files from the house. I talked to him. It was civilized conversation until he told me he was right across the street and he wanted them. And I said absolutely not. You can do it tomorrow. You cannot do it today. Tomorrow I will put those files right outside the front gate, but you can not come in the house. So, that was the last time that I ever spoke to him.

Survivor 16 ("intermediate" group), an Asian American woman, who had been completely controlled by her husband, had gone back and forth to the shelter several times. She recounted this incident that happened during one of the times she had returned home from the shelter.

> Monday, I told him . . . like today, I'm going to pick up kids. . . . He said, "No, I'll go with you." I said no . . . I said, "Don't control me." . . . 'Cuz I came from shelter so they gave me counseling . . . at the shelter. . . . So I became little, I mean not too much, strong but I think I because five percentage strong. But, after a brief honeymoon period, the abuse started again. . . . Again, I went [back] straight to shelter . . . so I filed restraining order and everything. . . . Then I got kick him out orders. . . . He left the house, I came back in the house. [And this went on until the end.] But this time I didn't let him come back. . . . That was my final decision. [At the time of the interview, she was in transitional housing for victims of domestic violence.]

Some of the survivors demonstrated determination, resourcefulness, and personal initiative in the steps they described they took to escape the violence. Reflecting back on her intimate partner violent experience, Survivor 2, a Caucasian woman whose violence was "abated" more than three years, says:

> He's going to go get drunk and come and kill me. So I started calling the police department and the district attorney's office and I started doing research. I would call anybody who would listen and say this

is my situation. How do I get out of here safely? And I really didn't want to go to a shelter, or give up my job or my life, I wanted him to be taken away, not me since I wasn't doing anything illegal. And that's how I met this district attorney that prosecuted him which ultimately was my salvation and then for the last six years I've been able to live without fear because he's been in prison. So, but I'm living in fear because he gets out soon. . . . But it's, um, it was, it was the tenacity of my search for how to get out and also luck that this woman [the district attorney]. . . . I don't know where I'd be if I hadn't. So, it wasn't, and then once I'd issued the no contact order through the probation officer, then I did go into hiding. I had to. I didn't want to take a shelter break, because I still had money. He hadn't taken quite all of it. And I immediately enrolled in a support group. The group support.

Survivor 23, another woman in the "fragile" group, describes how she decided to finally leave the relationship after both had met with a counselor:

Anyway, so the main thing that got me to leave is the night prior to me leaving, I had written down a list of the things that I felt were wrong with our relationship. . . . The communication, the respect issue, what have you . . . about different concerns that I had and goals and I sat down and I went through everything with him. I wanted to know how he felt. I wanted to know about what he had planned to do about coming to a, a conclusion as far as what we were gonna do about these specific problems. He could not come up with anything . . . not so much because he couldn't, because he just really didn't feel like putting in the brain power to do so. So, I said, well, you know what? I know what I want to do. I know what my goals are. I know what, what things I would like to accomplish in my life. And I don't see you helping me. I don't see you helping me or standing behind me or just supporting me, with words. Not money and not anything else. But with your verbal support. . . . So therefore I'm gonna, ha, I'm gonna do it all myself. And it, it was done. But the next day, um, he had, he was giving me a lot of trouble in trying to leave. So what I had ended up doing is, I have a cordless phone. So I was outside trying to talk on the phone. And I had just enough time to dial 911 and say I need some assistance. He unplugged the phone. They came. They came. I, I am so thankful. Because I had called them before, they knew where I was calling from. And they were there. And they took me, and my two girls, and everything that I could carry, to the police station. That's where, um, the shelter came and picked me up. But I still have not even gotten any of my other stuff . . . two months later.

FOR THE SAKE OF THEIR CHILDREN

Another common theme heard in the interviews was the survivors' drive to pro-tect their children from the violence. In the words of Survivor 3 (a Caucasian woman in the "intermediate" group):

> Because I knew I was not going to die, I was not going to have him kill me and have, you know. . . . My son needs a mother. You know he needs somebody more than . . . it's scary because I don't have that income.

A similar refrain is heard from Survivor 21, an African American woman ("fragile"). When asked what prompted her to separate from her first abuser, she said:

> One day, I just woke up and decided enough was enough. . . . And I didn't care what nobody else, it to me, something was wrong. . . . Didn't feel right. And then too, my daughter . . . my oldest daughter, she would have a habit of like scratching herself, in like inner arms and behind her legs and on her neck and stuff . . . and she was getting a really bad rash and I could not figure out why . . . I'd, um, changed—switched soaps, detergents, everything . . . I just couldn't figure out what the problem was. . . . And I, finally, I was reading something 'cuz I love to read a lot. . . . And it . . . something about . . . about nerve disorders or something. . . . So I was wondering, I wonder if this could be it. . . . And then one day we were arguing really bad . . . and, she was in the kitchen, she was . . . [under five] at the time. . . . And picked up the phone . . . and . . . her dad asked her what was she doing? She said, "I'm calling 911 because you're abusing my mom and I don't like it." . . . And that was what she had picked up at school. . . . So that's when it dawned on me, well, maybe that's the problem. . . . Well, one day I told him that I wasn't, I wouldn't put up with him. . . . And I'd given him a day, said I was gonna move out.

That no sacrifice is too big for the sake of their children was evident in the story of Survivor 10 ("intermediate" group). She was willing to let go of her chil-dren, if that was the only way to leave the violent relationship. As she reflects on giving up custody of her children to her abuser husband's parents, she recounts:

> I would let it be that way because my children have been through enough. That's how far gone I was. That's how, how, how much I needed to find myself was that I would even let go of my own chil-dren, which is not ever, ever, ever been anything that I'm about. I would never leave without my children before.

CAUTIOUS OPTIMISM AND HOPEFULNESS

Even if events may not fully materialize as they foresee it, the survivors are hopeful about a future for themselves and their children that will not include violence.

In the words of Survivor 3, a Caucasian woman, whose violent experience had been more than a year old ("intermediate" group):

> I'm working my butt off so I can make a better life for my son and . . . not have to depend on a man. And my next man that I get in my life will be there because I want him there and not because I need him there and that's not been the case in a lot of my relation—in most of my relationships. So I think, you know, this way I can help women. I can, and that's what I want to do . . . I'm way more cautious. I see any drinking and I'm just really going to watch it very closely. And, and, I mean I'm still a hopeless romantic. I still believe in love. . . . But I gotta be cautious. It's not like, okay well, make excuses for everybody. And I think, I'm not going to put my life on hold for anybody. Somebody who is the next man who's going to be right for me is going to be somebody who's going to be able to fit into my life. I'm not doing all the work. And they are going to have to, you know, they are going to have to earn me, in a way type of thing. I'm not going to be so easy, easily to get into things.

Another "intermediate" group survivor, Survivor 10, a Caucasian woman, said,

> [M]y plans, I'm going to pursue my relationship with . . . [new boyfriend] a little at a time, learn how to protect myself, I'm gonna get my children back, get them into therapy. . . . Uh huh. I plan to move not out of state, I just plan to move inaccessible to his family.

Even those survivors whose violent experiences were less than a year old ("fragile" group), were hopeful. Here are two examples.

Survivor 14 is a Caucasian woman, who like many of the interviewees had experienced a lot of moves, geographically and in relationships. Yet her realistic hopes for a better life for her and her children are undeniable.

> That's my number one goal. . . . Unless I get housing, even if it's, uh, an apartment . . . I don't care. We can all bunk in one room . . . I don't care. As long as we got a, a, a roof over our head, we'll never go hungry and my children . . . I'll never make my, my children have never gone hungry. Uh, 'cuz there are a lot of resource places around. . . . We've gone to the . . . in . . . gooood meals. We're not talking like a bowl of soup or something.

In the words of "fragile" group Survivor 8, a Hispanic woman who, after her son disclosed to her that he had been molested by his stepfather, who was also her abuser, filed a police complaint and left with help from her parents and siblings. She goes on to say,

> And our divorce is finalized. . . . But I'm an adult and you know, I certainly know how to protect myself if anybody ever tried that again . . . and, you know, now I'm just real careful about, you know, looking over my shoulder, watching my mirror, and . . .

REFLECTING ON THE VIOLENT EXPERIENCES AND THEIR FUTURE

Despite the traumatic experiences these survivors have been through, many were often thoughtfully reflective on the past and their future. The words of a few of the survivors at different stages in their dealing with the violent experiences follow.

Survivor 33, a Caucasian woman from the "abated violence" group, said:

> Nuh uh. I have done a lot of thinking about this and I'm convinced the alcohol was just part of the picture . . . I would say it, it probably got worse when he was drunk. . . . But the alcohol was almost always there. . . . But the man was underneath the alcohol. I don't think, if you had stopped him from drinking . . . he just would've found another addiction.

Even some in the "fragile" group provided their reflections. Below are four examples. In the words of Survivor 18, a Hispanic woman:

> When we first started going back and forth with the children, visitation, it was, it was . . . both of us screaming at the top of our lungs, my trying to defend myself and . . . and, uh, all in front of the kids. . . . And so working with the counselors, you know, it helped me to see that even my part in it wasn't good for the kids. . . . So I had to change the way I was reacting to him, and kind of distance myself . . . and they gave me a lot of tools to do that. [When asked whether it was helpful, she responded,] Oh, yeah. I was able to distance myself, so I, I wouldn't engage and totally go into that whole process where he would take me. . . . And, I'm able to apply it to bosses or other coworkers that, you know, have a tendency to be aggressive . . . so it has helped in more than one, one place . . . one part of my life.

Another Hispanic woman, Survivor 19, says:

> If I'm penniless but happy and free . . . I mean truly free, my mind,
> my soul, my body, everything, then it's, it's worth it. . . . And he
> succeeded but in the end, you know, I succeeded because I got the
> custody of my son. . . . And he did get visitations but he, he never
> did it and he, he would do violent things when the visitation was
> supposed to happen, so . . . And so I take the baby there and then
> she'd call me an hour later saying, "You know, he's not here, he's
> not coming, just come get your baby." So, I went back to court and
> I started asking for supervised visits. . . . By then I knew that, you
> know, he couldn't behave . . . anymore. . . . You know, so I went to
> the counselor only because I wanted to have a responsible relation-
> ship for the sake of our sons.

Or the case of Survivor 29, a Caucasian woman, who was married for about
five years but separated at the time of the interview and has a daughter with
her abuser. Reflecting on violence in her extended family, she says, her cousins
endured physical abuse.

> I think they drink because of all of this, you know. And then the vio-
> lence comes out in them. But even when they, these people weren't
> drinking, they'd have violence. Yeah, without drinking, they had it
> in them. Yeah. 'Cuz I'm not, I don't want to say, oh, the alcohol
> made them. . . . And I want to stop this cycle now. So she doesn't
> grow up like me.

And finally Survivor 1, a Caucasian woman, sees an optimistic future:

> And so I started meeting some healthy people that I had forgotten
> what it was like to know somebody healthy, and umm, so that was
> a big change, too, is remembering and saying I don't have to live
> this way. There are other people who care about me. I'm not a lone
> ranger. She [her mom] is a social worker and in charge of the kids at
> the school district.

SEEING THE IRONY AND LAUGHING GENTLY AS SHE
RECOLLECTS HER PAINFUL PAST

That the women are able to see the irony in their past is yet another testimony
to their inner strength.

Survivor 20, an African American woman in the "abated violence" group,
was in her second healthy marriage, has a teenage son from the previous marriage
in which the abuse occurred. She said:

But I eventually was able to, you know, get back with my family again, which I'm happy about. . . . You know, back about the late 80s, he said, well, you can leave anytime as long as you don't take. . . . That's our son . . . and he felt that, um, you know, he was my main spokesperson [laugh]. Except that he owned me too. . . . So I guess . . . so I turned forty and I got a more assertive [laugh].

Or Survivor 25 ("intermediate" group), a Japanese American, said:

And then I woke up, and he was out on the front porch. Um, and, he kept saying, "Don't make me hurt you. I don't want to hurt you. You know, and . . . I just want to talk, I just want to get back together." And I go, "You need to leave. And you need to leave here now. I'm calling the police." He goes, "Call me a cab." And so I called him a cab [laugh].

Even someone in the "fragile" group was able to see the irony in her past with her abuser. Survivor 22 is a Caucasian woman, married for over two years with two infant children, and was living in transitional housing at the time of the interview. When asked about her wedding, she said:

Uh, it was, it was terrible. Actually, we had fought the whole time. . . . Yeah. We just fought. And I don't, you know, and I look back now, I'm all, oh god, that was so stupid [laugh] 'cuz we weren't getting along before we had actually got married. We were fighting, we had fought afterwards . . . 'cuz I needed someone to say "I love you" because I never had that growing up.

TENUOUS AND WEARY

Lest we overdraw this portrayal of personal strength, there were also those who seemed quite weary and tenuous. Two examples follow.

Survivor 24, an African American in the "fragile" group, married for about twenty years, had three teenage children, and had been with her abuser since she was a teenager herself. She claims her parents "emancipated" [her words] her to him [who introduced her to prostitution and drugs]. She reflects:

After going through so much that I've went through with my husband . . . and it's just, you know, me getting older . . . I was just, I was tired. . . . You know, I was too young to be so tired. . . . You know . . . I was just truly tired of this same, same old, same old . . . just tired. . . . And I started, um, I was actually to the point where I'm listen . . . you know, I want, I was listening to other, other ideas . . . I've been with

my batterer for so many years . . . that's all I knew. [And so she went
to a shelter that provided her with some services.]

Survivor 12 ("intermediate" group) claims she has given up on men and

I'm really into my animal causes now, and I think, I've always been
into animals and this is kind of like, you know, my cat, I'm really
into. . . . [She continued to reflect on animals saying they are very
family-oriented and that] . . . They're, they don't . . . don't rape each
other . . . don't beat each other up. They kill, they attack each other,
but they take in alone . . . there isn't that sick dysfunction.

AND YET THEY SEEM WILLING TO GIVE BACK TO THE COMMUNITY

Despite their own personal experiences, three of the "abated" violence women
were working with other victims of domestic violence. One worked as a victim
advocate, another worked with the battered women's agency, and a third gives
lectures about domestic violence at local universities. Even a "fragile" violence
survivor hoped to work as an advocate for victims of intimate partner violence,
once her situation was resolved.

Conclusion

The portrait that emerges in this chapter is one that suggests that the women in
the agency samples are quite comparable to women nationally who have experienced intimate partner violence, with exceptions that capture the uniqueness
of Northern California. Second, the women seemed resilient, and had access
to social and personal resources which, with appropriate assistance, could be
marshaled into "encounters" within a restorative justice program, and ultimately
healing and preventing future violence in their intimate relationships.

Interestingly enough, there was not much difference in the social and personal resources the women reported being available to them, irrespective of how
much time had elapsed since they had experienced the violence. These survivors
typically reported support from family and/or friends who are part of their communities of care. Despite their recent traumatic violent experiences (even some
of the "fragile" and "intermediate" survivors), many were cautiously optimistic
and thoughtful in their reflections on the violence they had encountered not
so long ago. This is certainly not to underplay the tenuousness and weariness
expressed by some, particularly in the "fragile" group. Nonetheless, the resiliency

heard in the voices of these survivors bodes well for the introduction and potential appeal as well as success of restorative justice type programs in the context of domestic violence.

In short, it is quite clear that these women are survivors manifesting their ecological agency through their personal resources; they are resilient, self-reflective, resolved, resourceful, and demonstrate personal initiative. They are hopeful, even when they sound fragile and weary, underscoring the ongoing support they need from their wide ranging communities of care. These communities include not only family and friends but also battered women's agencies, shelters, support groups, district attorneys, legal and other service systems, faith communities, and even other victims.

On balance, what do these survivors' narratives tell us about the stakeholders to be involved in a restorative justice setting? In addition to the survivor and her care communities, the stakeholders might include the children, the batterer, his parents, and his support network. In keeping with the restorative justice principle of informed voluntary participation, survivors will have to be assisted in making informed choices about the key stakeholders and communities of care to be involved in a restorative justice framework. And such decisions will have to be made in the context of a thorough review of their histories of violent experiences. It is to this task that we turn in the next chapter.

Notes

1. As per the 2000 census data for SC County from which the samples were drawn (U.S Census Bureau, American FactFinder 2000), 59.5 percent of the county residents were white, 32.4 percent Hispanic or Latino, 10.9 percent Asian, 6.7 percent African American, and 0.3 percent American Indian/Hawaiian.

2. In 2000, 82.4 percent of female SC county residents had at least a high school degree; 36.6 percent had at least a bachelor's degree (U.S Census Bureau, American FactFinder 2000).

3. As was noted in chapter 2, the analysis will be disaggregated for three groups of battered women. Group 1, the "abated violence" group (an adaptation of Cherlin et al.'s (2004) "abated unions"), depicts cases where domestic violence had occurred three or more years prior to the interview; group 2 is the "intermediate" group (violence occurred between one and two years before the interview); and group 3 is the "fragile" group (less than one year with some in a shelter at the time of the interview and others outside shelters).

CHAPTER 4

Power and Control Dynamics in the Batterer-Battered Relationships

Introduction

As was noted in chapter 1, the social problem that is the focus of this manuscript is the violence that has occurred in intimate partner relationships, particularly violence that has been enacted by the batterer in the service of exercising power and control over the woman (Pence and Paymar 1993). We follow Johnson's (2008) operationalization of power and control in violence. Systematic battering (Johnson's "coercive control") is defined as when the batterer uses "a wide variety of tactics to control his or her partner, then it is reasonable to assume that the violence itself is being enacted in the service of that control" (13). In other words, the violence in systematic battering is not an isolated event, but a pattern of violent behavior that extends over a prolonged period of time and in a variety of situations.

The goal of domestic violence interventions, particularly of the restorative justice type, is to help the victim-survivors transform the power and control dynamics in their violent intimate relationships into an "equality model." A review of the survivors' violent case histories is imperative in order to identify the victims' needs (for information, telling their story, empowerment, and restitution and vindication), the harms to be addressed, and the causes of the harms so that the batterer can be held accountable (primary restorative justice goals, Van Ness and Strong 2006; Zehr 2002). It is in this personal historical context that the specifics of any programmatic intervention need to be located. Using case histories of victims' violence experiences and their insights into how they can heal is in line with restorative praxis (Umbreit et al. 2003; Zehr 2001).

In ecological terms, the focus in this chapter is on the micro-system. The systematic violent relationships between the batterer and the woman victim, who comprise the micro-system, will be outlined to illustrate the power and control dynamics. In the process, the other stakeholders as well the care communities will be highlighted. In the interest of giving voice and personal agency to the victim-survivors, we turn, in this chapter, to their personal narratives presented in their own voices.

Data from the survey (Service Utilization Survey) and interviews will be used in an iterative fashion. That is, the survey data will be used to draw the broad numeric outlines of the power and control dynamics. The narrative qualitative interviews will be used to flesh out the numeric outlines.

Power and Control Dynamics

The wheel of power and control presented by Pence and Paymar (1993) provides an excellent framework for outlining the variety of violence tactics that together have come to represent power and control dynamics. Intimate partner violence is not just physical, but includes coercion and threats, intimidation, emotional abuse, minimizing, economic abuse, and using children and male privilege. Coercion and threats range from threats to harm the victim, to leave her, or to commit suicide, employed as a way to force her into doing his wishes. Sometimes, batterers use intimidation as a control tactic to frighten the victim through looks, gestures, smashing things or property, or displaying weapons. Another control tactic might be emotional abuse (putting the victim down, calling her names, making her think she is crazy or guilty, humiliating her), minimizing/denying the abuse (making light of the abuse), or blaming the victim for the abuse. Isolating the victim from contact (be it verbal or physical) with other family members and friends, and monitoring or limiting her movements is yet another power and control tactic. Batterers might also exert male privilege, including sexual abuse, and use children (using visitation as an opportunity to harass her or threaten to take the children away) as tactics to control the victim. And finally, the violence might include economic abuse ranging from preventing her keeping or getting a job to controlling her access to financial resources, even when she earns a salary. In both the survey and interview data sets specific probes were used to gather information on the different control tactics as outlined in the power and control wheel.

Portrait of Power and Control Dynamics In the Lives of the Survey Utilization and Interview Samples

To trace the history of violence, the women in the survey and interview samples were asked about their first experience with abuse as an adult, the most severe abuse incident, the most recent incident of abuse, and, when relevant, the abuse they might have experienced in their childhood. As will be evident in this chapter, the violence, even in a single incident, was not a single slap or threat but included a series of control tactics that are emblematic of the batterer using his power in order to control the victim.

THE MOST SEVERE INCIDENT: A BRIEF REVIEW OF TIMING AND LOCATION (TABLES 4.1.1–4.1.3)

In order to establish a common reference point for the discussion of power and control in intimate partner violence, the primary focus in this chapter will be on the violence in the most severe incident of abuse the victims had ever experienced and sometimes in the most recent incident (vis-à-vis the interview date), which often was not as severe as the severe incident.

The most severe experience with domestic violence for the majority (63.6 percent) in the survey sample occurred three or more years before the survey date ("abated" violence). Another third (between one and two years) were in the "intermediate" group as far as the timing of the most severe violence incident goes. Only 7.1 percent of the survey women had experienced the most severe violence within one year of the interview.

Table 4.1. Most Severe Experience with Domestic Violence, Survey Sample

1. *When did the most severe incidence of violence occur?*	
Within the past year ("fragile")	7.1% (n=113)
Between 1 and 2 years ago ("intermediate")	29.2
3 or more years ago ("abated")	63.6
2. *Where were you when this happened?*	
Home	73.8% (n=103)
Victim's mom's home	1.9
Abuser's mom's home	1.9
On the street by car	1.9
Parking lot at work	1.0
Other	19.5
3. *How long did this most severe incident last?*	
Several seconds	3.0% (n=100)
Several minutes	19.0
Several hours	30.0
An evening	14.0
A day or more	24.0
Week or more	3.0
A month or more	6.0
Cannot remember	1.0

*Note: Percentages may not total 100 because of rounding.

A majority of the most severe incidents occurred at home (73.8 percent), with another 4 percent of the incidents occurring at a parent's home (his or her mother's home). The typical severe incident lasted between several hours (30.0 percent) to a day or more (24.0 percent). For another fifth (19.0 percent) of the victims, the most severe violence lasted a few minutes, but for others (14.0 percent) it lasted an entire evening. For another 9 percent, the most severe incident lasted a week or more.

POWER AND CONTROL TACTICS (TABLES 4.2.1–4.2.5)

As is evident in table 4.2.1, the victims report a wide range of abuse in the most severe incident. Physical and emotional abuse and intimidation were the most common power and control tactics used by the abusers. Around 92 percent

Table 4.2. Prevalence of Power and Control Tactics

1. *In the most severe incident, what did the batterer do?*	
Physical abuse	91.7 (n=108)
Emotional abuse	91.7
Intimidation	80.6
Psychological abuse	74.8
Minimizing, denying, blaming	74.5
Coercion and threats	64.2
Male privilege	64.2
Isolation	58.1
Economic abuse	40.6
Using children	34.9
Sexual abuse	34.6
Other	12.4
2. *Did the batterer threaten to harm you or anyone else?*	
Yes	63.8% (n=116)
No	36.2
3. *Did you believe these threats?*	
Yes	82.9% (n=76)
No	17.1
4. *Were you afraid that the batterer might kill you?*	
Yes	52.5% (n=118)
Yes and No	15.3
No	32.2
5. *Are you currently afraid that the batterer might kill you?*	
Yes	30.0% (n=117)
Yes and no	11.1
No	59.0

*Note: Percentages may not total 100 because of rounding.

(91.7 percent) said that they were physically abused; 91.7 percent said that they were emotionally abused, and 80.6 percent indicated that they were intimidated. Three-quarters said that they were psychologically abused (74.8 percent), and that the abuser minimized, denied, and blamed the victim (74.5 percent). In addition, 64.2 percent stated that the abuser used coercion and threats and directly or indirectly cited male privilege as his justification for his violent behavior. Finally, 58.1 percent indicated that they were isolated from family and friend, 40.6 percent experienced economic abuse, 34.9 percent indicated that children were used in the abuse situation, and 34.6 percent said that they were sexually abused.

In addition to these control tactics, 63.8 percent of the women indicated that the batterer threatened to harm them (table 4.2.2) or other people, with 82.9 percent of the women reporting that they believed these threats at the time they were made (table 4.2.3). That the power and control tactics had the desired effect is evident in the 52.5 percent of the women who feared that the batterer would kill them at the time of the most severe incident; another 15.3 percent considered the threat a possibility ("yes and no"). Only a third (32.2 percent) did not fear being killed by the batterer. In fact, at the time of the interview, 30 percent of the women continued to fear that the batterer will kill them (table 4.2.5); 11 percent were not sure ("yes and no"). However, 59 percent did not have this fear at the time of the survey, perhaps because sufficient time had elapsed since the incident.

Power and Control Narrative: Voices of Victims

While the victims in the survey are not the same as the victims in the interview samples, the voices[1] of the victims in the interview sample help fill in the broad numeric outlines provided above by the survey sample.

All, except two, of the thirty-five victims in the interview sample described in vivid detail the violence they had been subjected to by their batterers. The victims were given a choice to start talking about their violence experiences at any point that they were comfortable with. Some started at the very beginning but many started with the last incident. Once they started, with minimal prompting, they described the physical, verbal, and emotional abuse they were subjected to by the batterer and the sense of isolation (partly self-imposed out of shame) they felt even when the violence happened in public. In the process, they, without necessarily using the terms, also described the "cycle of violence" and "dependency" captured by Walker (1979, 1984). The victims often explained the batterer's abusive behavior as the product of status inconsistency (she is working while he was not, differences in family status), alcohol and drug use, or even history of family violence. Many of the women had, at the time of the interviews, terminated their abusive relationships, some permanently while others more temporarily.

As will be evident in the narratives detailed below, batterers used a package of violent tactics, that is, several violent tactics in conjunction with each other. We will start with one woman's narrative in which she recalls the violent events as they unfolded at different times in her relationship. This will be followed by specific examples of different "tropes" or patterns of tactics in other women's narratives. Since the narratives more often than not included a mix of violent tactics, the specific tactic will be highlighted if it is mentioned by the victim herself and if not, the tactic will be indicated in highlighted brackets [ ]. Also, rather than summarize the women's experiences, the victims will be allowed to speak through their narratives. In keeping with the naming conventions outlined in chapter 2, the women will be referred to as "victims" in this chapter in which their experiences with violence are analyzed.

A VICTIM RECALLS THE CYCLE OF VIOLENCE IN HER RELATIONSHIP

That the violence tactics often came as a package is illustrated in the experience of Victim 4.

> *The beginning:* We started out living together . . . when I first met him we both worked together for a local organization. . . . We lived together and the first time he ever hit me *[Physical]* was we were driving. . . . Driving somewhere with my supervisor at that time. . . . And, we were talking and he was saying something . . . I called him . . . which is kinda like saying idiot or stupid in . . . [his language] It's used affectionately or it could just be. It's not a real harsh word. . . . That's the first time he hit me. . . . Yeah, with [the supervisor] right there. This all went on. . . . In the car . . . [the supervisor] just laughed and I was in shock because I had always thought that if any-one had ever hit me I would kill them. I would leave the relationship. I wouldn't put up with it, kind of the rug was pulled out from under me. I didn't, you know. Know what to do. Yeah. And that wasn't severe. That was the very beginning.

> *The middle:* [When the victim was asked what he said after he hit her that first time in the car, she responded,] "Don't talk to me like that. . . . Don't talk to me like that. . . . Don't use those words with me. . . . Don't use that tone with me. You'll see" . . . that was the first time he hit me and then. . . . Oh no, no, I didn't tell anybody, I

didn't, no, I didn't *[Isolation]*. It was just, it was unreal. It was like
it didn't happen. . . . And then the, the abuse was . . . He was always
very critical of me . . . always making me feel like I wasn't fulfilling
or meeting the standards of a woman *[Male Privilege]* . . . like all
these other women were doing so much more than me . . . and those
were the periods of more intense abuse. And everybody [in the trailer
complex] knew about it. People heard it . . . you know, hit me in
public . . . I had been doing laundry and then I went to visit a friend
in a trailer and then I went back home and it was about nine o'clock
and I walked. . . . And I walked into the bedroom and he was laying
on the bed and he started you know, slapping *[Physical]* me mostly
in my face. Asking me where I had been. And I told him I had been
doing laundry and he says he looked for me over at the laundry place
and I was lying and who was I with and that was a lot of what he
did *[Isolation]*. He grabbed me by my arm, like by my wrist. And
I think I constantly had purple marks on my wrists. Shake me, pull
me by my hair. That was another thing. Pull me across the room by
my hair and throw me into the wall and he try and strangle me and
that night was pretty bad. I remember because . . . I kept saying that
I'm going to leave and every time that I would try and get out of the
room, he wouldn't let me. He'd drag me over to the bed. He would
sit on top of me. He would hold me down. He would put his hand
on my mouth. . . . And somehow, I don't know, but I got out and
I went next door. And banged on the door. . . . There's just a bil-
lion examples. I ran out and, I kinda felt like . . . some of the guys
[coworkers] had said to me that I had driven him crazy. That I had
mistreated him . . . well, there are a lot of things I just wouldn't do.
I mean, I remember him kicking me when I was in bed one morning
and I didn't want to get up at five o'clock and make him breakfast.
All the other men who had wives or women living with them, they
would make their meals and they would serve them. . . . And I
wouldn't do that and he, I think he felt humiliated. I think he felt a
lot of social pressure that possibly they were thinking that he wasn't
a man or he wasn't able to control me because you know, he would
have to make his own food or he wouldn't eat *[Male Privilege]*.
. . . And so I'm thinking, well, who, where am I going to go? I just
felt cornered. I felt like I had no options *[Dependency]*. I felt like
I just wanted it to be okay with him, but I was so, my adrenaline, I
remember was going so fast. I ran to the trailer of some friends I had
there. Well, I didn't know them that well, but I considered them
friends. They were the only other young people there and ran into
the arms of my friend and sobbing. And you know he was asking me,
"Did he hit you?" There were other people there too. And I, I said,
no, we were just fighting. Well, you know, obviously, I mean, they
knew I was lying. I couldn't ever, ever, come out and say yeah. That

he hit you. Yeah, I never, never could do that. And, so he showed up at the door and he said . . . and I went back with him. . . . Humm . . . well, a lot of mixed emotion . . . I felt comforted . . . by him, by being back with him. Going back to our place. . . . Kind of thinking that, I really did think that I could prevent this from happening *[Emotional]*. I really thought that he could change. I really thought that if I just could explain things to him. . . . And if I could be more affectionate and, just help him with his life. . . . To the extent back then I thought that he had a lot of problems in life and I felt sorry for him for that and I thought that if I could help him through those problems we could work on our relationship and he wouldn't do this. I thought it was out of frustration that he did this . . . I just remember him grabbing me by the back of my hair and dragging me and I'm screaming and I just remember getting dragged down the hall by my hair into the bedroom *[Physical]* . . . it would be, you know, I would be sore, I wish my mother was here. . . . And him saying, you know, fuck your parents, this and that. Really saying bad things about my father and you know just cussing at him. And, so you know that lasted throughout the day that he would, I mean I went to sleep, I remember going to sleep on the bed and I remember he actually made eggs for dinner. It was weird because I was in the room and didn't want to leave . . . because I didn't want to see the other people. . . . And, remember him bringing eggs into the room. He had scrambled some eggs. I remembered thinking he'd never cooked for me before. And, just thinking, like, it's going to be okay *[Cycle of Violence]*. . . . And then, I think he went out that evening for a little bit with his cousin. And his cousin, they didn't know anything was going on, but the people we lived with did. And nobody would talk about it. No, no one would talk about it. One time his friend told me that, his one friend . . . actually, kept telling me that I was making him crazy . . . when he came home and he wanted to sleep and I was trying to read. He turned off the lights while I'm laying in bed with a book open and I went and turned the light back on and he said, "I have to sleep. Turn off the light." I said, okay, I'll go read in the living room, and he said, "You will not go read in the living room." . . . He always thought that I wanted to be showing my body off to them [to other men in the trailer complex]. Like I remember once I was wearing shorts and he thought I was doing it for their benefit *[Isolation]*. He, it was just horrible and, he wouldn't let me out of the room and we started fighting, and . . . Verbally, yeah, it was always verbal along with physical.

And then the end: So what had happened was our relationship was going to end because I had had time to be away from him, started feeling better about myself and, and it was just tense. . . . And, what had happened was we were arguing because well he was living with a family. And it was dinner[time] and I kinda jokingly mouthed at him, you know, make your own food. And, I had embarrassed him in front of his friends that he lived with and he gave me that look like you know you'll . . . I really knew then that I had really said the wrong thing to him *[Intimidation]*. I couldn't joke with him. Sometimes I could, sometimes I couldn't . . . so at that time it was just a look. . . . Yeah, it was just a look. And then when it was time to go to bed, he would say, "How many times have I told you not to do that? You're no good. . . . You're not a woman. All you do is . . ." *[Emotional]* and I started saying things back. It's really hard to pinpoint but you know at one point he just smacked, me. . . . Hit me across the face *[Physical]* and . . . my response was to hit him back which was, of course, led to him basically getting on top of me . . . on my chest. . . . Well, that was, you know, after years of abuse and after I'd had time to think. It was, I had broken away, I think, at least enough emotionally to feel tremendous anger. . . . And this hatred that I hadn't had before. To tell you the truth, disgust . . . at him . . . but he apologized profusely. . . . Oh, right after. The same night. He'd get tired of hitting and I was sobbing and he would hold me while I'm crying *[Cycle of Violence]*. Like as if I'd gone to another person to cry on their shoulder. . . . And I thought I would just never talk to him again. . . . But, no, I stayed. I had one more day to stay. I stayed and then I left.

VIOLENT BEGINNINGS

Similar to Victim 4's experience, for many other victims, the violence often started early on in the relationship and continued for a while. Here are some narratives that illustrate the violent beginnings.

Victim 9 recalled:

Uh, at the beginning of the marriage there was the physical abuse. . . . But the first time of physical abuse . . . was, like four or five weeks before we got married. . . . And that's when he pushed me against the wall *[Physical]*. . . . And then the second time was two months after we were married and it was at . . . [amusement park]. . . . And I was asking him what programs do you want to see and do you not want to do and so he felt I was taking over, and pushing him and moving him along *[Male Privilege]*. . . . And he would just jerk my arm and once we got off the park, we decided to have lunch out of the park and then in the parking lot . . . he threw a Coke at me, which surprised me . . . and I threw a Coke back at him and then he started to hit me. . . . Very hurt. I have pictures . . . I started to scream for help. We were right by the street . . . I mean the main street, but no one stopped, no one helped. . . . No. Oh no. I mean I just I . . . I wandered around the parking lot by myself. . . . No, it was like he was looking at me, you know, I really don't know . . . because I was just wandering, you know, 'cuz I was just wandering around . . . just, just, oh, and I was like, and, and I remember a little bit of like, just help me, help me, but it was a really low voice. . . . Help me, someone, help me. . . . And then it felt like I couldn't go any place, there was no phone that was nearby, I just felt and it was just like, and then I was so scared. It was like the only thing to do is just to get in the car and have him drive me home *[Cycle of Violence]*. . . . But then once I got home, and I went to the bathroom and I saw all these bruises on me, it was like, I can't stay here. . . . So I called an elderly woman that I stayed with before I got married . . . and I asked if I could spend the night there and she said yes, and she saw all of these bruises . . . and she didn't say anything about it. . . . So . . . Well, the next day, my only reaction was I need to go back to my husband. . . . So, and, that was a Saturday and then the next day was a Sunday and we went to church together, uh huh, right. And then I remember the pastor say, "Give the person next to you a hug," and I remember, I, and that was the first time that I went to and I turned to him and I said, don't you touch me. . . . You know, and it was like it was automatic like and I was surprised that I even said that, and then he said, "Too bad." So. Uh huh, he hugged me *[Male Privilege]*. And I remember wearing long sleeves . . . then the physical abuse stopped . . . for a while . . . but the *intimidation*, the *verbal* abuse, the . . . Oh, that I was psychotic *[Minimizing]*. Oh, it, it could be, whether or it, it was like him consistently coming home late and not accounting for what, you know, what was going on . . . he was probably still at work . . . just so I wanted to know. . . . Yeah, that kind of thing, so you know, and I would say something, you know, if you're at work, you know, just let me know . . . or you're spending a few minutes . . . friends, talking whatever . . . it doesn't matter to me . . . oh, you know, "you're just psychotic" *[Minimizing, Blaming]* and stuff like that. And "you're always depressed, you want somebody here all the time," you know, kind of . . . that type of thing. . . . And it was always, he's used those words a lot with me. . . . "psychotic and depressed" . . . I was working . . . working as a high school counselor at the time. . . . And I would go with bruises and work. . . . To work, yeah . . . the other ones were not as severe as that one. That was the worst . . . the time when in the [amusement park] . . . much of the abuse came around holidays, birthdays . . . well, his, no. . . . His birthday, no, not ever. But, my birthdays . . . yeah, I've been, I've been called a bitch, you know, my birthdays, it would be because I wanted to go out and have dinner at a certain place. . . . You know, oh, you're just being a bitch about it, why don't we go here and I'm like . . .

Or as Victim 11 remembered,

[Y]ou know, I've, I couldn't forgive, but this was before we were married. . . . And he didn't hit me but he picked me up and threw me *[Physical]*. . . . Yeah. He did. But you know, you keep . . . at that time I didn't, I didn't see no warning signs, you know . . . I just thought he was upset. You know, didn't know what he was doing.

Talking about the first time her batterer hit her, Victim 12 recalled:

[H]e gave me a black eye a week before my wedding *[Physical]*. . . . Yeah. And because I'm the oldest, and, I'm, I did, I didn't want to, oh, he, he cried. That was the one time he cried *[Cycle of Violence]* . . . after he gave me that black eye . . . and hit me on the mouth and I still have a flap of skin. . . . And I totally hid it. He didn't and he's so dysfunctional, and so backward and how can I say it, ignorant in the way of psychology . . . even though he took psychology courses and he used to always like to say, "I'm so much smarter than you" *[Minimizing]*. See, it's that thing too, you know . . . It's his insecurity that he didn't go to school, blah blah blah, that kind of thing. . . . He finally got his AA. And that's why he's gonna go to the university in [out of state]. . . . To go and try to make something out of himself. . . . He was a construction worker. Iron worker. Very strong.

When Victim 18 was asked how her relationship with the batterer started, she recounted:

[W]e met at a party and he never left. . . . It was very slow and subtle. He'd be **controlling**. He wouldn't want me to, if he didn't want me to go somewhere or do something, then he would voice that and be almost forceful about it *[Isolation]*. And then it got a little worse when he wouldn't let me leave the room. Like no, you're not leaving. Actually, it'd start with an argument. We would be arguing and then I'd want to leave to cool off. And he wouldn't allow me to do that. I guess he wasn't finished *[Coercion]*.

ALCOHOL OR DRUG USE MADE THE PHYSICAL ABUSE, THREATS, INTIMIDATION, AND ECONOMIC ABUSE EVEN WORSE

More often than not, there was alcohol or drug use associated with the violence, which intensified the violent experiences. In some cases, alcohol was involved from the very beginning.

As Victim 18 remembered,

> [A]nd then he introduced me to some ***drugs and alcohol*** and then that just blew everything out of proportion. He'd been using for years. So he knew what he was doing, I guess. I think it [the violence] subsided when he was high but when he was coming down, then it was really, really bad. But alcohol made it worse.

Victim 1 described the role of alcohol and drugs in her battering relationship thusly:

> So it started soon after marriage. . . . Yes, yeah. Once again it wasn't, I'm not sure what to relate it to. I think it was a pattern of life for him already established. . . . He did many things. He's thrown me down three flights of stairs *[Physical]*, he's come home because he couldn't find his ***cocaine [Drug Use]***, he had left it at the place that he was at, and he'd wake our son and I up and [son] was young at the time, and I was nursing him and he'd wake us up and then break every light fixture in the house *[Intimidation]*. I would have glass, you know, all over my body. And he was bad. He was bad news. One time we took the jeep and he was driving and he decided he, he had forgotten his cigarettes and so he was going to turn really quickly and so he slammed into a guard rail and I was thrown out of the jeep after my head hitting, you know, the windshield. He thought I was faking it and just trying to create a scene *[Minimizing]*. Which really what happened is I didn't know who I was. You know, the ambulance came. They asked me, "Who are you?" Oh, I know I just can't think of it right now. "How old are you?" I can't think of that either right now but I know it, don't worry. Where do you live? Oh, this way. The opposite direction. So, of course, they took me and then they found him [the batterer] and his brother also who had taken off and left me there. And they took us all to the hospital. And even the next morning I couldn't remember who I was. . . . But he would actually leave for sometimes weeks at a time and you never knew where he was. But those times were peaceful compared to when he was at home because then you never knew when he was going to explode . . . I would have to say that anything could lead him to explode, but everything was magnified because he was ***drinking*** all the time and he was doing ***drugs*** all the time, right. And so it could just be a bad day at work or he might have had something said to him that he didn't care to hear or the house wasn't perfect or the dinner wasn't on the table at six o'clock *[Male Privilege]*. Doesn't matter if he didn't come home for a week, but it better be on the table at six o'clock. Oh, he did that to me one time, too. Oh, I'm, my grandmother was visiting me. And he says, you know, I'm going to be home and I'd

like such and such and such to eat for dinner. I didn't see him for a week and a half later. And then he calls me up and he's in another state in the hospital. And he says, "Well, aren't you concerned about me?" and I say, well, you're all right. At least now I know where you are. And I'm thinking, and how I'm really feeling is that I'm glad you are gone. So, you know, then, I was safe . . . when he wasn't there.

Similarly, Victim 28 describing the first violence incident recalled:

The first started right after we were married. Um, he just, he came home one evening, was *drunk*, and started fighting with me, pushing me around *[Physical]*, he was military, so I called for the military to come pick him up, they promised to take him and let him stay the night at the barracks. But instead, they took him out and got him more drunk, and he came home and held a bat over my head and said he would kill me. I called the police, they came out, he ran away. Just, we were arguing because he was drunk. And he didn't tell me where he was and I was studying for finals and everything, so, we just started arguing. He did a lot of shoving. He never really hit me at that point. That pretty much stopped and there was nothing else until, um, five years later. And we were in California at this time and his brother had moved in for temporary stay with us. The baby was crying in the middle of the night. She was very sick. He told me if I didn't shut her up, he'd break my nose *[Verbal; Threats]*. At that point, he came at me and was trying to hit me in the face. And he did hit me. He tried to break my hand when I fought him off. I didn't call the police at that time, because the last time, no one did anything. I stayed there and was afraid, but didn't do anything.

Victim 34 met her current batterer about five years before the interview date. She was living with her parents; the batterer was their neighbor. She recalls him being very nice, very friendly. They got to know each other for about a year and then they moved in with each other in an apartment they found together.

And he, in the beginning it was nice, but within the year, he started becoming *physically* and *verbally* abusive, particularly when he was *drinking*, as well as when he was on *drugs* . . . "whore and so called, um, b b-i-t-c-h" *[Verbal, Emotional]*. When he was drinking, it was horrible. I would have to put up with it for like five hours straight, on just any little thing he was nit-picky. Very angry towards me. Saying I couldn't do, I couldn't do anything right *[Male Privilege]*. . . . I thought that if I quit drinking and quit doing the drugs, maybe the fighting and the arguing would stop. Three years . . . after that, after I quit drinking and doing drugs, I, I went cold turkey. My children were more important to me than the party lifestyle that he want, wanted to live. But then it started getting worse. The **verbal** abuse, where I couldn't, like I said, I couldn't do anything right. Didn't matter, the toilet paper, I couldn't, I didn't put the toilet paper, it was a big deal, a big argument on which way the toilet paper is to be put on the roll *[Male Privilege]* . . . there was times where he was yanking me out of the house. Dragging me like a cave woman out the door, throwing me outside, locking the door, or vice versa, where I would do the same just to try to get rid of, to get rid of it. I didn't want to deal with it anymore. No. I didn't, I didn't tell anybody anything *[Isolation]* . . . only my girlfriend. One time I had told her about the key incident. He was drinking and he wanted the keys to the, to the car. And I had the keys. And I didn't want to give them to him because I didn't want him to hurt himself. And that's when he ripped the keys out of my hands and threw me to the floor.

SEXUAL VIOLENCE ADDS INSULT TO INJURY

In addition to the intimidation, minimizing, physical violence, and other emotional types of violent tactics that the batterer used, some women spoke about the sexual violence they were subjected to by their batterer. Some examples are presented below in the victims' voices.

Victim 24 started out her interview with

> [Y]ou're gonna be very interested in my story. . . . When, okay. My mom emancipated me when I was eleven to my husband. She sold me, basically signed me over and sold me, for $ . . . He was seventeen that time. So and knowing his background, he's a pimp, he's drug seller. So I got to that life. I got into the drug selling, the drug using, the prostitution, the madam, I was everything in that category at a very young age. I did have my three kids. Every time I had a child, I'd give it to my mom. I have no idea why I always give it to our mom, but my mom, my mom had feared us big time. So I knew she would never do to my kids what she did to me. [Interviewer: "Why do you think she feared you?"] Oh, threat, death threats. My husband would constantly death threat her . . . I went to prison for approximately four years. . . . An accessory to a . . . [felony]. . . . With my husband . . . he only served two and a half. And he was caught on camera . . . doing that . . . a matter of fact, he, he was on camera, he killed someone. Had witnesses and everything. . . . He only spent seven months for that [because he had a good lawyer with his parents' help].
>
> [Speaking of her first incident, Victim 24 continued,] the abuse first started when I was sixteen. He approached me with selling my body *[Sexual]*. And you know, I was young and no way, you know,

no way. You know, I was not married to him at that time. He, he looked at me with such a look *[Intimidation]*, and he just slapped me *[Physical]* and I hit the back wall. And he grabbed me up by my neck and he told me I'm gonna do what he says. That's how it first started. Let me tell you, I had been with him for already five years; he basically was like a father, a father type. So I didn't know how to feel. I felt, okay, if that's what you say, okay. You know, I didn't know to be scared of him, I didn't know to, I didn't know any of that because he was all I knew. I thought what he told me was right. I was young. And that continued.

Victim 10, when asked to describe the sexual violence that she said she had experienced, recalled:

I waited for this ride for hours . . . I used to have a pager from my work saying that I was able to, they were able to get somebody to come pick me up. That's how I waited by the store, and here comes the police. And I'm arrested for supposedly hitting my husband in the shoulder with a toy. . . . He called. And had me arrested. I spent two days humiliating myself, two days . . . for something that I didn't do. . . . I didn't touch him. I left . . . I didn't care. . . . [When asked whether he had physically assaulted before, she replied,] Not physically. . . . No. . . . Yeah. Everything else. . . . No, no. No, no, no. He bailed me out and I didn't want to go with him but I didn't really have a choice. I didn't feel I had a choice. I refused to come home. He wanted me to come home but I had emergency restraining order on me. So I told him I wanted to stay at a motel, alone. . . . And I did. He took me to the local inn. . . . And I spent the night there, alone. . . . In shock. He spent several days, kissing up, I will call it *[Cycle of Violence]*. . . . I came home, well, to his home. I still was not living there . . . had not lived there. I stayed there one night because I didn't have any money on hand, you know. . . . He slept in the living room, I slept in the bedroom, and he was a perfect gentleman . . . Mother's Day, I got to have the kids. By myself. I told him that's what I wanted for Mother's Day. It was just my two children and me alone, to do whatever we want, without any pressure. . . . I even took them to a motel and we spent the night and had a campout, then the next day we went to the beach and I came home, went to his home, I brought the children home, and, he insisted like that the kids could go out and play and he'd go out and watch them outside. And he insisted that I take a shower, 'cuz I was, he went, I was filthy. And so, all my clothes being there, I went ahead and went for that. . . . Thinking he was going outside like he said. . . . He ended up back in the shower and he **raped** *[Sexual]* me that day. I haven't really dealt with it, so it doesn't yet affect me, because so many things have happened since. It's almost like it didn't happen. Just, it's, it's not time for me to handle it.

For Victim 27, the violence included sexual and other emotional abuse:

> My husband, he would shake me and he would push me. But he would never, and he threaten with, make a fist and threaten to hit me *[Threats]* but he never give me black eyes or nothing. Maybe just a bruise on my arm. And he did, he did mostly, very, very violent person. He would throw toys, he would yell at me, scream *[Intimidation]* and, and if he didn't get his way, he would actually, he would want to force me to have **sex** *[Sexual]* with him when I didn't want to. And, one time he, one time he tried to **rape** me but I didn't let him. Didn't work. So he got very, very angry and he left. And then he would leave for a little while and then come back and apologize, cry, hug me, tell me I'm sorry and, and, and, and I just thought that he you know, was really, really sorry because he would cry *[Cycle of Violence]* and he was shaking me.

Victim 33's abuser was a medical professional.

> So, the abuse started I'd say within two or three months of getting married. And then, against my will really, I, I didn't know as much about it, I was pregnant the first, you know, within just a month or two of marriage. And then I, I had a total of five children, and I had a total of eight abortions. Five of which he, he did. With no anesthesia, on the kitchen table. So, that just gives you kind of a, so this tells you that, I mean, he used pregnancy as a way of controlling me. And, it also was a way of just beating me down. So I mean he not only used beating, and over the years, rather than going to an individual incident, well, well, let's see, when I was pregnant with my second child, once he choked me unconscious *[Physical]*. And threw water in my face and I've found that talking didn't always work so I just sort of sat there and just stared. And he was **verbally** abusing me and I wasn't responding at all and that made him absolutely furious. And he said, told me I was crazy and he threatened *[Threats, Minimizing]* to commit me. And being a . . . [medical professional], I really thought he could. And so I had the threat of, over the thirty years, I had the threat of being committed, of having my children taken away from me, of taking all the money, of killing me, he said it would be really easy. As a matter of fact, in my final deposition thirty years later, that was part of it, is that he said as a [medical professional], it would be easy for him to kill me and no one would know. You know, these threats went over all the years.

When Victim 18 was asked to elaborate about what she meant about getting tired of him forcing her to do things, she responded:

> He was great at manipulation *[Emotional]*. He's, he's used the kids as pawns and . . . because, before I had custody of him [son], he'd say, you know, well, if you're going to leave me, you know, I'll give him to a foster home or you don't know what I'll do to him *[Using Children]*. And so I'd, you know, do whatever he wanted me to do to a certain extent and, there was, there was a lot of *sexual* abuse. I did things that I would never have done had he not manipulated from self-perspective but I know, in my heart. When you're afraid that someone's gonna flip out at anything, you just, you behave differently around that person. And so I mean I understand it now better than I did. Uh huh.

VIOLENCE AROUND ISSUES RELATED TO CHILDREN

As would be predicted by the power and control dynamics of violence, some batterers used children as pawns to control the victim. Custody battles or child visitation became contexts in which the batterer continued to victimize the victim. Victim 3's narrative went this way:

> So, anyway, he wanted to talk about this legal issue with our son. And I had told him no. I will only talk with him about these kinds of issues when he's *sober*. And he got all bent out of shape and yelled at me *[Verbal]*, was threatening *[Threats]* me and I just was, like, just stay on the phone [with a friend] with me please. And he'd leave and come back. Finally he came in and he grabbed the phone. Hung the phone up. And he, I was sitting in my bed. And he grabbed me by the throat and laid down on top of me *[Physical]* and held my head, hair back with his other hand and *threatened* to kill me if I didn't sign . . . he threatened, yeah, he just kept threatening he'd kill me. I didn't know who I was screwing with. He could have me killed. He knew people. And, he knows how the system works [batterer is an attorney] and I don't, and he was just . . . You know, I believed him. I was so *scared*. You've got a *drunken* maniac. And, I've never felt like that before. I felt like I was going to die. And, I was so afraid. I was so afraid. I just couldn't, I really thought I was going to die. I really felt this close to death. You know there's nothing I could do. I mean, I didn't really want to really fight with him. He was laying on top of me. I couldn't move *[Physical]*. He was *threatening* me. I didn't want to make him more mad. I was dealing with a *drunk*.

And so finally . . . I don't know what it was, but something said to me, just agree with him. You're not going to be the next Nicole Brown Simpson. So just agree with him. Tell him what he wants to hear, sign what he wants you to sign, do whatever he wants you to do right now. When he gets out of the room, dial 911 . . . I got off the phone. I just finally started crying. I'm like okay, okay, you know. I stood up. He let me stood up and he was like yelling at me and I was looking down and I was just scared. And he popped, smacked my head up. "You look at me now, you look at me, bitch, when I'm talking to you. You just look at me when I'm talking to you, bitch" *[Physical and Verbal]*. Those are the words he was using to me. And I said okay. He goes, "You're going to sign it and you're going to like it, aren't you?" I'll sign it, I'll like it, I'm sorry, I'm horrible, I'm just a bad person and . . . And he says, "I'm going to go write it up and I'll have it ready for you in the morning." I'm like, okay fine. And he walked out.

But the violence only continued:

[T]hat's when I called the police . . . he walked into the front room. He was sleeping in the front room at that time. We were, we were separated pretty much. It was, he was really, it was a financial thing. Why I was still there. I just wanted to try at least make it through [community college] before I transferred and then I was going to try to, and it didn't work that way, but that was kind of my plan. . . . He heard me and then he unhooked the phone *[Isolation]*. I was on the cordless. He unhooked the phone and they called me right back. I ran in my son's room. Thank God, my son was sleeping through this whole thing. And, I said I'm really sorry and they said, "Are you okay?" and I said no, I'm not. But you know he's out there, he's walking around and . . . So the police came. And they asked him. He was all *drunk*, you know, acting like he's Mr. Wonderful . . . he answered the door, and I was in the bedroom just shaking, talking to the 911 lady. And she goes just stay on the phone with me 'til the police get in here. And so then finally they came in and the officer came in and said, "Are you okay?" I said yes. And he said, "I want you to stay in here for a minute and I'm going to go talk with, you know, [the batterer]." . . . He went out and talked with him.

Victim 9 spoke of the verbal and physical abuse, threats and intimidation around the care her son needed:

Most recent was probably, there was one after that and I don't know, but I mean it was like, three weeks after that. . . . But the most recent one was, it happened on April . . . I can even tell you the date . . .

April. . . . And that is when he became extremely **verbally** abusive . . . it was what triggered it; my son was going to be two years old, it was his birthday party that day. And he was in charge of bringing the container for the punch . . . and it was not clean and I had said to him, I have lots of things to do because he had asked me if I would clean it. I said, no, I can't. . . . And then he said God damn it, that kind of a thing. . . . And I said, I think you need to leave. And then it was F-you F-you F-you . . . and I'm gonna call CPS on you *[Using Children]* . . . and threatened to take my son, and it was like, I don't need this, get out, you know. . . . And so that was it. But there was another incident similar to that after that. . . . It was the same thing . . . oh, since my son is ill . . . he had forgot to bring his medication and I said, you know, what about the medication . . . and he said, "Well, it was my choice not to give it to him," and I said, well, he needs that medication . . . because it's in regards to his heart . . . and, and you know, he kept on. I said, please, don't play these mind games with me . . . it was like he needs this medication and then it was just like "damn it, you, you can't even take care of your son, I'm gonna call CPS" . . . but it was the **intimidation** 'cuz he, he does a lot of intimidating. Like coming right at your face and . . . then backing out. . . . And I just like . . . it just really, just scares you. . . . That kind of intimidation. . . . So, I called the police and I said, you know, they said, "Do you want it written up?" And I had never known before that time that I can have something written up . . . and I said yes.

Victim 19's batterer used her son to *threaten and taunt* her:

[T]he worst incident, I would say was when he, he tried to kidnap my son, and he said that he wanted me to spend the night with him and I didn't want to. And he was so mad that he took my son in his arms and he kept taunting me and saying, "How does it feel to not be able to touch your son?" and stuff, and he's walking around the house and, and saying, you know, "Go ahead, call the police," you know, we were at his house. But he didn't have a phone. His phone didn't work so he was just saying, you know, saying that because he knew that it would frustrate me more. And then he was grabbing personal parts of my body, and when I would hit his hands away, he would tell my son, "Look what your mother's doing to me."

ISOLATION AS A VIOLENT TACTIC

Being isolated from their family and friends was another common trope in the victims' narratives. Here are some poignant examples.

Victim 18, speaking of the stalking and isolation she had experienced, remembered:

> Uh huh. Uh huh. In fact, the last time I left to the shelter, he went all the way to, he went out of state to my parents' house. He had the police. So, yeah. He threatened all his friends, and my friends. Of course, I didn't have any at that point *[Isolation]* but his friends, you know, "if you know anything about where she's at," yeah, he really tried to hunt me down. Well, yeah. I had brought friends home from work and he, if he didn't like them, which was most of the time he didn't, he was rude to them. So they didn't want to be my friends. And my family, the same way. They'd come to visit and he was completely obnoxious. And we'd go to family functions and he'd do the same thing. So, they, my family, quit visiting me at one point. Plus they've seen how he treated me. You know. And they didn't like it. And, and I'd get, got tired of being embarrassed. And it was embarrassing being down all the time and not having my life the way I wanted to so, you know, I didn't want to share the, you know, I didn't like myself, why would I want to share it with anybody.

Victim 19 spoke about her isolation as she described her first incident of violence:

> The first one was when we were just living together. He, I remember, he hit me with a jug of milk *[Physical]*. A full gallon of milk. Ahh, I believe he was **drunk**. Yeah. And on **drugs**. And I, I believe I hit him back too. And I, I remember he was holding me against somewhere and I had, I don't know, the thing you smash potatoes with or beans with, and I hit him with that to get him away from me. And you know, then they just, he was always sorry *[Cycle of Violence]* and I was kind of embarrassed because it was, you know, my first month with him and I kept it pretty much a secret *[Isolation]*.

ECONOMIC ABUSE: WHAT DOES IT LOOK LIKE?

Along with verbal, physical, sexual, and isolation violence tactics, some women's violence experiences had economic dimensions.

Sometimes, the batterer's drug use was financed by the victim's finances *[Economic Abuse]*. For example, Victim 11, who had left her husband/batterer three times, reported that he did not work because he could not pass a drug test to get a job. She worked, but he controlled the money; he gave her an allowance. In her words:

[H]e would take the money and spend the bills, he would give me what I needed for the house . . . and he would take what he figured he could have, you know, so that he wouldn't be all on edge all the time . . . he was stealing, robbing me . . . as soon as I closed my eyes, he would take the money . . . he was waking my children up in the middle of the night for their allowances . . . he was selling the food out of the home, he would take all of the food stamps. . . . This is so that he can get the money for his drug habit.

Victim 8's batterer was her work supervisor and held the threat of having her fired *[Economic]* in case she talked to anyone about the abuse.

For, he's violated the restraining order. We've been separated since last June. . . . And now we're divorced. . . . I didn't divorce him due to the battery. I divorced him due to the fact that he molested my older son [his stepson] and that's the time my child chose to disclose, on this particular night . . . we had been you know, having a *verbal* stay away argument . . . and then, basically ignoring each other. . . . Well, I had set up a bedpost in the living room . . . so I could be out there with the children. . . . And I had the portable phone in the living room with me . . . there was also a phone in the master bedroom . . . Well, he came out and took the phone from me . . . he had a phone call and I knocked on the bedroom door, I told him that he had a phone call. . . . But rather than him take the phone in the bedroom where he was . . . he had to come out and get the portable phone from me. . . . And I asked him if he could please return the phone when he was done . . . and then he shouted obscene words *[Verbal]* at me and he, of course, did not bring it back. . . . So when I went to retrieve it . . . then he, you know, he started acting ballistic. . . . He came out, slammed me against the hallway wall *[Physical]* . . . with my herniated disk . . . held me by my throat . . . had his other fist, hand cocked back in a fist . . . and said, "I will fuck you up, cunt" *[Threats]*. . . . And I was terrified in fear of my life because this was the first time that we had had progressed from *verbal* abuse to, you know, actual real *physical* violence. . . . And he acts, you know, seeing his fist cock at me as if I was a male . . . was just incredible. So I was terrified.

Victim 19, describing one of many violent episodes, remembers:

[H]appened on my honeymoon. He ripped apart all of my clothes and he did that because we were in . . . [resort], and he was *drunk*, and he just began to be angry with me and mean and I didn't do anything. We, we had a motel or hotel close to the casinos, so, it was probably all five o'clock in the morning already. He didn't want to come home, he just wanted to keep partying and, and gambling. And I think I'm not sure if this is the episode or not but I think they kicked him out of the casino. Yeah. It was time for him to go 'cuz he was getting loud and, and violent. And so I was walking home in front of him and he was just yelling and saying, you know, bad things to me *[Verbal]*. And he wanted the money *[Economic]* that I had 'cuz he wanted to gamble more. And I wouldn't give it to him, and it was in my shoe, but, you know, and the process of looking for it, he ripped apart everything that I had in my suitcase. We came back to the room and I thought you know, we might just go to sleep. He, he was still very angry and I believe that probably the alcohol was the main ingredient that kept the anger . . . no, he didn't hurt me too bad. Maybe pushed me around and grab things, but it wasn't, wasn't too bad. . . . There's been so many episodes and that was like that.

Victim 23 talked about the economic abuse, in addition to psychological and physical violence, in her relationship:

[T]he AFDC checks would come in my fiancé's name, he was considered to be head, head of household and he had not had an income, so they would come in his name. So come the first of the month, when I had none, he received the check and he cashed it, left me with not any money *[Economic]*. And the last check that I received from work, 'cuz I ended up getting fired because of the, the problems that I was having. And first time ever in my life have I ever been fired without a reason why. And my last check I had cashed and I put the money away, he still, he took it. And so that left me with absolutely nothing. And so that only left me with a little over a $100 for the entire month. Now, this next month on the very first will be the very first time that I've ever received a full check. But it's been so hard.

RARE CASES OF PRIMARILY PHYSICAL VIOLENCE IN THE BATTERING RELATIONSHIP

Victim 5:

I had known him briefly for about three years . . . he was a neighbor. And I knew him, I knew of him and he would tell me hello and we would have a brief conversation and then I had been dating and involved with him. . . . When this incident happened, it caught me totally unaware . . . I never was around profanity and I wasn't going to listen to him fume around and I was walking out of the room . . . he grabbed me and threw me to the floor *[Physical]* and after I landed on carpet and I didn't hit all the hard objects that were around. . . . As I was lying on the carpet he leaned over me and he would continue to scream in my face. I couldn't see. But I could hear what he was saying. I could even smell his breath and I don't . . . but I must have kinda gotten on my knees, but I got up the stairs and I locked the door. . . . And I went in there and I was putting . . . on the black eye . . . I was up there for like two hours and then I heard him, he tapped on the door. And he said that he was sorry that he had done that *[Cycle of Violence]*, would I talk to him so that we could work things out? And I said maybe, but . . . But after about five minutes or so I went downstairs, as I walked in the room he started the abuse again. . . . And . . . I jumped for the telephone and called 911 . . . I think I truly believe what you psychologically call you are so stunned that you are absolutely not thinking.

Victim 7:

So the next day was Christmas Eve . . . and I proceeded to go run around, buy more preparations and have them [his family] over . . . and then he decided to work until like, 7:00 or 8:00. And not help me at all. . . . And I'd talked to him at work, and I said, well, you know, this is your family. And I think you should come home and help. . . . And he obviously had talked to his parents during the day because he was in a very agitated state. And I can tell the difference when he's talked to them and he hasn't. . . . He came home at approximately 4:30. He wasn't in the house five minutes. . . . And he started calling me, you know, "a f-ing bitch" . . . and this is all your fault, dadda dadda da. And then he just took me and he just threw me across the room *[Physical]*. And which resulted in me hitting the coffee table. . . . And the way I fell, I had twisted my back and I had bruised up . . . my hand, which I still have scars today from it. . . . From that. . . . And it knocked the wind out of me, and what he did is he went, we have a den and where he pushed me from was right there and he closed the doors, went back in the den, and first he said, "Oh, get up, you're not hurt" *[Minimizing]*. . . . And I was scared, I was very scared. And my child was in the house who happened to be in his bed. . . . Asleep, for some reason he fell asleep . . . I was really, really scared. . . . So as soon as I got up and he went in the den, I called 911 . . . I was scared for my safety and my son's . . . because the November before that, I had to leave the house with my son [young] . . . and I just thought it was just progressing. . . . He had come home at 9:00 at night. . . . And wanted, insisted, he put on a . . . outfit. He didn't want to, he was tired, which he should've been going to bed. . . . And then that made him more mad, and then he yelled, and then he said you would put this outfit on, and then he picked him up by both hands and took him in his room and just shoved him in his bed and I can hear him crying . . . a different cry than he normally cries. So I knew something was going on. And then I heard like a smacking sound. Like he was probably spanking him.

Victim 10:

Well yeah, I was mad at him because he [husband] said I couldn't take the car after I got home *[Isolation]*. After I got to his house, I couldn't take the car. I had to stay with the kids and he was gonna go do and I know his go do, he don't ever come back. . . . And here I would not have anywhere to take the children 'cuz I'm not supposed to or it wasn't agreed upon thing. And on that night, he attacked me with a hammer *[Physical]*. . . . When I was in the bedroom. I went into the master bathroom, because it was habit. . . . It hadn't been that long since I had lived there. . . . That's just the one I always used. . . . And when I came out of the bathroom, he was in front of the door with the door locked. And I told him that I didn't want to stay, and that I just thought it would be best if I just left, wouldn't take a car, just, I'll just go and handle it. And he wouldn't get out of the way, and he had his hands behind his back like he was holding onto the door knob. And so I went over to the phone to try to call the police and he took the plug out of the back of the phone, the AC adapter. . . . I put the phone back down and he hit me like three times, three or four times in the head with the hammer, and then he tried to twist my head so I would break my neck . . . and when that didn't work, because I've been wrestling with him for six years, on a play level sometimes, he was a wrestler in high school. . . . He's gonna win. He outweighs me by about forty pounds, there's no way I could win. And he laid on top me on my waterbed, it was my face down, pushing with his hands on my airways. He wanted me to die. And, and he told me that—that, if I wasn't gonna be with him, then I just wasn't gonna be, and this was yet a separate moment in the ordeal where he was on top of me, on my chest with my elbows under his knees, and he just he was trying to cover my mouth and my son was hitting on the door, "don't hurt my mom." . . . And I screamed to for him to call the police, and he did.

[And the violence just continued.] And I have a four poster waterbed so I grabbed a hold of one of the post on the end of bed and it was the furthest away from the door. And he came back and he took his knee and just his hand and he shoved my head into his knee *[Physical]*. And then he went back to the door. And then he came back. And he did it again. And every time, I was like screaming. And trying to, no, no, no, no, no. I can remember thinking, it's not gonna, he's not gonna do it again, he's not gonna do it again and then he did it. Every time. And then, the door bell rang. I guess my husband got scared. So he opened up the door and went running down the hallway. And, like this adrenaline rush hit me, and I knew it was my only chance while the front door was open and to take him by surprise, to run out. I went and I looked in my purse, because I had a taser. It was gone. It was just gone. And my car key was gone. And I, I just ran and made it. He grabbed for me but he didn't get a good enough hold on me. They found the hammer in the garbage dumpster right outside the door where we live in the garbage shoot. And from what I've heard of the reports there was blood all over the place. But that wasn't mine. Because when I ran out of my apartment, I went to the left. Down the hallway to try to find help because I was not doing okay. I was not okay. My head was hurt so bad I couldn't even think. My eye was swelling so bad I couldn't, all I could do was scream and my husband turned around and said to the kids, "Mommy hit me with a hammer."

Or as Victim 12 remembers:

I never had a broken bone in my body until this. . . . That was me running upstairs, trying to get him to talk to me. And he literally jumped on me, and I felt something crack *[Physical]*. . . . And he wasn't even supportive when I went to the doctor that day and I called in sick and I tried to hide the whole thing. I told them that I was moving a chest of drawers upstairs. . . . It was that simple. That easy to hide. . . . No. Nope. But, see, when I came forward with that doctor, forget it. People in the emergency room, they, like, abused me. They were trying to. . . . Oh, 'cuz I said I fell, fell down on the beach. And they were like, yeah, right, sure. Look at that bruise. You can tell that's hand marks and this and that. And you—they wonder why people don't come forward. . . . You know. It's like, there's no way. And I don't think I'll be going in to a hospital anytime soon either.

RARE CASES OF PRIMARILY EMOTIONAL ABUSE

Victim 13 has been abused in two relationships. Speaking of the most recent relationship, she says:

[B]ut the [recent relationship] was very, he was awful. He was very, very, demeaning *[Minimizing]*. I mean the way he spoke to me and . . . Oh, he's a paramedic . . . where he'd say, this is a totem pole and he's not really intelligent but his, his degree in paramedic, firefighter certificate, whatever he has, meant so much to him but because I hadn't gone to college or had any educational background, I was considered to be low on the totem pole. His status was high. His family was from . . . and he had lots of money, and he would constantly say these things to me and it may seem trivial but, I mean, it just over and over and over . . . it was like, he'd say if I broke up with you, it would be different. And I mean it was just and he'd call and he'd leave these mean, mean messages and my daughter was listening to them and I changed my number . . . and then he'd show up wherever I was *[Threats and Stalking]*. . . . When I went to court for restraining order, he had an attorney. I did not . . . I couldn't afford one. I mean, I was losing my apartment and he wouldn't even help me out with day care so I could continue to work. . . . And at that time, I had to go on welfare. Well, that was the lowest thing I could ever do . . . I mean, I was the scum of the earth then. . . . Well, he was informed that if the child was his, he was going to have to pay. . . . So then I was a threat to him. I was going to sue him and I wasn't. I just wanted to get on with my life . . . no, he didn't physically abuse me. . . . Yes. . . . But when I went into, I know in my interviews, I told them I don't have any bruises on the outside, all my scars are on the inside. And I honestly thought my chances were very slim.

Victim 21 described her first husband's possessiveness and emotional violence:

My husband, he wasn't a physically abuser, he was an emotion, *emotional* batterer. . . . Like with him, he would always used to accuse me of cheating or whatever. . . . Or just . . . put me down about . . . I was married eight years but separated four. One day, I just woke up and decided enough was enough. And I didn't care what nobody else said to me, something was wrong. Didn't feel right. . . . [When asked about the divorce from her husband, she said,] Yes. I think that's why he hasn't filed for divorce. 'Cuz he could've filed it a long time ago. But he didn't. Because he knows once you go to court and we get, we get the court order established, I don't have to speak to him. Or really have any contact with him. He's asking me if I would, if I would ever get back with him. He has a girlfriend now . . . that lives with him. . . . But he still wants to get back together with me. . . . [Interviewer: "How about you?"] No. . . . Never. . . . [Interviewer: "If you had to give one reason why, why you say never, what would that be?"] The emotional abuse.

She had two children from her marriage. And had a third child with her current boyfriend who is physically violent (see below in section on abuse in multiple serial relationships).

SOMETIMES THE VIOLENCE STARTED OUT EMOTIONAL AND THEN TURNED PHYSICAL

Here is Victim 31 describing the evolution of her battering relationship from emotional to physical:

> I'd only known the man for not quite three years. I had married him six months after I met him. Strangely enough, I was coming from a very abusive ten-year relationship. . . . And he seemed very different. Anyway, but he wasn't, and his abuse started out as *verbal, emotional,* Well I left him the first time because he telling me I was worthless and old hag and I mean it made me feel. . . . He's three years older than I am. He badgered me to the point that I was worthless, and useless. And he later told me that it was because he felt he couldn't take care of me. We were both on the streets at this point. I ended up on the streets because of my injury. I was kind of out of it when this started and, and so all of a sudden I found myself in a position where I had no money. No income whatsoever. And so forth and so on. I'd been looking for a job when I found him, and he helped me, took care of me, every time when I needed. He's on SSI. He's a little bit, he's mentally disturbed. But it didn't really seem that way, at beginning. Anyway, it started out, but due to his own insecurities and his own problems, the *verbal and emotional abuse turned to physical abuse* a month or so after we were married. It's funny because I kind of took care of him, but then the intimidation and the physical abuse, which was not overwhelming or not great, started. He punched me, and because he thought I was, he, because of jealousy, he thought I was, had been with or whatever, a friend of ours. And that's been the pattern. Just ever since he's tremendously, tremendously insecure. And he feels that I am a lying slut, whore, bitch *[Verbal].* Yeah, after a while when you feel like fucking bitch is your name. Um, anyway, and there'd be sporadic episodes of violence.

Victim 20, whose abuse experience was primarily emotional, psychological, and financial until it became physical:

> [H]e was pretty violent. I remember my son wanted to baptized. . . .You know, he was of the age and at my church, you know, being a . . . kids decide on their own. And so he was going to a Catholic school so he decided that, you know, it was time for him . . . to become a part of church and everything, so he decided it. And that's when I really saw this side 'cuz my son really liked to be with my family when he had the chance to be, and my ex-husband said no. "Well,

it's okay as long as they don't come to the baptism." And I said, well, that's kind of ridiculous. So my family honored his request, although they later gave my son presents and things like that *[Isolation]*. But, you know, they said if he doesn't want us around, we won't come around. So anyway, he got very angry with me though and he took the car keys and so one of my friends picked me up and . . . I spent the night with her. . . . He just got angry at me because I said, you know, I am tired of this, you're trying to run everything. . . . He says, "No, I don't want them there, they're not gonna show up," he just . . . he just wanted me to be at his . . . and I said no, I'm tired of this *[Verbal, Controlling]*. . . . I said, well, I think I can go back . . . because my brother as well, one of my older brothers told me, you know, "Divorce is like war so you might not want to go into this right now, so think about it. . . . And if he's not hurting you physically, let's see if, you know, you can work it out." So I tried it. And, you know, I stayed for about another three months. . . . And then he just got really violent on me. He manhandled me *[Physical]*. And that scared me.

THE BATTERER KNEW THE DOS AND DON'TS ABOUT VIOLENCE

Victim 18, describing the worst incident of violence, said:

[B]ecause it was the most humiliating is when he drove me down the street. And that started with an argument and I was leaving. And was gonna walk down the street. And then I heard his footsteps chasing me behind me, so I started running but I couldn't outrun him, so he grabbed me and drew me back and I started to say, okay, okay, I'm coming with you. I'm coming home. And then I started struggling again, so he was choking me and pulling my hair *[Physical]*. . . . Out in the street. And I think that the witnesses were mostly kids, neighborhood kids. So I remember trying to calm myself that he wouldn't be so bad. Because I didn't want them to see it. And, but I, I didn't want to be forced in the house and I remember trying to pr—prop it up my legs and he was, I had called the police on him a couple of times. So he knew the rules about leaving marks. So he'd pick me up and throw me and he'd choke me but he's never happened to leave any marks. You know, and he hit me in the head, I mean he . . . He learned really quick. Yeah. And he'd say, "Go ahead and call them 'cuz I didn't do anything anyways." *[Intimidation and Coercion]*

FEELING TRAPPED: LEAVING AND RETURNING, AND THE CYCLE CONTINUED

Victim 16 is a well-educated person with technical training (so was the batterer) and described the sense of being trapped in a relationship that was violent at the physical, sexual, emotional, intimidation, and financial levels.

> And first he used to come on like **verbal**. And then from verbal he became physical . . . the violence started from very beginning. . . . I found out he didn't have any job and . . . so I, I was hiding everything from my family . . . I thought it will be very painful because I'm the youngest. . . . So I didn't want to hurt their feelings. . . . [She said that she helped him with his job search and he finally found a job] . . . first he started . . . giving me like **mental** abuse . . . every time he was trying to put me down. . . . Oh, "you don't know how to speak English" and this and that. Every time he was putting me down with English. . . . Oh, "you're dead, you're ugly, you're dead . . . you're dark" *[Emotional]* . . . then he started to abuse me like he started counting things in the house. . . . Counted, like, one day he came back from work . . . he said, "When I left, we had five bananas. How come we have four bananas?" . . . and he didn't let me talk to my family. He kept me **isolated** . . . have permission to watch TV . . . I didn't have permission to do anything in my house . . . and like when I was even coming back from work, first thing he used to look, look through window, but I mean about me like, whatever I'm doing. . . . And if I'm in the bathroom, if he's knocking on the door, if he stays like one minute or two minutes, oh, then after that he used to put me deep trouble . . . "fucking bitch" and this and that, "what were you doing?" and this . . . dirty, dirty things. . . . Then he used to touch TV. . . . 'Cuz then it's hot or cold . . . If it's hot, it means I was watching TV *[Isolation]*. . . . One day he came home and he made so scared, I, I was so scared of him. . . . One day I was watching TV. The minute he came, I turned it off. But he touched the TV and started beating me up . . . "you told lie" . . . that was my favorite program.

In addition, here is how the victim described the economic and sexual dimensions of the violence:

> If I wanted to, if I was getting some job from somewhere, he was creating so many problems. He didn't let me apply for work anywhere, he didn't let me go to college *[Economic]* . . . like a slave and then slowly, slowly, he came on to sexual abuse, started **raping** me twice a day *[Sexual]*. Oh, yeah. I was pregnant and then he was so cruel.

. . . During pregnancy, I was so tired because I, I had evening sickness . . . I mean, touching me, I used to feel, throw up . . . he didn't let me learn any single thing. . . . In seven and a half years, I didn't know how to, how to use checks, how to use credit card, I didn't know how to use ATM cards *[Economic]* . . . and then how to fill gas tanks . . . he used to beat me up when he was teaching me driving. . . . So I took for granted to die. And then I became pregnant, so I said, oh, because of him, I don't want to kill another person. . . . So I said forget it . . . "Did you mop the floor?" I say, yeah, I did. And then he will say, "How come this floor is still dirty?" And then I'll say, no I cleaned it. . . . "So your mom didn't teach you how to clean" and this and that *[Male Privilege]*. . . . Oh, yeah . . . I mean one time he hit my older kid very badly. He hit his head on the bed frame. And every single day, like at least three, four times, he used to hit him. . . . Hitting them for nothing. . . . One day, he couldn't find his soccer gloves. So he said, "Now this is your punishment. You stay outside and keep outside and you do not get food tonight." He locked the house from outside, and left from there. Me and my kids was, we stayed outside and no food, no water, nothing. And, uh, no shoes. [The neighbor helped her with some food and water and she decided that day to leave him but did not have money to hire a lawyer until two neighbors took her to a shelter] . . . I was at the shelter for fifteen days.

And the cycle of violence continued:

When I came back [from the shelter] for like three, four days, he was nice. He apologizing and said, oh, I wouldn't do anything, this and that. And then he forgot, after one week, he forgot *[Cycle]*. After one week, he started doing same thing he did to my older kid. . . . So, my older kid said, "Mom, this is your fault. Why did you bring us back from shelter? We were happy over there." So I felt so terrible. I said, oh, I should go back. So somehow, I, I had to spend Saturday and Sunday over there, Monday I told him like today, I'm going to pick up kids. He said, "No, I'll go with you." I said no. I said don't control me. 'Cuz I came from shelter so they gave me counseling at the shelter. So I became little, I mean not too much strong but I think I became five percentage strong. So I told him no, today I'm going to pick them up. He said okay. I picked up my both kids, told their teachers they're not going to come because I'm going to go back to shelter. And then I left. Again, I went straight to shelter, I filed restraining order and everything. He left the house, I came back in the house. But he kept on sending friends, made me guilty, saying he's going to change, he's going to change, he's going to change . . . he's going to work . . . he's going to do this . . . so slowly, slowly, he trapped me again. He came back again. [She did leave him; see below in "The Last Straw?" section.]

Victim 26:

[M]y dealings with the police is whenever he was using *drugs* . . . I knew that he was under the influence and I would, when he'd get out of hand, I'd call the police. On my part, that could've been a control mechanism but I thought I was trying to set boundaries 'cuz I did not want him to use *drugs*. And I did not like the way he acted when he came off the drugs. Now, there was two questions in my mind at this time. First off, he was someone I loved. Second off, I was fearful of him going to jail *[Dependence]*. So that had to be a choice that I had to make. So I would call them and they would come out and I would not mention that he was on, under the influence. I just would want him to leave so they would talk to him and then we'd work things out between us. And by the time the police got there and I had told the police are coming, you need to leave, and that was a tight control of situation. Now, a lot of the times, he would greet them when they came up the hill and they would talk . . . and one time he said I was on my period, that I was really having a PMS problem *[Minimizing]* and one of the officers even told me, "You know, you need to go to the doctor and have something done about that. It was just making you act hysterical." So I, I had bad dealings with the police and that was my choice not to call that night. But the next day, I had to do what I had to do. Uh, he went to jail and he was there for two weeks.

And the dependence continued:

And during this time, I tried to get a lot of help from some organizations because my rent was coming, was I needed money. I had animals. I had no transportation because he was angry that I had him arrested and he had his family come and get his truck, and it was in his name. So there was a lot of punishment, towards me. And the need for him was really desperate. I mean, I needed him there. I needed the money, I needed the support, I needed the help *[Dependence]*. So I was frightened of my security. So I worked to get him out of jail. Well, I talked to friends and had someone raise up money. And bailed him out, because . . . first couple of days he didn't call. Then after that, he was very apologetic, felt bad for what he had done, and, of course, I believed this. And we'd been together prior, a good two and a half years before this incident had happened, without being hit. Now he by nature is a loud person. There's a lot of reasons that added up to the fighting. He's having problems in his business, I had lost a baby . . . [he had] taken a woman who ended up being our friend who betrays me and slept with him. She ends up having a baby for him. And there was a lot of consequences to this. . . . What I found mostly is, when I did call the agencies, funds are very low. I would've had to, if I went to a shelter, instead of trying to educate me, they said, "Well, leave him. He has no respect for you." I mean, it's kind of hard 'cuz people do bond with their attackers. Okay? And I needed to be good, needed to know that I was good for him. Instead of not wanting him, I did want him. I wanted to know, wanted to mend, I wanted to patch up *[Dependence]*. And the need there, was severe, you know. I didn't want them to tell me that he was never gonna care about me, that he was never gonna respect me, that I needed to come to this shelter, I needed to get all my things out of that house and leave. And that was giving up everything to me. I didn't want to sacrifice that. . . . So he and I agreed to work harder, said that he would quit drugs but he didn't. I did call the police on him numerous times afterwards. To the point to where his *drug* problem and his *verbal* abuse became very suicidal for myself. I felt very degraded, I lost self-confidence . . . he was more *verbal*. Very *verbal*. So I end up in the hospital couple different times. Tried to hurt myself but not so much as wanting to die. But so much just to show him what he was doing to me. I never really wanted to die and I wanted to strike back at him, but I had my own boundaries on myself. So instead of hurting him physically, I hurt myself. I took it out on myself.

"AND I GO BACK FOR MORE" (VICTIM 14): ABUSE IN MULTIPLE SERIAL RELATIONSHIPS

Victim 14 has a son and two daughters. At the outset she clarified that her son had a different father than her two girls whom she had with her ex-husband. There was violence in both relationships. Describing the abuse in her first marriage, she says:

[M]y husband was not physical . . . his father left his family at an early age. His father was an alcoholic. His mother and sisters, he was like the man of the family. Okay? So he's seen with his mother and father and so the *cycle* just kept going with him. He's the only boy, he's got two other sisters and, of course, being he was the man, he saw how his father was, he . . . followed in his father's footsteps. . . . So, like I said, the cycle has to be broken somewhere and it didn't break with him. . . . And, it started off with, you know, hitting, punching walls, holes in the walls and the doors *[Intimidation]* . . . just anything. Just, just anything. You know . . . it didn't have to be anything major. . . . Just you know, either he would snap you and, of course,

he would say that's the Italian in me. . . . It's not . . . That's yelling
and screaming. Uh, yeah, he's half Italian, half Irish . . . But, his only
way of communicating is through yelling and screaming. So is my
children, that's the only way they communicate and . . . I'm, I've
got myself doing that, you know. . . . So I'm trying to, when I catch
myself, I, just try to stop him. . . . Well, after that, he never did hit me
and . . . but, the *verbal* abuse was getting worse and worse and like
I said, it started back again, after our daughter was born, and then
we had another daughter in. . . . And I should've probably left him
before she was born, but you know, like many other women, I didn't
. . . because I knew it wouldn't get any better. He always kept saying
it, I'll change, I'll change *[Cycle]*. . . . He didn't want to hold a job
down . . . you know, he'd go out get a job for a couple of weeks, trying to make. . . . He's a roofer . . . construction, you know. There're
plenty of jobs. . . . And, he would just go out and get a job, to make
it look good. And he'd fall right back in that same pattern . . . when
he is not working, he would just lie around, watch TV. He wasn't a
drug abuser, he wasn't an alcoholic, so I can't blame it on that . . .
he's not a hard liquor drinker. This is why I can't understand. . . .
But his father was an alcoholic.

In her second relationship (boyfriend), the violence was decidedly physical,
verbal, and emotional. She had just left her relationship when she was interviewed.

There is no relationship anymore. . . . But, very abusive, still. . . . A
lot of *verbal* abuse. He's on probation already for domestic violence
for previous girlfriend . . . he's actually tried to choke me, he's pick
me up off of a coffee table, trying to choke me *[Physical]*. . . . He's
left me in . . . when we were camping. And I go back for more. . . .
And, this last time, I just, I couldn't, I can't do it. The *verbal* abuse,
I mean, is so bad. He would call me an asshole. I'm stupid. I don't
have. . . . But I mean, it got to the point where my self-esteem was
getting about this big, you know. . . . Because I was starting to feel
like, well, maybe I am stupid, you know *[Emotional]*. . . . But, I
just kept going back for more punishment 'cuz I don't, I mean, love
is blind, they say, and . . . it's like, boy, I must really be blind and
[laugh] opened my eyes up this time.

Victim 21's first relationship (with husband) was primarily emotional (see
section on emotional abuse). However, abuse in her next relationship was not
only emotional but decidedly physical. Describing the first incidence, she recounts:

[T]he first incident when I was staying with a friend of my mother,
and she used to have a lot of company coming in and out, in and
out. And he would accuse me of having them coming over to see

me *[Controlling, Emotional]*. . . . When, when most of the time
when I wasn't, when he wasn't there, I wasn't there either most of
the time. . . . And I think I tried, we were arguing, I tried to walk
off, and that was the first time he hit me *[Physical]*. [Interviewer:
"And what did you do?"] Mostly I was in shock. It took a couple of
minutes for it to penetrate. That he had actually hit me. And then
I, I hit him back. Yes, escalated it. . . . sometimes, I wouldn't hit
him back, but he would still keep, keep at it. Didn't, basically didn't
matter whether I hit him back or not. But when I did hit him back,
it wouldn't last as long as if when I didn't hit him back. . . . At first
he did [leave bruises], well, he always did, but at first he left them
where everybody could see 'em. And afterwards, he started leaving
where nobody else but him. [Interviewer: "Did you call the police?"]
No. Because I didn't have a lot of faith in police. 'Cuz watching them
when I was growing up and everything . . . by the time they came,
it would be, be too late. So why bother, right? He went to jail for
about almost the entire time I was pregnant with my son, he was in
jail. For a parole viol . . . for probation violation. He was on probation when I met him. . . . For weapon possession. When he got out,
moved in with his mother. . . . But he was, he was jealous of me and
her friendship *[Controlling]*. So, me and her became pretty good
friends. So, he became even jealous of that, and he would accuse me
of messing with his younger brothers, who are all underage *[Male
Privilege]*. So we recently, we just moved into our own place. [The
batterer did not work.]

Victim 18's violence experiences included physical, sexual, verbal, and psychological abuse, as well as alcohol, manipulation, and cycles of repeated leaving
and returning out of perceived necessity.

[F]irst of all, I, I had left, I had left him, you know, a handful of
times already so my family had already, I felt that I had exhausted
them. Okay, well, sure you can come and stay, but are you gonna
go back to him? . . . My family would absolutely disapprove of me
going back to him. . . . They knew it was a bad situation but they
knew they couldn't tell me what to do . . . I was gonna do what I
was going to do. And it was then and only then that I started saying,
you know, well, I want to leave but where do I go? I have no job. I
just quit my job. I have no car because my car died. And here I am
in a situation, he's got me just where he wanted me and that's when
it escalated, when I had no job and no car. So I was like, oh, gosh. I,
I gotta get out. [When asked when the abuse escalated, she recalls,]
He was choking my son and, and yeah, throwing him against the wall
and, and throwing me across the room and, um, he dragged me down
the street when I tried to run from him in front of a bunch of people.

He choked me and violence, violence *[Physical]*. Yeah. As well as the daily, almost the daily ritual of throwing the dinner I cooked down the sink. Because I was an awful cook *[Male Privilege, Emotional]*. I was this, I was that. And you know, all of this, most of it in front of the kids. Most of it.

Victim 22, talking about her ongoing relationship with her (adult) batterer where she could not see a way out:

I moved out when I was eighteen. I was supposed to go to college. I ended up staying behind 'cuz I fell in love [with someone she worked with]. . . . I, I just told my dad I wasn't ready, he now knows the truth but not when he was upset. And then a year later, and that never came of anything, and then a year later, when I was nineteen, I had started, yeah, I guess I was nineteen, I started dating my batterer [who worked at the same grocery store] . . . there were signs now that I look back from when I first started dating him . . . he was really overprotective and jealous *[Isolation, Male Privilege]*. But at that time, I wanted someone to be overprotective and jealous. You know. I wanted that, I think. And, he was just, I mean, if I even talked to another guy, he would get mad. Anybody, anybody he didn't know, he'd get upset, you know. I'd have a customer come up, a male customer would come up and just start talking. And then, it'd start changing to "Why did you talk to him like that? Why were you smiling at him like that?" You know, I was like, oh, come on, you know. There were just many signs like that. . . . So, then we started living together and then I got pregnant right away. He wanted me to get pregnant. He said that he wanted me to get pregnant. And I did. I thought I loved him. . . . Yeah. He wanted to marry me like a week after we met. But I still had some sense, you know, when I first met him. But then after I got pregnant, the series of the batter, the battering, the abuse started. . . . Right when I, he found out I was pregnant. He did not want a girl. He told me he would not, he didn't want me to have a girl, if it was a girl, he'd be upset. . . . He wanted a boy *[Male Privilege]*. And this goes back, I married my mother [she said that her mother physically abused her as a child]. Anyways, I did, you know, a lot of people say that you'll marry your father. I married a man who was exactly like my mother . . . and then after that, a lot of shoving, he had find reasons to shove me. Or hit me *[Physical]*.

And the violence just escalated with the cycle continuing. She goes on to say:

And then the biggest thing where I knew I was in trouble happened in August. . . . I was at work and we had argued *[Verbal]* right before he had dropped me off at work. And I went in to work and his sister was calling, saying she didn't know where he was. He dropped off his son. He had a son from a previous relationship. And they didn't know where he was. Well, he came in about one o'clock in the morning, my shift was 'til two. And he started yelling, cussing at me. Throwing things *[Intimidation]*. And I worked in a, they had a glass door that locked. And I wouldn't let him in. And we had some of the guys come and he beat up some of the guys pretty bad. Him and his friend. And he was cussing at me, telling me he's gonna kill me, and I was asking for it *[Coercion, Threats]*. And it was just terrible. And he lost his job. And that was the starting of more abuse. So it just followed that pattern and . . . And I had left him actually for about a month [stayed at a friend's house]. But it was just being pregnant and knowing I'm carrying his baby and I could never do it on my own. And I needed him. So, of course, I went back *[Cycle of Violence]*.

Over time, the violence only got even worse but she became more emotionally dependent on the batterer even though he did not support her financially when she needed it the most:

So then we moved to another apartment and it only got worse. 'Cuz then he started drinking more. He drank before but now he was drinking all the time *[Alcohol]*. And he went to jail once since then for some [car] tickets he had and for what he did at work [a grocery store]. . . . Only for like three or four days [in jail] 'cuz his family bailed him out. And he used to call me every time from jail and I used to, for some reason, just accepted every call *[Cycle, Dependency]*. I don't know why he'd call and say I was dead, but, you know, he was gonna kick my ass, he was gonna kill me and I'm a bitch and I'm stupid and I'm crazy and I'm lying *[Verbal, Threats, Emotional]*. Even though I wasn't lying . . . I was probably like five months, six months pregnant. And then he came out of jail and I locked all the doors and I was so scared 'cuz he threatened to kill me. You know, his friend was in the car, listening to this. And then he came in, he started yelling at me and then he said, "Okay, well, I forgive you this time" *[Male privilege]*. I didn't do anything. But you know, and then every day, I think for the rest of our relationship, I heard how I got him fired from [the grocery store], how it was my fault, how it was my fault that he went to jail, that before he met me he never went to jail or had problems *[Blaming]*. . . . And I was about seven, eight months pregnant. And something had happened, and I don't remember what. But I was lying down and he put his fist over my face and he asked me if I would like to see tomorrow. 'Cuz he had been *drinking*. Always drinking. . . . And my neighbors had called 911 'cuz they could hear the screaming. And he had, before they had come, he had al—already opened the door, and he had dragged me out while I was pregnant. You know, and he was just sort of stomping my belly, that "I don't want this," and all that. It was just terrible. And the police came. Of course, I denied anything happened. And they were just like, "Are you sure?" and I denied it *[Dependency]*. . . . Didn't want him to go to jail. And I think in my head, he had already gone to jail. And I didn't want to hear about it again and so I didn't want him to come back, even more mad. And then, let's see, and then eventually I had my daughter that March. And, you know, he wasn't even there. Well, he was when I went into labor and I wanted to call my friend or someone to come help 'cuz he was like, I could just tell he was gonna do something and I asked for my friends to be there. But, no, no, he wouldn't let me have the phone. And when I actually had started pushing, he left. He didn't come back. He didn't come back to see his daughter . . . it was okay for a while and then the abuse started again. And he would, he would go to his ex-girlfriend's house or her parents' house. And leave me alone. That I had a baby and he left me, I wasn't working. He made me quit [work] right after I had my daughter *[Economic]*. . . . I couldn't work. He left, he would leave me with no money and my dad wouldn't help me. I had nothing. I had to live off, I had, we had a jar of quarters, nickels, dimes, and pennies and stuff. I'd just live off that for like weeks. And then he would decide to come back. Then he would leave again. And then he'd come back.

ONE EPISODE OF VIOLENCE LASTING SEVERAL DAYS

While systematic battering typically occurs over the length of the relationship, some episodes can last several days.

Here is Victim 26's experience:

The first, there was one incident of actual hitting, this was with a current guy that I am with. Where prior to that, he had been under the influence of *drugs* and a lot of stress, I guess which prompted him to react in the way that he did. . . . That's how I conceive it. He doesn't really understand why, he just lost it. It was a very excited moment, we live up on top of a mountain . . . self-contained. . . . And we have a generator. And, he couldn't get it started and I had came out the back door, I had brought groceries in and got my, I have a grandchild, I brought him in the house and I was asking him was everything okay? And he became infuriated by that. Yelled at me, how the hell would I know, stupid f-in' B-I-T-C-H *[Verbal, Emotional]*. And there's no lights on. So this upset me, I felt hurt. I felt that there was no need for him to react that way. I knew he was upset. About the mountain lion thing. They had gotten to, 'cuz we had had a pig that had recently been attacked by a mountain lion and it died. So I knew that he was upset, and I, I was hurt by his comments. So he eventually got the lights on and then he came into the house and asked me was I going to help him, or was I gonna lay up and not do anything *[Male Privilege]*. And I was crying 'cuz my feelings had been hurt, and I told him that no, I didn't feel that he should talk to me the way he was. And I thought that he was mean. And he said do I want to see mean? And he punched me *[Physical]*. And he started hitting me, numerous times after that. I didn't leave right away. The next day, I went to bed very upset, I didn't call the police on him. The next day, he continued with, I guess, I don't know . . . but he totally blamed me for it *[Emotional]* . . . said that he hadn't had nothing to eat all day. 'Cuz I had slept through the night and I had slept most of the day 'til like six in the afternoon. I believe that I, my injuries might have made me sleep, 'cuz I had a lot of head injuries. And from him hitting me in the head. He'd given me two black eyes, punched right in the middle of the forehead, burnt me with a cigarette. Yeah, that night.

The victim attempted to leave temporarily, but it only made matters worse, and she felt trapped:

So the next morning, he told me he was hungry and that he hadn't had nothing to eat and I was lazy and I slept all day *[Male Privilege]*. And I told him that at that time I feared that he would abuse me again, so I picked up the phone and dialed 911 and let the phone dangle. 'Cuz he started yelling at me. And I told him he had no right to treat me like that. And I went to walk past him, and he started kicking me, knocked me down, and the police recorded this and the police came and arrested him. And he got charged with domestic violence. That same day. That morning. It was a two-day incident. . . . Then after that . . . him dealing with himself, I think made it worse. Because after he beat me up, it's like he really just became down degrading on me. Oh, "you're so stupid" *[Minimizing]* . . . when he'd first do his drugs, he was fine. As soon as he was tired, he'd get up. "What the hell are you gonna do? Lay up on your ass all day long?" And he was just really mean. I was scared. If I didn't get up and make his breakfast, he would be angry at me. I let this go for like a day or so until I got to the point to where I'd leave. I'd leave for a day. I'd go get a hotel room. Stay gone. 'Cuz I was just fearful that he would hit me. Because he'd just start arguing with me and cussing at me and calling names. And I couldn't talk, I'd cry and get upset and he'd tell me I'm stupid and, and I didn't want to believe it so I'd leave. And I had to wait for him to calm down. 'Cuz I knew he was just tired. I knew he was upset. But I mean enough of that. And it did get to be hard for me. I hated him at times, wished I wasn't with him. Then I'd leave him and I'd miss him when I was gone. Just terrible feeling. 'Cuz I did love him. I still do love him. But I didn't know how *[Dependency]*.

FIGHTING BACK: RULED MUTUAL COMBAT BY THE LEGAL SYSTEM

Lest we portray the victims as completely helpless, some did fight back. Contrary to the predictions of the "dependency" perspective, some women did try to respond to the violence, at least physically. Often, though, it was ruled as "mutual combat" by the legal system. Some examples follow.

Victim 8 described one incident thusly:

> So, a few minutes later I went back in there and asked him what, you know, the blank was his problem . . . and in this fight, he obtained one sixteenth of an inch scratch on his forehead. . . . And the district attorney ruled a *mutual combat.* . . . Because after twenty-four hours, they decided to interview him and apparently he had some self-inflicted injury on his leg . . . which was not there before . . . what happened was he was in the bedroom in bed and that's when I went to go ask him what had happened. . . . He sat up in bed, and this is why I don't know what could have happened to his leg because he was covered up, with covers. . . . And he sat up and reached out with an open hand and slapped me across my face *[Physical]*. It gave me instant black eyes . . . I've never had a black eye, and I've never had any kind of relationship with anybody like that . . . because if we tried to leave, he'd put a loaded gun to his head, and into his mouth in the presence of my ten-year-old son then *[Coercion and Threats]*.

Victim 23:

> You know, and he would just say such terrible, awful things, using extremely bad language *[Verbal]*, and being very abusive. I, I hung in there for a very long period of time. But there was one incident where I came home, and I was late, of course, and he was so angry at me because I had called him from work right before I left, and said today was an extremely busy day, they want me to stay a half hour later. And he did not agree with me working to begin with because it was at a liquor store, but it was just an in-between job, and he didn't agree with me working there. And he was just so angry that he kicked the most stuff around the house that, you know, at that point, that was a breaking point for me, he didn't hit me or anything like

that but he kicked our baby swings *[Intimidation]*. I was, of course, holding the baby. He would never hit, hurt any children ever, ever. But he, he was very abusive to the things around the house and so I ended up calling the police on him and having him taken away from the property. But yet no report was filed, no anything. He was just to leave the premises but to return whenever he wanted. Which was extremely frustrating. And then the weekend after, I had gotten permission from him *[Isolation]* to go out with a girlfriend and I ended up going and having a couple of drinks, which is not a normal thing for me, very rarely. And, I came home and he, he ended up being extremely angry because I was so late, when he said that it was okay for me to do this, and he was angry anyway, and we got into a very heated argument *[Verbal]*, and he ended shoving me with his chest, so I shoved him back, and he pushed me and I pushed him back, and he pushed me yet even harder, I fell back and landed in our garbage can in the kitchen *[Mutual Combat]*. I wasn't so angry of the fact that he pushed me, but where I was, I was in a garbage can, I was really mad. So I ended up charging at him to restrain him. I put my hand on his neck, not hard enough to leave any bruises but there were red marks. I said, you know, I'm gonna go outside and I am going to go and call the police because this kind of thing is just not supposed to happen. And so as I went outside, I just stood outside for a little while, I didn't go and call the police. I came back and he was already on the phone with the police. And the police came, they handcuffed me. And I ended up going to jail for four days and I'm still going to court on this issue of domestic violence. Now, I am the batterer. I ended up going and doing time for the very first time in my life.

Here is Victim 24, describing her most severe experience and how she fought back:

[M]y husband threw me off a five-story bedroom *[Physical]*. We were at a friend's house. We got into an argument. And during this time, you know, I was fighting back. Now, I'm fighting back. I didn't care now, I was fighting back. Still . . . but still . . . whatever he said was right . . . it cost in a flaming, flaming argument *[Verbal]*. I don't even remember. I'm gonna tell you, because if I didn't have hospital papers and court documents, I don't even remember the incident. I always look at the hospital papers, the police reports . . . 'cuz I still do not remember that. But I have court, I have all the papers. So, well, when he threw me, all I remember is him throwing me over. I don't remember anything else. I remember the fight, I remember the fight . . . and I was hitting him, I was hitting him and I picked up a chair *[Mutual Combat]*. And he pushed me and the chair, and lost my balance and I went over. That was it. I was pronounced dead twice, dead in the ambulance, and I was pronounced dead on the operating table. . . . I was in a coma for six months, now from what I have, the police papers, the court papers, the whole nine yards, my husband did five months for that. He only did five months for that. Because when I woke in my sixth month, he was there. He's the only face I see when I woke up from my coma. I mean, he was there when I woke up from my coma. [She was sent to rehab for one year that was paid for by his parents. Even at rehab,] I really, you know, I was still hearing him, above anything and everything else. Oh, he would just say things like "Just get his done, get this over with so you can come home, be my wife again. You don't need all these folks talking to you. They don't know, they ain't gonna take care of you the way I'm gonna take care of you." You know, just things like that, and . . . 'Cuz he is all I have.

THE LAST STRAW? PROCESS OF ENDING THE VIOLENT RELATIONSHIP, TEMPORARILY OR PERMANENTLY

To varying degrees and over a period of time, the victims had come to the decision to leave the relationship with their batterer. After the prolonged history of abuse, finally, "enough was enough." Here is how they explained their process of attempting to end the relationship.

In the words of Victim 2:

It was my ex-husband and it was August. . . . It was the last time that he beat me up. . . . Hopefully, for sure the last time. . . . And it wasn't the worst time. . . . It was just the time that made me leave . . . there was yelling and screaming and threatening and then eventually grabbing. I remember I had finger wounds from his hands on my arms. And then he was shoving me around on the balcony and I almost fell down the stairs *[Physical]*. . . . I think we were arguing about his drinking. Because all through our relationship, our whole relationship is eighteen months. And he misrepresented how much he *drank [Alcohol]* when we met and then when I found out [about the drinking] we constantly argued about it because I couldn't understand how you could say I love you and then when you'd wake up from being drunk, seeing that you'd hurt the person you love, how you could drink again. I didn't understand alcoholism at all. . . . And when we first met and did that part of the relationship where you are discovering each other, I told him that I'd been in some really bad car accidents where I've had serious skull fractures and I'm not supposed to bump my head. And he took that very seriously and then after we got married all he ever did was hit me in the head. And I think that those accidents and those skull fractures actually saved my life because I really thought that he was going to kill me. And I think most people don't really get down to the fact that he told me that he was going to kill me if I left so I was going to die trying *[Threats]*. . . . I promised I would leave him and then I had to lie to everybody for seven months because I gave him another chance *[Isolation; Cycle of Violence]*. That was, that was, God, that is complicated stuff, but he had. He had been beating me up. It was at Christmastime and he had started beating me up two weeks before Christmas. And the night in question was two days after Christmas. And he had me on the ground and he was kicking me in my back and really mad and picked me up and threw me across the bathroom *[Physical]*. He was **drunk** and strong. And I landed on my head in the bathtub, unconscious. And I don't remember coming to. The next thing I remember was I was on the phone to 911. But I had to be taken to urgent care. My ankle was all screwed up. They thought I had all this internal injuries. They x-rayed me from head to toe. I had a concussion. And that's when I decided to leave him and that's when I told everybody and yet he still convinced me to give him another chance. . . . That was the first time, that was the first time I called the crisis line. I got the cards from the police before, but I never read them or used them. . . . [Interviewer: "What made you call this time?"] Because I was going to end my marriage and I had nothing else to do except for to heal and I wanted out and I wanted to figure out how to get out and I called the crisis line and it was just unbelievable to me learning that it was not my behavior that was in question. Learning that five million women a year go through this a year in our country. That four to six women a day are being killed by it and that we have thousands of buildings in this country called shelters where women and children have to hide from their husbands and fathers.

Victim 18 talks about her tipping point when he physically abused her son:

So I think one of the episodes is when, you know, I watched him because I had told him that I was yelling at . . . [our son] for not listening to me. And he, he got involved in the discipline and it escalated to choking him *[Physical]* and no! And as soon as he was gone from the house is I started calling. I got the telephone book out and I called the [shelter] place and they gave me, they had must had a list 'cuz they gave me, well, what you need to do is you need to go to a shelter. And I had no idea that they had shelters for battered women. I just thought a shelter was a place that had a series of beds, that there were hobos and just a whole slew of different types of homeless people. I had no idea they had shelters that centered around counseling for the kids and for me and all. You know, that really, and that was safe places that he couldn't get into. I had no idea. So we all packed while he was at work, and he must have come home to an empty house 'cuz we ran to the shelter.

For Victim 11:

[H]e was all upset because I called the police. So he threw, uh, uh, a couch on me *[Physical]* . . . in front of the children. . . . And, I did, I, I'd told him it had to stop, he was throwing things around the house *[Intimidation]* . . . he had finally reached the point where he felt comfortable enough to hit me. . . . I've, I, I, I didn't do anything . . . you know, but, that's when I began to make arrangements to leave . . . oh, I called, a hotline for domestic violence and . . .

Victim 16's ending went this way:

But he kept on sending friends, made me guilty, saying he's going to change, he's going to change, he's going to change . . . he's going to work . . . he's going to do this . . . so slowly, slowly, he trapped me again. He came back again *[Cycle]*. This time again, he started doing after I think one month, And then one day, then it was too, it became again too much. One of my friends has kids and my kids used go to same school. She gave me a ride, I went to attorney. And I hired her. And I took out money from joint account and paid her. So when we went to court, he was shocked. He said, well, "you fucking bitch, you this, you that." [He continued to harass her at work, **stalked** her for two years, until she filed for divorce and did not let him back into the house. At the time of the telephone interview she was at an anonymous safe house arranged by her lawyer.]

Victim 20 described the lead-up to the day she left thusly:

[T]hat whole day was like a whole weekend of terror. In fact, he came home, and my son knew how he could be, he was like sick that whole week. He didn't go to work, my ex-husband. . . . And so, he asked my son to go upstairs, he demands that he go upstairs, and so my son was kind of like looking back because it was weird, you know. My ex-husband went outside, he got this hammer, and I didn't know if he was going to repair something or what, but he started closing all the windows *[Intimidation]* . . . so my son [under ten] was going upstairs but looking back all at the same time. . . . He's looking back. And so, you know, I stayed downstairs, see what was gonna happen here, and then my ex came back and, yeah, he didn't really do anything to me. So then I noticed that whole week, he [the batterer] was just lying down, he didn't talk to me. . . . And he came back one night, it was like a Thursday night when this whole thing kind of started happening. My son woke up that Friday, he said, "Mom, I had a dream that, uh, Dad, um, he, Daddy killed you. . . ." And he said, "He killed you three different ways," and I said what, he says, "Yeah, he stabbed you and then he, you know, he shot you." I said, oh my God, even my son's starting to dream like this. . . . And so that Saturday, I wasn't home all day and I came back and he demanded that I go get him some chicken from the colonel. . . . And I said, well, I don't really want to go. You know, I just got home from somewhere. He says, well, if you're gonna have my name, you need to do things for me *[Male Privilege]*, and I said, well, you can have your name back, you know [laugh]. So [laugh]. My son says, "Mom, just do it so you can keep peace." . . . And I said, well, uh huh. I said, no, I'm not gonna do this. . . . So I don't think I did it. And so I guess he went to sleep and I said I'm just gonna stay downstairs, at least I can hear him upstairs if he does anything. But you know, I started sleeping in one of the guest rooms and I'd lock my door 'cuz I just imagined he's gonna come breaking in one of these times. . . . Because he was starting to get that violent. . . . Just even the arguments *[Verbal]*. He would raise his voice and it was like he did not want anybody to disagree with him. . . . So I said he's not the same person. You know, one thing he started **drinking** and he'd be drunk every night by about nine o'clock and I kept asking, I said, "Why do you drink so much?" "Oh, I don't drink that much." But his voice would be all [laugh] slurred speech and everything. I said, well, it seems to be quite a bit as far as I'm concerned. . . . But he didn't want to do anything about it.

[And then, with help from friends, relatives, and a neighbor, she made the move to leave.] So I remember, like the Sunday, that all this happened. . . . I went to church and one of my friends, she says, "You know, you're shaking like a leaf, what's the matter?" And I said, oh, you know, this has been one weekend. And she goes, "Well, you have to do something about that"; so I went home, after church and I was talking to him and he was angry the whole time, he says, I'm going to rent a car, he was still very demanding *[Controlling]*. . . . One of my nieces called for me, he hung up on the phone her *[Isolation]*, and I finally called her back and that's one of the things my friends was telling me, I didn't understand it. . . . But this friend said, "Every time I call for you, he would pretend you weren't home." She goes, "Boy, I didn't know you went through that much . . . it's like he never wanted me to have contact with you" *[Isolation]*. . . . So it was these little things that started adding up and then, like I said, that day, I was gradually trying to sneak my son out 'cuz I could see things were kind of starting to escalate and . . . I said, I don't like this picture. I knew I had to get out of that relationship. In fact, one of my nieces called me, she says, "You don't sound too good" and I said, no, I'm not, kind of really in a bad mood here. She goes, "Well, you gotta do something. I'll come down." She lived out of town. She says, "I'll come visit you." . . . And so I said, well, if anything, I'm gonna have to get my son with me. If we can get out of here, 'cuz he manhandled me in a chair . . . I just assumed he was gonna kill me. After I got loose from that, then I decided to . . . I grabbed my son, and we went running. He finally came running after us and this neighbor saw me trying to hide behind the shrubbery there and he said, "Ma'am, may I help you?" and I said yes. You know, can you give me some shelter for a few minutes and so the neighbor let me come into his house.

Speaking of the worst set of incidents of domestic violence in her relationship, Victim 21 remembered making plans to leave.

That would be the time when he had left for a while, and one of his friends had came over, and I told him he wasn't there, closed the door, and . . . he [his friend who had come over] told him that there's somebody in there, when I didn't. And when he came home that day, he acted like he couldn't find the keys or whatever, but he had me open the door, as soon as I opened it, then he hit *[Physical]* me. That day he hit me everywhere you can think of. . . . 'Cuz then I felt I had to hide that feeling from him, I couldn't let him stay otherwise. It would've been even worse. I waited my time and, well, couple of weeks later, he got arrested for. . . . So I was thinking, okay, he's gonna be in jail for a while. I have a little time. So I would go to court and see what, so I would know what was happening. And what happened was they let him go and I didn't know that they had let him go because they couldn't find an impartial jury. And they let him go and one night at twelve o'clock, he popped up at home. And I'm thinking, man, if I would've, if I would've known he was getting out, I would've left while he was gone. But I didn't know. So for six more weeks, I was stuck there. And for weeks, he didn't go anywhere. He just stayed at home every day. He would, he would want to stay up all night and sleep all day. Watch TV. Yeah he was into **drugs**. At the time, I didn't know. I found out like a couple of months afterwards. [Interviewer: "So, when did you finally decide to leave? What happened that prompted you to leave again?"] Well, I'd already made my decision. I was biding my time to wait. But what made me decide that, that was enough, 'cuz it was getting to be where we, we would have, uh, um, a battery incident everyday. And I noticed that it was taking effect on my son who was . . . [a toddler then]. Even when we weren't **yelling or screaming, or hitting**, or when we were upset with each other, he would just sit there and scream. No reason. And I figured that might, that might be the cause of it. Then, on New Year's

Eve . . . New Year's resolution, mine was, the next time it happened, I was leaving no matter what. And it happened the next day, I left the next day. Went to that shelter. . . . And I haven't seen him since.

Finally, after many cycles of break-ups and getting back together with her batterer, Victim 22 recalls:

Well, finally in October, he beat me up so bad *[Physical]*. So bad. The neighbors had called the police, the landlords, you know, we lived on a mobile home park, who ran the place called the police. They knew he had been abusing me. He beat me up so bad. He chipped my tooth, my head was bleeding 'cuz he took his ha—hand and slammed my head into the floor so bad. And I had bruises up and down my arms, and all over. That's when the police just said you're going to jail. So he went to jail, for I don't even know how long, 'cuz when he got out, he wouldn't even come. He used to call me from jail but as soon as he got out, he went to his ex-girlfriend's family's house again. That was pretty bad. It was just horrible and I got emergency restraining order. But at the same time, I needed him to come back because I needed money *[Dependency]*. . . . And so November, December, my daughter was still infant, and there were days where she would literally starve. And I would have to feed her water. Just, it was just terrible. He didn't care. He didn't care about her. Nothing . . . I ended up having to sell the mobile home and I got nothing out of it. And I had no money. . . . And then I lived in a person's house and on the weekends, I'd clean her house, and then I'd live there for rent free. I had no child support at the time, so. And I had to buy a car. I ended up buying a brand new car and with the car payment, you know, and her day care cost, I was just making it. And I was starting to do good and I, you know, I was starting to get on my feet a little. And then I just saw him, somewhere, I forget, and, you know, he started talking. And then he found out I was doing okay, I think, and he wanted to get back together. Well, I'd do a lot better financially if I was with him. I couldn't afford to do more. So, of course, I went back *[Cycle]*. And this only lasted about a month and that's when I got pregnant with my son. Again. And I stayed with my friend for about two or three days and while he was gone from the apartment I went and took a lot of my stuff. And that's when I had entered the shelter.

WHY DID THE WOMEN STAY WITH THE ABUSERS FOR SO LONG?

Some of the interview victims gave the abusers many second chances because they felt they loved them (for example, Victims 2 or 26) while for others it was financial issues (as with Victim 22 or Victim 3) that kept victims with abusers. For yet others, it was buying time until child custody issues were settled (see Victim 18). Similarly, the survey respondents cited financial concerns (48 percent), their children (44 percent), fear of the batterer (38 percent), and concern for security (32 percent) as reasons why they did not leave sooner. An additional 30 percent indicated that they were concerned about their marital status, with 24 percent indicating that love was a major factor. Pressure from the family (23 percent) and religion (15 percent) were also mentioned.

The narrative of Victim 25 lends an agonizing voice to the long, confusing, and difficult process of trying to end the relationship with the batterer. Remembering the most recent and last incident in their relationship, Victim 25 described the history of drug use; verbal, physical, and emotional abuse; the cycle of violence and co-dependency in her relationship; and finally her decision to file for a restraining order.

The calm before the final storm:

> [T]hat's the freshest one in my memory, that happened about prob-
> ably two years and three months ago. This was the incident that
> pretty much changed my life. That was the last one. . . . Well, every-
> thing was going fantastic. Better than I had ever seen it before and
> I finally thought, wow, he, he's grown up. He has changed and we
> finally have gotten to the point where, you know, where I've always
> wanted us to be. Really happy. He's never treated me any better in
> our whole entire relationship. And I even went back to work. And
> my mom came back . . . she owns the house that we live at but she's
> taking care of her mother. . . . And so I'm watching her house, which
> works out perfect for us. And I had gone back to work. I was working
> . . . and also baby-sitting during the day. And [husband] was helping
> me with the baby-sitting since I was away until seven o'clock in the
> morning with . . . work. And he was baby-sitting my kids and also I
> was watching three other kids. All in my home. . . . And, my mom
> told me that [husband] was staying awake all night while I was gone
> and he'd go to bed when I went to bed at night but he'd get up as
> soon as I left to go to work and then he was out in the garage all night
> long. And I told her, you know, he's depressed and she goes, "No,
> I've seen this before." She goes, "He's on drugs." *[Drugs]* And I go,
> Mom, you don't understand depression. He's depressed. You know,
> I've done drugs. And I, I know what and I know the type of drugs
> that he's doing, um, methamphetamine. And I know all the signs
> *[Co-dependency]*. But I was so convinced, I mean, there was even
> needles. He was shooting up drugs in my garage. There was needles
> all over the garage and I thought that he was using them to inject,
> um, oil into his skates. You know, and to make models. All these in-
> nocent little things I totally denied that he was using drugs. I thought

for sure he was depressed. And 'cuz I've seen him depressed before. I thought he was depressed but maybe it was drugs all along but he gets sweaty looking, he smells different, he looks real haggard and I thought those were signs of depression, that you chemically become different. I thought he was a very sick person *[Co-dependency]*.

The confrontation:

So that night that he was taken out of the home [to the hospital by the police] I had brought it up to him. "If you're using drugs, I need to know." I, I go, "We need to talk." He didn't want to talk, he wanted to go and play music at a friend's house. I go, "You know . . . I've been really reasonable about all of this and I've let you at the bars, all I want you to do is be happy and whatever that takes, that's what I want you to be. And do. But tonight I want to talk to you." And he did not want to talk. And this guy came over to pick him up and I didn't know it but that was the guy that was supplying him with the *drugs*. And he lost control and he grabbed me, in front of my mom, in front of my children *[Physical]*. And after all of these years, that was enough. And plus, after I had told my mom, you don't have to worry about me anymore, he's fine and we're gonna be okay, and he did that again. And my kids are too old for, they were getting too old for me to say, well, your dad doesn't feel well, you know, explain things away. You know, or ignore things. I, I knew that if I kept doing this, my kids were gonna do the same thing or live through the same stuff. And I had to show them that, hey, this is ter—terribly wrong. This is really wrong. And even if, even if I loved [him, her husband], I didn't feel like I'd do it for myself, I had to do it for them. And I was hoping that soon, I would feel this, that I could do it for me. But I did it for them first. And so I took them, I told my mom, "Take the kids, and get out of the house, now. Go to the neighbors." And I was gonna call the police and [he] grabbed the phone and smashed it and broke it. So I walked out of the house, was able to get out, and I called the police from next door. And they came and I told them that he's dangerous. The police came, it was five squad cars. They came up to the house and saw him pacing back and forth in the house; then he took off into the garage. And they said [to the victim], "He was in the garage and he said that you're gonna have to kill me. You're gonna have to do me. I'm not going with you" . . . and he barricades himself in the garage. They tried talking to him for about, I'd say, forty-five minutes and couldn't get him to come out of the garage. He was very agitated and upset. So they came back over next door and talked to me some more and told me to say whatever it took to get him to calm down, that you loved him and that you'd help him through this again and that he needs to go to a hospital and get help. And so, I did that; they said it would be okay to lie. And so I lied and I told him what he needed to hear and he calmed down and they put the cuffs on him and took him away. And he was in that hospital for about a month.

But she still continued to hope:

And I was still working on it. With him. You know, I was willing to work on it, if he got help. And I told him too, "I need to know . . . that I want to hear you say that you were taking drugs." And he would never admit it. And on the day of his release from the hospital, they had to have to release him to somebody, and to be responsible for him, whether he had a place to go. So his counselor called. I go, you know, "I'll take [him] back as long as I know what's on his toxicology report. And, and what has been going on with his counseling." And she goes, "Well, [he] said he wouldn't disclose anything to you of what was on his toxicology report." I go, "Well, then he can't come home." . . . we hung up and then right away, [husband] calls back and says, "They're gonna try to tell you that I was on methamphetamine." I go [with irony in her voice], "It's a conspiracy. You know. It's a conspiracy. Everybody's against you." And I just hung up. I go, "Don't bother me anymore." And so he tried calling me back and I ignored it and then I started to talk to him again *[Cycle of Violence]*. And I go, "You need help." And so he agreed to go to a halfway house, where which he really didn't want to go to but it was the only way actually for him to get out of that hospital.

And things only got worse:

So he went to a halfway house for drug rehabilitation. And I was still kind of sticking with him there, and once he got out of the halfway house, he went straight downhill. And he got completely back into crank *[Drugs]*, he never came home. And he just went got sicker and sicker and sicker. I still wouldn't let him come back. And he got so sick that he became violent again. And he came to the house and he wanted to work things out. He was determined. Well, see, what happened was he would, he would go on a binge. And once he was done doing what he wanted to do, and he was tired, and all of his friends were sick of him crashing at their house, and they wanted him out, and his resources out there were getting thin, he would want to come back and get well. And have me take care of him. I told him, "No way. No way. You're not coming back here." He wanted to see the kids *[Using Children]*. . . . I had to go, my truck was broken down again and so I needed to go get a battery. And so I let him take the kids and he still not being, not of the right mind yet, because this person could not take care of himself, let alone my children. You know, he was very sick. I let him take them to . . . [fast food place]. He took them there and I had walked with my girlfriend to the store to go get a new battery . . . and we came back and she said, "I'm not going to your house." Because he had already threatened to murder her. . . . And so I dropped her off at the store and I came back home, and [abuser] had broken into my house and, of course, rifled through all my things *[Stalking]*. I have condoms at the house, I bought because of him. Because I didn't trust him. And he counted them. You know, to make sure that there was still the same amount as when he left and there was. He went through my things and he broke into the house and he said because the kids had to go to the bathroom. And then right when I got in the house, he started going crazy. He said, "I want to talk to you." And I said, "There's really, there's really nothing to talk about." Because his idea of talking is "I get my way, you just do what I say" *[Controlling]*. And I wouldn't talk to him so he said, "I want to talk to you out in the garage." I said there's no way I'm going out there. Because he wanted to have the privacy to do what he wanted or say what he wanted without being, looking that way in front of the children. And I said there's no way I'm going out there. And we were in the kitchen and he started to grab me *[Physical]*. And I started to twist and turn away from him, and he had me. And I looked out towards the living room and I told [daughter], "Go get help." And he was yelling at her, "No, everything's fine, don't go get help" *[Using Children]*. I go, fuck you . . . I was so crazy and scared by this point. He could practically yell at me, I'd fall down and start having anxiety attacks *[Verbal]* and I got out of control and I just started screaming at her, "Go get help." And [daughter] was listening to her father. She was torn, she didn't know what to do *[Using Children]*. And so she just stood there, and I tried to rip her away from [him] and start running and he, I got to about almost the front door and he dived on top of me *[Physical]*. And knocked me down to the ground. He had one knee in my chest and one knee on the back of his fingers while he strangled me until I lost consciousness. And then I woke up, and he was out on the front porch. He kept saying, "I, you, I, don't you make me hurt you" *[Minimizing]*. "I don't want to hurt you. . . . I just want to talk, I just want to get back together." And I go, "You need to leave. And you need to leave here now." And he reached down into his travel bag. And I told him, "You know, I really don't feel comfortable with you, even doing that in front of, I don't know what you're gonna do." He goes, "You think I'm going for my gun? Well, let me tell you. I don't need a gun. I'd just snap your throat" *[Intimidation]*. I was just "Wow, you know, if you don't leave, I'm calling the police." He goes, "Call me a cab." And so I called him a cab [laugh]. Right. I'll go call you a cab. So I called him a cab and he left.

And finally, the restraining order application:

> [T]hen my girlfriend came back to the house and she said, "You didn't call the police?" 'Cuz I had marks around my neck and I had bruises on my arms and I had a broken blood vessel in my eye. And she goes, "If you don't call the police, I'm never gonna see you again." She was staying at the house with me. She goes, "I have to move out. This is, too dangerous for me." So I called the police and while they were there, they took pictures of my throat and the police officer was really nice to me. . . . Then on [daughter's] birthday, I got my restraining order. It was, I was like a robot. Kind of walking through all of this and it was funny, I was standing in a line for restraining orders and over here was another line for divorce. You know. And, and marriage certificates.

VICTIMS' EXPERIENCES OF CHILDHOOD ABUSE

As they tried to make sense of their experiences, some of the victims also talked about the abuse they had suffered as children in their natal families. Often, this disclosure was unprompted by the interviewer.

Victim 13, reflecting on the abuse she experienced in her natal family:

> Some of us, you know, our abuse goes way back. Mine, you know, I mean I started off in this life . . . well, yeah. I mean, with my past as a child, I mean, I was abused as a young girl and [Interviewer: "By whom?"] . . . by a member of my family . . . *sexual abuse* . . . So I never really knew what was right, what was low, you know . . . and I, I grew up with this attitude that you, you know, men, but [laugh]. Anyway . . . I was really, I was really confused. But there was, there was something, you know, in my spirit that kept me going.

Victim 25, who said:

> I come from, I was raised with, uh, my father was a *child molester*. I thought everybody's father did that to them. And I, through a lot of counseling realized why, every relationship I've ever been in was bad. Men abused me all along. And I realized that finally, I mean this just, this just doesn't happen by accident. I, I kind of realize now why this

is happening, or happened to me. I was trying to make this crazy guy love me. And if I could make, if I could just love that person enough, they would stop hurting me.

For Victim 22, the abuser was her mother; the abuse was physical and emotional. When asked to start talking about her experience with violence, she chose to start with the violence in her childhood.

> I think it's important when I talk about being a battered woman, to go back to my childhood because that's where it really started. I was, I grew up right down in [local city]. We're middle upper class, really nice area, I went to the best schools, and but that didn't really matter when it came down to . . . I had parents. One, my father who was never there. He's a workaholic as I like to call it and . . . He managed [a big corporation] . . . and he liked to shut his family out. He never . . . the only person he cared about was my mother. He didn't care really about any of the kids. I'm his only daughter. I have two half sisters and brothers that aren't his. But he didn't, he never listened to me, he never cared, really. And so then I had my mother who was very abusive towards me. And my brother. She used to, I like to call it torture. I can look back at this now and, you know, my mom used to lock up me in a closet, she used to beat me *[Physical]*, you know, like I was a slave. She used to get out a belt and not on my butt. You know, it would go everywhere but my back. And it hurt. It's, it's a pattern. My grandmother and her brother, I guess, sort of abused her. And her father . . . my grandmother was abused so it's a line. You know, that's followed down. So yeah, she used to do a lot of terrible things. She, she's like a light switch. She could be really great and nice woman one minute, the next minute she'd split. And it's really . . . You know, you never knew, you could walk in the house and she could have a smile on her face but if you say something, she could take it the wrong way and just you'd flip out. . . . She worked on and off. . . . My mother. She was going after money. She married him so he would help her raise her three kids. . . . And I was sort of a surprise and back in . . . when I was born . . . I was always told I was a mistake or I should've been a boy, so that, you know, that really did not please my mother that I was born *[Emotional]*. So, yeah. There, that was terrible. And then they got divorced . . . I was sixteen years old at the time. . . . And she tried to hit me and I stopped it and she kicked me out. So I had to go live with my father. But then when I got to go live with my father, we ended up talking, getting to know each other, I mean, for sixteen years of my life, I didn't know this man.

THE BATTERER'S CHILDHOOD EXPERIENCES AS REPORTED BY THE VICTIM

Sometimes one heard the victims explain the batterer's violent behavior as a product of the abuse he had experienced as a child. For example, Victim 14 said:

> [H]e's seen his father slap his mother around . . . you know, all women are cunts, you know. That's his favorite word. . . . Oh, yeah. That's his favorite word. I'm a slut, I'm a tramp, I've screwed every-body from . . . to . . . *[Verbal, Minimizing]*. So I told him one time, I said okay. I said, you know what, honey? I said next time we're out somewhere and the first man that approaches us, I said I'm gonna ask him if I slept with him before. And if he tells me no, I'm gonna tell him, "Hell, he must be new to town" [laugh]. He said that wasn't funny at all. Oh, yeah [laugh].

Or as Victim 28 recalled:

> He came from that situation. His mo—his real mother abandoned him. And gave him to his father when he was six. Then his father abused his stepmother, severely, *physically* abused him. The dad was on *drugs*, and ended up in jail. And he chose to live with his step-mom, who also has been a little bit *alcoholic*, um, so he came from that background.

IS THAT THE END TO THE BATTERING RELATIONSHIP?

As was noted earlier, none of the victims in the interview sample were living with the batterer at the time of the interview. Some had legally (even if not emotion-ally) terminated their relationship. Others were separated and were living with friends or shelters. Similarly, in the survey sample, two-thirds (66 percent) of the women said that they were either divorced, separated, or have no relationship with the abuser at the time of the survey (which may explain why most of the women did not fear being killed by the batterer).

However, 36 percent indicated that they are married or living with the bat-terer at the time of the interview. Seven percent indicated that the batterer has visitation rights with their children, and 3 percent stated that they were still see-ing the batterer of the most severe incident in a casual/dating relationship. (The percentages add up to more than 100 percent because women gave multiple responses, such as divorced and no relationship.) For many of these women, whether the battering relationship had ended at the time of the interview is questionable. If their past experience is an indicator, the probability of violence in the relationship is reasonably high. For example, for two-thirds (68 percent) of the victims in the survey sample, there had been another recent incident of violence since the most severe incident.

Conclusion

The victims' narratives are vivid illustrations of the power and control dynamics in the micro-system of intimate partner relationships. While the violence experiences are horrific, all of the women had sought assistance from the many programs available in the county that have become their care communities.[2] Some had sought help from the legal system (police, probation department, court system) while others had received help from programs, such as shelters, offered by the local battered women's community programs. A careful review of their narratives makes quite clear what the harms are (from the victim's perspective), the causes of the harm, and the victims' yearning to transform the power and control dynamics in their intimate relationships into one based on equality. Restated in Zehr's victim needs terminology (2002), the narratives make clear victims' need for information about the offense (why it happened and what has happened since), for telling the truth about happened (so that healing can happen), for reclaiming the control they have lost (empowerment), and restitution (either real or symbolic) for the losses as a means of vindication. The case histories also point to potential stakeholders who need to be involved in a restorative justice intervention so that the batterer can be held accountable. In addition to the victim and her batterer, relevant stakeholders might include their children, her family and friends, the batterer's family and friends, and even service providers.

Thus, obtaining case histories of the violence seems essential in outlining the contours of a restorative justice intervention for these victims of intimate partner violence; this is in line with effective restorative justice practice (for examples, see Zehr 2001; Umbreit et al. 2003). Such case histories could also get at the kinds of potential outcomes she hopes for, which might range from wanting to reunite with the batterer on a more equal footing to maintaining a healthy connection that will be helpful for their children, to terminate the relationship, to secure "closure" even though the relationship has been legally terminated, and to ultimately reintegrate into their care communities. Knowledge of the victims' case histories will enable the service providers in helping them make informed choices about the process and outcomes.

The case histories also reveal the types of services the victims have already accessed from the extant service community. However, some victims were able to access many more services than others. Why is this the case? This is the question we next turn to in chapter 5.

Notes

1. The interviews were tape-recorded and transcribed, and are presented verbatim, except for potentially identifying information and the numerous occurrences of "umm," "uh," and "you know" that were edited out because they did not add anything to the victims' violence narratives; rather, they distracted from the readability of the poignant stories. Also, the victims' narratives are presented in smaller font than the rest of the text only in the interest of space and presentation style.

2. As noted in chapter 2, all the women in the interview and survey samples were contacted through the service agencies that they had used.

CHAPTER 5

Help-Seeking Patterns

ARE WOMEN VICTIMS OR SURVIVORS?

Marilyn Fernandez with Kichiro Iwamoto

Introduction: Intensity of Violence and Seeking Interventions

"How can we expect a woman, who has been physically and emotionally battered into submission, to have the courage (personal agency) to seek help?" "Will a victim seek services even when it means that her intimate partner might be convicted and removed from the home?" "Will she have the staying power to engage in the restorative work needed to repair the harm caused by the violence?" "Would she be able to face, even if indirectly, those stakeholders that have caused her harm and need to be held accountable?" These are some of the questions raised in popular discussions about funding and provision of domestic violence services. This chapter seeks to address such questions by examining the impact of women's domestic violence histories on their probability of seeking interventions to deal with their violent relationships.

At least two types of formal institutional services are currently available to victims of intimate partner violence in the county under consideration: law enforcement and battered women's agencies. Studies have shown that many of these services are quite effective, if implemented and used, in improving quality of life and reducing the future incidence of violence in the lives of women who seek help (Campbell, Rose, Kub, and Nedd 1998; Ferraro 1997; Kirkwood 1993; Schechter 1982; Sullivan and Bybee 1999; Sutherland, Bybee, and Sullivan 2002). As has already been noted, restorative justice–principled programs are not offered in the county in which the victims reside; hence the victims were not directly asked about them. Yet, as is being documented in this book, if the women are survivors, there is hope for restorative justice principled programs that might help them repair the harm caused by the violence, transform their relationships, and reintegrate them into their communities. With appropriate assistance and safeguards, women survivors might have the personal agency to engage in some type of restorative encounter with the batterer and their communities.

Unlike the "passive" victim often portrayed in popular media, women who experience violence in their intimate relationships have been known to respond and cope in many ways. Most women do not simply pack up and leave at the first sign of trouble. As we saw in chapter 4, this is often because the violence, when it happens, occurs in a relationship that was, and perhaps still is, a loving relationship. Research (Bachman and Carmody 1994; Browne 1987; Burke et al. 2001; Campbell et al. 1998; Dobash and Dobash 1979, 1992; Ferraro 1997; Kirkwood 1993; Leone, Johnson, and Cohan 2007; Miller 2005; Pagelow 1981; Schechter 1982; Stark 2007; Walker 1984) confirms the variety of coping strategies, often used in stages, that women rely on to deal with the violence in their intimate relationships. The coping strategies might range from reasoning and confronting the violent partner, changing one's own behavior (particularly potential triggers) to accommodate him, seeking help from friends, family, professionals, the police, and the courts. Johnson (2008) has also shown that sometimes the woman's resistance might turn violent.

As was noted in chapter 1, there is disagreement in the literature about the causes of intimate partner violence as well as the factors that lead women to seek interventions and the way they seek interventions. In this chapter, we use two sets of competing theoretical models—(a) dependency model that draws from theories of gendered violence, cycle of violence, and learned helplessness versus (b) the survivor model—to predict intervention-seeking patterns.

Academicians and practitioners have increasingly recognized that domestic violence or the violence against women by their intimate partners poses a serious social and public health risk to women (Roberts 1996; Johnson 2008). To reiterate some of the reported statistics about domestic violence: one in every four women will experience domestic violence in her lifetime (Tjaden and Thoennes 2000); females represent about 84 percent of spousal abuse victims and 86 percent of victims of boyfriends (U.S. Department of Justice 2005). A wide variety of domestic violence interventions are currently available (Johnson 2008; Roberts 1996). Some institutional examples of services designed directly for battered women include hotlines for crisis counseling and information, temporary shelters and safe houses, support groups, assistance with courts and welfare systems, temporary and permanent restraining orders against the abusers, and assistance with material resources of income, housing, food, and health care to empower women to leave the abusive relationship, if they choose. Other types of domestic violence interventions have an indirect impact on battered women. Some examples are direct intervention programs for batterers; special training of judges, police, medical personnel, lawyers, and others who deal with domestic violence cases; and educational and advocacy programs to change cultural beliefs, values, laws, and practices that tolerate, if not promote, violence against women. Their intended outcomes also differentiate among these different programs. Some, like crisis intervention, seek to provide temporary relief from violence. Others, like the permanent restraining orders, couples' counseling, and batterers' services are intended to move couples toward a more permanent resolution of violence.

Factors Associated With Domestic Violence

A review of the scholarly and advocacy literature on domestic violence presented in chapter 1 suggests agreement on some issues but not on others. To recap, Johnson (2008) helps make sense of the disagreements by disaggregating the findings by whether the violence is of the systematic, battering kind (what he refers to as intimate terrorism) or of the situational couple violence kind. We use Johnson's distinction to define the dynamics of battering to include the general, systematic, controlling, and cumulative types of abuse enacted in the service of power and control (and is not random) over the abuser's partner. In contrast, situational couple violence arises from the escalation of specific conflicts but the conflict, even if chronic, is not a central feature of the couple's relationship. Of course, both types of abuse might result in serious injuries and consequences. But situational couple violence typically is not about control and might involve a single incident or might be chronic but without the range of different types of abuse captured in a power and control dynamics.

In this chapter, we conceptualize violence on a continuum that ranges from systematic battering to situational couple violence. We use intensity of abuse as an indicator that captures this range. Intensity of abuse is measured by the number of abuse tactics used by the batterer in the most severe abuse incident experienced by the woman and can range from battering to situational couple violence. Simply put, the more abuse tactics used, the more likely that the violence is of the systematic and battering type. Conversely, the less intense abuse represents Johnson's situational couple violence.

The rich volume of research on the status characteristics and relational dynamics associated with incidents of domestic violence and the consequences of such violence have already been outlined in chapter 1. To set the context for the discussion in this chapter, only a brief review of those findings is presented here.

Scholars like Johnson (2008), Johnson and Ferraro (2000), and Stith et al. (2000) have disaggregated the impact of factors that increase the risk of intimate partner violence by specifying whether the risk markers are predictors of systematic battering or situational couple violence. Since the primary predictor of help-seeking in this chapter might span a spectrum that ranges from situational couple violence to systematic battering, it is useful to review this research here.

Under what conditions have scholars found systematic battering? It is not just the fact of being married, as Stets and Straus had identified in 1989, which is linked to systematic battering. Rather, couples experiencing relationship challenges that might arise from disagreements about child-rearing or status inconsistency (say, between the husbands' education and occupation or between the husband and wife) or who have had childhood exposure to family violence are at higher risk for systematic battering (Gelles 1974; Finkelhor 1983; Johnson and Ferraro 2000; Hotaling and Sugarman 1986; Straus, Gelles, and Steinmetz 1980; Johnson 2008). More recently, scholars have identified skill deficits (Feldman and Ridley 2000; Holtzworth-Munroe et al. 1994, 2003) rather than just personality traits (Wodarski 1987) that are associated with battering but not with situational couple violence. On the other hand, some conditions that have been found to precipitate situational couple violence are when the couple is not married (Macmillan and Gartner 1999), when couples face economic challenges (Johnson and Ferraro 2000; Kantor and Jasinski 1998; Straus, Gelles, and Steinmetz 1980), or when there are arguments over the partner's heavy drinking (Kantor and Jasinski 1998; Kantor and Straus 1989).

Researchers have also documented some of the human and financial consequences of violence and the impact of violence on the relationships between the victim and the batterer. As might be expected, the severity of the consequences varies by the type of violence. While physical injuries and psychological trauma (posttraumatic stress, fear, anxiety, depression, and diminished self-esteem) are substantially more pronounced in systematic battering relationships, these negative consequences do also occur in situational couple violence (Johnson and Ferraro 2000; Stets and Straus 1989). Nonetheless, in battering relationships, they often include injuries or severe injuries requiring emergency room treatment (Johnson 2006; Johnson and Leone 2005; Leone, Johnson, Cohan, and Lloyd 2004; Rosenbaum and O'Leary 1981), high rates of suicide and homicide for women (Holtz and Furniss 1993), and economic challenges such as economic dependency, lack of economic resources, and worker absenteeism (Lloyd and Taluc 1999; New York Victims Services Agency 1987; Riger, Ahrens, and Blickenstaff 2001). In addition, researchers have looked at women who continue to stay in violent relationships and even report relatively happy marriages; it is these women who typically experience situational couple violence. Johnson (2008) suggests this is the case because in situational violence, violence is not a central feature of the relationship and both partners might be violent. Many women do also escape systematic battering relationships, albeit over a long period of time, either by leaving their partners or by changing their partners' behavior (Campbell et al. 1998; Ferraro 1997).

These varied research findings about the causes of domestic violence and the manner in which women deal with violence can be better understood by examining the different methodological and related theoretical assumptions that guide domestic violence research. During the last three decades, two major theories—the "family violence" versus "feminist" theories—have provided contrasting explanations of the causes of violence against women by their partners. As was noted in chapter 1, the family violence group has typically relied on general survey data while the feminist theories on agency samples. Two additional sets of theoretical perspectives—cycle of violence and learned helplessness versus survivor theory—document different processes of violence against women and divergent coping styles.

On a methodological level, Johnson, Stith, Ferraro, and their colleagues have documented that large-scale survey research (such as the National Violence Against Women Survey or the National Family Violence Survey) that samples the general population includes both men and women respondents and captures violence perpetrated in the family. Agency samples, on the other hand, typically include women victims who visit agencies such as shelters, courts, police, and emergency rooms for help with their violence situations. Johnson (2008) uses survey and agency data to demonstrate that survey samples tap more into situational couple violence while agency samples capture battering (or intimate terrorism) and violent resistance by women.

Theoretical proponents of the family violence perspective who argue that wife abuse is part of a pattern of violence that occurs among all family members have drawn on national survey research (Gelles 1980; McNeely and Mann 1990; Shupe, Stacey, and Hazelwood 1987; Straus 1973; Straus, Gelles, and Steinmetz 1980; Steinmetz 1977/1978). In this perspective, family violence is conceptualized as an outcome of the violent environment that occurs and is reinforced at the individual, family, and societal levels in the social system. The problem becomes not wife-beating by violent men, but "violent couples" and "violent people."

This "sexual symmetry" in violence thesis has been criticized by the feminist perspective of gendered violence (Dobash, Dobash, Wilson, and Daly 1992). The feminist theories focus on the unique nature of the violence experienced by women that sets it apart from male experiences of violence. Women are more likely to suffer injury and serious injury in the violent encounter than men, even if women use weapons. When women engage in acts of violence, it is often out of self-defense or retaliation. Women, on average, engage in one-time violent behavior while men engage in more repetitive or battering types of violence (Dobash and Dobash 1979; Dobash et al. 1992; Murphy 1992).

The feminist theory, by attempting to clarify gender differences in the types and severity of violence, offers a perspective different from that of the family violence model. Researchers in this tradition focus on the context in which domestic violence occurs—societal norms of male dominance and male entitlement, and the resulting inequalities in the structure of husband-wife roles. They contend that not recognizing these structured inequalities has unfortunate theoretical and practical implications. Not considering gendered inequalities has the potential for locating the source of the problem in the individual's characteristics and prior history and results in solely blaming the aggressor and the abused woman (Dutton 1992; Dutton and Goodman 2005; Fine 1989; Hart 1993). There is also the danger of considering the women's coping strategies as pathological (Herbert, Silver, and Ellard 1991). For example, police officers, who often do not have an appreciation for women's subordinate status in their families, are generally unsympathetic toward women, particularly when they are ambivalent about pressing criminal charges against their partners (Ferraro 1993). Or as Warshaw (1989) discovered, physicians and nurses "medicalize" the violence and treat the physical injuries as decontextualized events, which often results in the true causes of the injury going unaddressed. In contrast, the gendered violence perspective would focus on the structural constraints that trap women in abusive relationships. It is the perceived sense of entrapment and dependency that sets women's experience with violence apart from the male's experience.

Another critical aspect of domestic violence is the process of violence. There is ample evidence to suggest that violence against women is cumulative (Walker 1979, 1984). Women often do not experience a continual barrage of verbal, psychological, or physical abuse. Rather, they experience abuse that follows periodic patterns. Lenore Walker's theory of the cycle of violence that captures these periodic patterns consists of three specific phases: phase 1, the "tension-building stage," which is followed by phase 2, the "acute battering incident" and phase 3, "kindness and contrite loving behavior." At phase 3, the male's kindness and love can be overwhelming; he poses no threat and therefore she becomes torn. It is during this phase that a woman receives all the rewards that this relationship has to offer. At this point, some women decide to seek help and leave. Yet most women decide to remain in and cope with the relationship and to give him the "second chance" he so desperately begged for. However, Walker (1984) also found that over time, the loving, contrite phase declined while the tension-building phase became more common (see chapter 4 for examples).

Lenore Walker (1979) applies Martin Seligman's theory of learned helplessness to demonstrate further how women cope with the violence. The woman believes that she does not have the power to control her partner's behavior or their relationship; she feels that the man will kill her, kill himself, or retaliate in some form toward children, family members, or close friends; she also believes that nothing can be done to alter her situation. As the woman becomes more helpless in the relationship, she seeks to cope rather than escape because she feels unable to predict her safety when she escapes. As a result of learned helplessness, the woman will choose the response that will have the highest predictability, while avoiding responses that are unpredictable. Thus, the theories of gendered violence, cycle of violence, and learned helplessness, together, suggest that domestic violence against women is cumulative over the life of women. The more severe the violence the more dependent the woman will be on the abuser and the less likely the woman is to seek intervention to address the violence. A study by Fernandez, Iwamoto, and Muscat (1997) found that severity of abuse and dependence on the abuser had a negative impact on women completing the restraining order application process.

In contrast, Gondolf and Fisher's (1988) survivor model has been presented as an alternative to the passive victims portrayed by the feminist theories. Walker's learned helplessness model was viewed as pathologizing battered women and discounting their survivor instinct. Gondolf and Fisher's (1988: 17–18) survivor hypothesis, on the other hand, suggested that "battered women increase their help seeking in the face of increased violence, rather than decrease help seeking as learned helplessness would suggest." As the women realize the increasing danger that accompanies mounting violence, they will logically attempt to protect and ensure their own survival and that of their children.

One way of reconciling the contradictory theoretical expectations is to investigate the relationship between the range of violence and the different types of interventions sought. For example, Gelles (1976) and Grau, Fagan, and Wexler (1985) have argued that, when examining the impact of abuse experiences on seeking interventions, it may be necessary to distinguish the acts of seeking immediate and temporary help from a more permanent break or resolution of the conflict in the relationship. Gelles (1976) found that women who experienced frequent abuse were more likely to seek immediate protection (like calling the police) while those who experienced less frequent abuse (perhaps situational couple violence) were more inclined to seek legal separation or divorce. Similarly, Grau et al. (1985) found that women who had experienced less severe violence were the most likely to obtain restraining orders. We will follow this approach and in Johnson's (2008) typology tradition to examine the range of violence, from situational couple violence to battering type of violence, experienced in the most severe incident.

Analysis Plans

In this analysis, we use data from the domestic violence service utilization survey (see chapter 2 for a description of the survey) to evaluate deductively two sets of competing hypothesis about the degree of overall services sought and the types of services, whether temporary or more legal and permanent. The dependency model based on the first set of theories—the gendered violence, cycle of violence, and learned helplessness—leads to the following predictions:

Hypothesis 1   The more violent the experience (of battering), the less likely the women are to seek services offered by law enforcement and battered women's agencies.

In contrast, the survivor theory would predict that because women are survivors,

Hypothesis 2   The more violent the experience (of battering), the more likely women are to seek as many services as possible.

SOME OPERATIONALIZATION ISSUES

Two types of services are included in the measurement of the dependent variable: law enforcement services (LES) and the services offered by battered women's agencies (BWAs).[1] Even though both these types of services offer immediate protection, they differ in the permanence/temporary nature of the resolution they potentially offer. For example, the outcomes associated with the services offered by law enforcement agencies are often different from those typically associated with the support services offered by battered women's agencies (BWAs). The police are often the first to arrive on the scene of domestic violence, particularly when the abuse is severe. Police involvement also sets in motion a lengthy process of involvement of the batterer and the victim in the court system. The local county policy is that the police must file a report for every domestic violence call they respond to. This report must be reviewed by the district attorney's office who then decides whether to file charges against the batterer. Court involvement could involve the following outcomes: criminal court proceedings and possible conviction of the batterer—if convicted, the batterer would receive a jail or prison sentence, electronic monitoring, probation (formal probation, which is supervised by a probation officer, or court probation, where the court is in charge of probation with no supervision by the probation department), diversion (to receive the court-ordered batterer's treatment program), and/or court-ordered counseling; family court proceedings when there are issues of child custody, visitation rights, child support, restraining orders, divorce, and/or separation. Law enforcement and the court system focus primarily on the batterer who is the main perpetrator of the violence and indirectly on the victim. Thus, while the police provide immediate protection to the woman during an abuse incident, seeking assistance from law enforcement provides women access to services (such as permanent restraining orders, conviction and sentencing of the batterer, batterer's treatment programs, court-mandated counseling) that are intended to move couples toward a more permanent resolution of violence.

The police often refer the victim to a BWA (battered women's agency) for services. However, women can also seek the assistance of the battered women's agency on their own. Examples of services offered by BWAs include access to a hotline, temporary shelters and transitional housing, support groups, and crisis counseling. Many of the services offered through BWAs offer a more temporary resolution to the violence for the victim than the court processes, because BWA services deal only with the victim and do not involve the perpetrator of the violence.

The two types of services are operationalized as follows:

(A) "Number of law enforcement services (LES) used" (more permanent): The variable is a composite of three indicators with the composite score ranging from 0 to 3. The specific indicators are (i) whether police were called (1=yes; 0=no); (ii) whether the respondent was the one to call the police (1=yes; 0=no); and (iii) whether the respondent made specific requests of the police when they arrived (1=yes; 0=no). The mean score on this index was 1.15 and a standard deviation of 0.94.

(B) "Number of BWA services used" (more temporary): The composite indicator score ranges from 0 to 8. The specific indicators are (i) whether respondent contacted a BWA (1=yes; 0=no); and (ii) the number of services offered by battered women's agencies that were used by the respondent. The services include shelters, legal assistance, support groups, individual counseling, hotlines, crisis counseling, and other unspecified services. This indicator ranges from 0 to 8, with a mean of 1.66 and a standard deviation of 1.92.

The primary independent variable was "the severity of violence index." This index was computed from the various types of violence a woman indicated she experienced during the most severe incident. The index includes physical abuse, emotional abuse, sexual abuse, intimidation, and other types of violent behavior outlined in the power and control model (Pence and Paymar 1993). A client was given one point for each of the twelve possible types, producing a score ranging from 0 to 12. The mean on this index was 6.4 and a standard deviation of 3.6; that is, the average victim had experienced at least six of the types of violence on the power and control wheel. It is worth noting here that that the survey data (from the domestic violence service utilization survey) used in this chapter included women who had sought services for their violence experiences. These experiences might cover both situational couple violence and battering. As Johnson (2008: 21–22) had found, his agency sample (women who sought services from agencies) included a considerable number of situational couple violence cases, underscoring the fact that situational couple violence also can have serious injuries associated with it.

In addition, several other indicators that potentially tap into the dependent relationship that the victim might have had with the batterer and might dampen the probability of seeking services are used. While just the presence of children might not necessarily put a woman at risk for violence (as was noted earlier), if violence occurs, a woman might be more likely to seek services to protect the children. The number of children that the respondents had ranged from "no children" to "nine children," with a mean of 2.2 and a standard deviation of 1.5. While status inconsistency between the couple might be a risk marker of violence, a woman's education, and the resources higher education make available, might indicate her ability to disrupt the escalation of violence, and also to seek services in the event violence occurs. On average, the respondent had completed 12.7 years of education (standard deviation = 3.8 and a range of "0 years" to "20 years." Also, age might bring a sense of strength and experience that might motivate older women to seek help. The respondent's age ranged from nineteen years to sixty-four years. The average respondent was thirty-seven years of age (standard deviation = 9.3).

IS RECALL AN ISSUE?

To reiterate, these hypotheses seek to understand why some abused women seek services from law enforcement and battered women's agencies while others do not, after experiencing their most severe abusive incident (as of the interview date). One might ask whether the time elapsed between the time of the severe incident and interview date might cloud respondents' memory about services used. In order to isolate the potential contamination of recall, time elapsed since the incidence of violence will be controlled for,[2] as we examine the various responses of battered women to the available legal and community agencies.

A NOTE ABOUT STATISTICAL SIGNIFICANCE

In the regression analyses that follow, we use a combination of traditional criteria of statistical significance and substantive significance (McCloskey 1985, 1998). Because the 120 women in the survey were not randomly selected, measures of statistical significance alone cannot be reliably used. Calculation of statistical significance is extremely sensitive to sample size, both large and small. With large samples, what is statistically significant might not necessarily be substantively significant (measured by size of the coefficient). Besides, all that statistical significance tells us is the probability of generalizing from a random sample to the population from which the sample was drawn. With small sample sizes, as in this case, most coefficients are not likely to be statistically significant. Hence, the size of the coefficients (an indicator of substantive significance), along with tests of statistical significance, are highlighted and used below to identify substantial findings.

Results

In the initial analyses (tables 5.1–5.4), linear regression analyses of total services used and then of the number of LES and BWA services used were run. The primary independent variable was the severity of violence index. Indicators of dependency—namely, the number of children, age of the woman, and her years of education—were used as additional predictors. Time elapsed since the most severe incident (tables 5.1–5.3) and an interaction term of time and intensity of violence (table 5.4) were also included to determine the need for separating the sample into the "abated violence" and "fragile" group.[3]

WOMEN ARE MORE LIKELY TO BE SURVIVORS THAN DEPENDENT VICTIMS

Results in table 5.1 indicate that, as predicted by the survivor hypothesis, the more intense the violence experienced (as in battering), the more services used by the women (Beta=.256; p=.01). However, the services women reach for when the violence is intense are more likely to be BWA services (Beta=.361; p=.00; table 5.3) and not LES (not significant in table 5.2), an indication that intensity of violence lead women to seek immediate and temporary help but not the more permanent types of services. Also, the more children the women have, the less likely they are to seek the temporary BWA services (Beta=-.143; p=.23; table 5.3). In contrast, it is older women who are more likely to seek the more permanent LES services (Beta=.218; p=.07; table 5.2).

What difference did time and recall make? The more time that had elapsed between the severe incident and interview date (abated violence), the less likely they were to report having used services (Beta=-.224; p=.05; table 5.1). This finding might suggest that recall/memory is an issue: the more time that separates the severe incident and interview date, the fewer services women report using or at least remember using—or the fragile group is more likely to report using more services. However, that is not the whole story because the effect of

Table 5.1. Linear Regression of Total Services Used on Index of Violence Experienced, Time Elapsed Since Severe Incident, and Socio-Demographic Characteristics of Respondents (n=93)

Indicators	Beta (Unstandardized Coefficient)	P-Value
Violence Index	.256 (.152)	.01
Time elapsed since most severe incident	−.224 (−.069)	.05
Number of Children	−.149 (−.226)	.21
Age	.097 (.023)	.395
Years of education	−.061 (−.033)	.565
R^2 (Adjusted R^2)	.154 (.106)	.01
Constant	2.034	.078

Table 5.2. Linear Regression of LES Services Used on Index of Violence Experienced, Time Elapsed Since Severe Incident, and Socio-Demographic Characteristics of Respondents (n=93)

Indicators	Beta (Unstandardized Coefficient)	P-Value
Violence Index	−.094 (−.025)	.363
Time elapsed since most severe incident	−.348 (−.048)	.01
Number of Children	.027 (.018)	.82
Age	.218 (.023)	.07
Years of education	−.029 (−.007)	.79
R^2 (Adjusted R^2)	.112 (.062)	.06
Constant	.775	.14

Table 5.3. Linear Regression of BWA Services Used on Index of Violence Experienced, Time Elapsed Since Severe Incident, and Socio-Demographic Characteristics of Respondents (n=94)

Indicators	Beta (Unstandardized Coefficient)	P-Value
Violence Index	.361 (.181)	.00
Time elapsed since most severe incident	−.085 (−.022)	.44
Number of Children	−.143 (−.166)	.23
Age	−.017 (−.003)	.88
Years of education	−.056 (−.025)	.60
R^2 (Adjusted R^2)	.167 (.121)	.01
Constant	1.198	.215

Table 5.4. Linear Regression of Total Services Used on Index of Violence Experienced, Time Elapsed Since Last Severe Incident, and Interaction Effect Between Violence Index and Time (n=99)

Indicators	Beta (Unstandardized Coefficient)	P-Value
Violence Index	.391 (.238)	.01
Time Elapsed	.078 (.021)	NA
Violence Index * Time	−0.232	.18
R²	0.114	.01
Constant	1.346	.02

time is not consistent for LES and BWA services. Time elapsed makes a difference only in the case of LES services (Beta=-.348, p=.01; table 5.2) but not for BWA services (Beta not significant). If recall/memory is an issue, the negative effect should be similar for both types of services. Because of this differential effect and also because the combined effect of time elapsed and intensity of violence (Beta=-.232; p=.18; table 5.4) is significant (suggesting that the more intense the violence and the more time that has passed by the time of the interview, the fewer services used), the sample will be disaggregated into the "abated" and "fragile" groups for the remainder of the analyses.

"ABATED" VERSUS "MORE FRAGILE" GROUPS

Again, the more intense the violence (battering violence), the more total services used, indicating a survivor effect (Beta=.394, p=.01; table 5.5), whether it is the "more fragile" (Beta=.394; table 5.5) or "abated" group (Beta=.189, p=.24; table 5.6). But, as is evident from the size of the coefficients, the survivor effect (compare Beta coefficients) of seeking services is double for the "fragile" group when compared to the "abated violence" group. On the hand, the number of children has a depressing effect on seeking services only for the "fragile" group (Beta=-226; p=.15).

In short, women are likely to seek services, particularly when they are battered, as the survivor model would predict. Perhaps the situational couple type of violence (as measured by lower score on the violence index) was not considered by the women to be severe enough to lead them to seek services. More children, on the contrary, might indicate a traditional sex role attitude, that might leave the "fragile" woman economically and emotionally dependent on the abuser and result in fewer services used.

Table 5.5. Linear Regression of Total Services Used on Index of Violence Experienced, Socio-Demographic Characteristics of Respondents; More Fragile Group (Less Than Three Years Elapsed Since Severe Violence Incident; n=48)

Indicators	Beta (Unstandardized Coefficient)	P-Value
Violence Index	**.394 (.248)**	**.01**
Number of Children	**−.226 (−.394)**	**.15**
Age	.158 (.038)	.33
Years of education	.018 (.01)	.90
R^2 (Adjusted R^2)	.219 (.148)	.03
Constant	0.70	.64

Table 5.6. Linear Regression of Total Services Used on Index of Violence Experienced, Socio-Demographic Characteristics of Respondents; Abated Violence (Three Or More Years Elapsed Since Severe Violence Incident; n=44)

Indicators	Beta (Unstandardized Coefficient)	P-Value
Violence Index	**.189 (.10)**	**.24**
Number of Children	−.097 (−.132)	.61
Age	−.10 (−.023)	.55
Years of education	−.14 (−.072)	.43
R^2 (Adjusted R^2)	.065 (−.029)	.60
Constant	3.549	.07

DID THE TYPE OF SERVICES USED MAKE A DIFFERENCE?

When the impact of violence on services used is disaggregated by whether the services sought were of the LES or BWA type, some interesting differences become evident. For example, when the focus is on LES services, women are equally likely to turn (or not) to law enforcement, irrespective of whether their violence is abated or fragile; the Beta coefficients for the effect of violence index on LES services used are not significant for either group (tables 5.7 and 5.8). On the other hand, the more intense the violence (battering), the more women are likely to turn to BWA services (table 5.9 and 5.10). The effects are stronger for the "fragile" group (Beta=.482; p=.001; table 5.9) than for the "abated" group (Beta=.243; p=.13; table 5.10).

Table 5.7.   Linear Regression of LES Services Used on Index of Violence Experienced, Socio-Demographic Characteristics of Respondents; Fragile Group (Less Than Three Years Elapsed Since Severe Violence Incident; n=48)

Indicators	Beta (Unstandardized Coefficient)	P-Value
Violence Index	−.035 (−.010)	.81
Number of Children	−.031 (−.025)	.85
Age	**.408 (.045)**	**.02**
Years of education	−.012 (−.003)	.94
R^2 (Adjusted R^2)	.153 (.076)	.11
Constant	−.032	.97

Table 5.8.   Linear Regression of LES Services Used on Index of Violence Experienced, Socio-Demographic Characteristics of Respondents; Abated Violence (Three Or More Years Elapsed Since Severe Violence Incident; n=44)

Indicators	Beta (Unstandardized Coefficient)	P-Value
Violence Index	−.052 (−.011)	.75
Number of Children	−.047 (−.026)	.80
Age	**−.163 (−.015)**	**.33**
Years of education	**−.185 (−.038)**	**.30**
R^2 (Adjusted R^2)	.063 (−.031)	.62
Constant	2.063	.01

Table 5.9.   Linear Regression of BWA Services Used on Index of Violence Experienced, Socio-Demographic Characteristics of Respondents; More Fragile Group (Less Than Three Years Elapsed Since Severe Violence Incident; n=48)

Indicators	Beta (Unstandardized Coefficient)	P-Value
Violence Index	**.482 (.258)**	**.001**
Number of Children	**−.249 (−.369)**	**.095**
Age	−.034 (−.007)	.82
Years of education	.028 (.013)	.84
R^2 (Adjusted R^2)	.311 (.248)	.01
Constant	.732	.54

Table 5.10. Linear Regression of BWA Services Used on Index of Violence Experienced, Socio-Demographic Characteristics of Respondents; Abated Violence (Three Or More Years Elapsed Since Severe Violence Incident; n=45)

Indicators	Beta (Unstandardized Coefficient)	P-Value
Violence Index	**.243 (.114)**	**.13**
Number of Children	−.017 (−.017)	.93
Age	−.056 (−.011)	.73
Years of education	−.067 (−.030)	.71
R^2 (Adjusted R^2)	.067 (−.024)	.57
Constant	1.362	.41

Further, age of the woman has conflicting effects in the "fragile" and "abated" groups. The positive effect of age on LES service use is statistically significant only for the "fragile" group (Beta=.408; p=.02; table 5.7); but this is countered by its negative effect in the "abated violence" group (Beta=-.163; p=.33; table 5.8). When their severe abuse incident was recent ("fragile"), older women were more likely to report using LES than younger women. On the other hand, the younger the woman, the more likely she was to use LES if her violence was abated (table 5.8). Also, education has a negative effect on LES service use for the abated violence group. The negative effect of children on services used is found only with the "fragile" group and their use of BWA services (Beta=-249; p=.095; table 5.9).

Conclusion

The evidence presented in this chapter indicates that if services are available and accessible, women will seek them, particularly when they face intense systematic battering violence. These findings lend support to the survivor model of help-seeking behavior. Unlike what the dependency perspective suggests, women are survivors and will seek services, particularly the nonlegal, community-oriented services that BWAs provide, even when they are severely battered. On the other hand, if there are injuries, women might not have a choice but also use law enforcement services, irrespective of how intense the violence is. For example, a number of states require medical personnel to report any signs of domestic abuse of patients they are treating.

Yet the ties that might bind women to the batterer through their children might restrict their willingness and ability to seek services. Also, the fact that children have a dampening effect on a woman's ability or desire to seek BWA services might speak more to the women's perceptions of how child-friendly these services are. That these findings are not fully consistent across the time dimension and types of services also lend some credence to the earlier contention that the effects are not completely clouded by memory or recall.

Finally, it is a hopeful signal that if restorative justice principled services, with their emphasis on holding the batterer accountable, repairing harms, and reintegration into the community, are available, the survivors might use them. Of course, intimate partner violence is too serious a crime to not have the stick of the legal system behind any intervention. Consequently, restorative justice programs will have to be a supplement to the existing legal and community programs. Including all the relevant stakeholders, such as children, the survivor, the batterer, their family, and friends, in a restorative framework might also be a way of overcoming the dampening effects of relationships on service seeking that was identified above.

We next turn to how satisfied these women are with the extant services they have used. In chapter 6, we will explore their satisfaction with the services they have used and their reasons for their satisfaction or dissatisfaction with the expectation that their opinions would provide clues about how to improve the services available to victims of domestic violence and also to their openness to restorative programs in the domestic violence context.

Notes

1. See chapter 6 for concrete examples of services the survivors have used.

2. The initial analyses will use an interval measure of years elapsed since the most severe incidence of violence. A subsequent set of analyses disaggregates the sample into two groups (following Cherlin et al., 2004): "abated unions" (where domestic violence had occurred three or more years prior to the interview) and "more fragile" group that combines (due to small sample size) Cherlin's "intermediate" group (violence occurred between one and two years prior to the interview) and "fragile" group (less than one year with some in a shelter at the time of the interview and others outside shelters).

3. The coefficients that are statistically and substantively (by size of coefficients) significant are highlighted in tables 5.1–5.10.

CHAPTER 6

How Well Do Extant Domestic Violence Services Serve Survivors?

SOME RESTORATIVE JUSTICE IMPLICATIONS

Marilyn Fernandez with Kichiro Iwamoto

Now that we have established (in chapters 4 and 5) that women victims of intimate partner violence are "survivors" and do use domestic violence services when they are available, the next step is to examine how well the existing formal service system meets victim needs. We will explore this question with data reported in the Service Utilization Survey (see appendix 2 for the survey instrument). This survey was conducted in order to gauge satisfaction with extant domestic violence services in the county from the perspective of victims who had used the services. Questions were asked about all the services available in the county; if the women had accessed the services, their views on the helpfulness of the services were ascertained. At the time of the study (or for that matter at the time of publication of this book), there were no restorative justice programs in the county for domestic violence victims. But comments will be made about elements of the current system that might be restorative (even if they are not termed as such) either in intent and/or in the survivors' perception. At the very least, the survivors' responses also provide clues to the need for supplemental restorative-type programs that set the dyadic survivor-batterer relationship in the context of the relevant stakeholders and their communities of care (see Van Ness and Strong 2006; Umbreit et al. 2003; Zehr 2002, 2005).

Brief Theoretical Notes

In this chapter, we will broaden our focus, beyond the victim and her batterer, and examine the survivor's relationship with the local service system. The ecological perspective (Bronfenbrenner 1979), with its nested systems approach and the role of human agency in shaping the interactions between and among the systems, will provide one theoretical context for this analysis. In the ecological analytical mode, the micro-system of the survivor and her batterer—that is, the focus of the power and control model[1]—is nested within their community. The domestic violence service system is part of this local community. While the legal and community domestic violence service systems are designed to ultimately impact, and perhaps transform, the violent relationships in the micro-system (that is, the batterer and the survivor), the more direct and immediate focus of these services are not the dyadic relationship between the survivor and her batterer. Rather, they are designed to deal with the survivor and her batterer as separate entities. The legal system is set up to litigate, adjudicate, and punish the violent crime that may have been perpetrated by the batterer. On the other hand, community agencies such as the battered women's agencies address the needs of the victim and her children. The ecological perspective also theorizes that both the batterer and the survivor have the agency to influence the service delivery system. In the process of analyzing the services the survivor used, we will tease out the survivor's relationship with the service systems.

Restorative justice theory provides the second frame for understanding the survivors' opinions of the services they have used. Unlike most of the extant legal and community services, restorative programs focus on the dyad, their communities of care, and other relevant stakeholders. Restorative justice practice is guided by concepts that include the following: identifying the harms, causes of the harms, and victims' needs; repairing the harms and healing the victims' wounds; involving those affected by the offense in the restorative process; encouraging offenders to take responsibility; and reintegrating the victim and batterer into their communities (see, for example, Van Ness and Strong 2006; Umbreit et al. 2003; Zehr 2001, 2002, 2005). We will indicate elements of the extant service system that might be restorative in spirit and might become important partners in restorative justice interventions.

A Typical Interface Between a Victim and the Extant Service Delivery System

The typical interface between a victim and the service delivery system had been outlined in previous chapters. However, a recap is helpful to set the context for this chapter. The police are often the first to arrive on the scene of domestic violence, particularly when the abuse is severe. Police involvement also sets in motion a lengthy process of involvement of the batterer and the victim in the court system. The local county policy is that a report must be filed by the police for every domestic violence call they respond to (Santa Clara County Probation

Department, n.d.). This report must be reviewed by the district attorney's office who then decides whether to file charges against the batterer. Court involvement could involve any of the following outcomes—criminal court proceedings and possible conviction of the batterer; if convicted, the batterer would receive any of the following sentences: a jail or prison sentence, or electronic monitoring, probation (formal probation, which is supervised by a probation officer, or court probation, where the court is in charge of probation with no supervision by the probation department), diversion (to attend the court ordered batterer's treatment program), and/or court-ordered counseling. When there are issues of child custody, visitation rights, child support, restraining orders, divorce, and/or separation, family court proceedings might be involved.

On balance, law enforcement and the criminal court system focus primarily on the batterer who is the main perpetrator of the violence and only indirectly on the victim. No doubt, the police offer immediate protection to the woman during their visit to an abuse incident. In addition, seeking assistance from law enforcement opens up access for the women to services (such as permanent restraining orders, conviction and sentencing of the batterer, batterer's treatment programs, court-mandated counseling) that are intended to move couples toward a more permanent, legal resolution of violence. The police often refer the victim to a battered women's agency (BWA) for services. But women can also seek assistance from the battered women's agency on their own. Examples of services offered by BWAs to the victims include access to a hotline, temporary shelters, transitional housing, support groups, and crisis counseling. Many of the services offered through BWAs offer a more temporary resolution to the violence for the victim than the court processes, because BWA services deal only with the victim and do not involve the perpetrator of the violence.

Programs founded on restorative justice principles, in contrast, have a dual focus on the batterer and the victim, as well as the relevant stakeholders. They also seek a more permanent resolution of the harm and reintegration of the victim and batterer into their communities of care (Van Ness and Strong 2006; Umbreit et al. 2003; Zehr 2002, 2005).

In the county under consideration, there were eleven formal services, legal and community agency–based, available to victims of domestic violence. Using data from the survey sample, we will examine how many services were used by the victims, how they felt about the responsiveness of service providers, and the extent to which these services met their needs. We will also attempt to tease out what possible next steps the women wish to take to resolve their experiences with violence.

In order to anchor the women's experiences with the services in common frames, they were asked about services used for two types of incidents: the most

Table 6.1.   Types of Abuse Experienced During the Incidents When the Police Were Called

	Most Severe Incident (n=61)	Recent Incident (n=39)
Physical abuse	93.4	66.7%
Emotional abuse	88.5	28.2
Intimidation	78.7	23.1
Psychological abuse	73.8	12.8
Minimizing, denying, blaming	70.5	0.0
Coercion and threats	63.3	20.5
Male privilege	59.3	0.0
Isolation	53.3	5.1
Economic abuse	39.3	0.0
Using children	31.1	15.4
Sexual abuse	29.5	0.0
Other	13.6	33.3

severe incident of violence and the most recent (relative to the date of the survey). A distinction was also made between whether or not the police were called for each of the two types of incidents. That the two types of incidents were qualitatively different is evident in table 6.1 above. The most severe incident in which the police were called was characterized by the use of multiple types of abuse reflecting the power and control dynamics in the abuse relationship. In contrast, the survey women characterized their most recent violent incident as one in which physical abuse was the primary type of violence they experienced. Yet, whether it was the most severe or more recent incident, physical abuse was the most common type of abuse (93 percent in the most severe incident and 67 percent in the most recent violent incident). But at least 50 percent of the women in the most severe incident reported other types of abuse, such as emotional abuse, intimidation, psychological abuse, minimizing/denying/ blaming, coercion and threats, male privilege, and isolation. In contrast, in the recent incident, in addition to physical abuse, under a third of the women had experienced emotional abuse (28.2 percent), intimidation (23.1 percent), and coercion/threat (20.5 percent).

Even when the police were not called, the pattern of abuse was similar. Emotional abuse, physical abuse, and intimidation occurred over 80 percent of the time in the most severe incident, with physical abuse being the only predominant type of abuse (66.7 percent) in the most recent violent incident. Thus, the violence in the most severe incident reflects the systematic battering type (or Johnson's "coercive control," 2008) and will be the focus in the rest of this chapter.

Table 6.2.   Types of Abuse in Incidents When the Police Were Not Called

	Most Severe Incident (n=46)	Recent Incident (n=6)
Emotional abuse	95.7	0.0%
Physical abuse	89.1	66.7
Intimidation	82.6	0.0
Minimizing, denying, blaming	76.1	0.0
Psychological abuse	73.9	0.0
Male privilege	69.6	16.7
Coercion and threats	63.0	0.0
Isolation	60.9	0.0
Economic abuse	39.1	16.7
Sexual abuse	39.1	0.0
Using children	37.0	0.0
Other	13.0	57.1

Types of Formal Community Services Used

As was discussed earlier, two types of formal community services are available to victims of domestic violence in the county in which the survivors live; services offered through law enforcement and the legal system and those offered by the battered women's agencies. Three broad questions are posed in this chapter: (1) Which services did the victims use? (2) What happened when they encountered a service? (3) How satisfied were they with the services? We will first examine details of the services used. We will then turn to the victims' assessments of the assistance they received and point out areas that have restorative implications.

Over 50 percent of all the women used at least eight of the available eleven community services when they experienced their most severe abuse. As for the law enforcement services, a little over half of the women (sixty-seven women, or 56.8 percent of the 118 surveyed; see table 6.3) reported that the police were called when their most severe incident occurred. About half of these sixty-seven women (55.2 percent, or thirty-seven women) used the criminal court system and a little over a tenth (11.9 percent, or eight women) used the family court system. One of the possible sentences the court can impose on a convicted batterer is probation. Of the thirty-seven women whose batterers were involved in the criminal court system, almost all (87.5 percent) indicated that the batterer was placed on probation.

As was noted before, women are often referred by the police to a battered women's agency (BWA) for services. On the other hand, women can also seek

Table 6.3.   Use of Domestic Violence Services

Type of Service	Most Severe (%) (n)
Legal and Law Enforcement:	
Police	56.8 (118)
Criminal court	55.2 (67)
Family court	11.9 (67)
Probation	87.5 (37)
Community Agencies (BWA):	47.6 (63)
Legal assistance	51.1 (30)
Support group	57.4 (30)
Individual counseling	59.6 (30)
Hotline	59.6 (30)
Crisis counseling	55.3 (30)
Shelter	38.3 (30)
Other	28.9 (30)

the assistance of the battered women's agency on their own. Almost half of the women (47.6 percent) contacted a community agency (battered women's agency) when they (sixty-three women) experienced their most severe incident. Examples of services offered by the BWA and used by more than half (59.6–51.1 percent) of the women include access to a hotline service, individual counseling, support groups, crisis counseling, and legal assistance services. About a third (38.3 percent) used temporary shelters and transitional housing. Once again, many of the services offered through BWAs offer a more temporary, nonlegal resolution to the violence for the victim than the court processes, because BWA services deal only with the victim and do not involve the perpetrator of the violence. However, because of their relationship with the victim, BWA staff members are very likely to have knowledgeable access to the harms resulting from the violence experienced by the victims, the causes of the harms, and to victim needs. Consequently, BWAs, which become part of the victims' community of care, could become critical partners in restorative justice interventions; among other types of assistance, they can help identify victim needs and assist survivors in making informed choices.

Survivors Encounter the Service System

In order to understand the services provided in the county from the perspective of the survivors, we will examine each of the services as they were encountered by the women after their most severe experience of abuse. In the interest of not letting the storylines about survivors' encounter with services be too cluttered by the percentages and numbers, we present the numbers sparingly in the text presented below.[2] Also, while the survey data cover two scenarios, services used after the most severe incident and after the most recent incident, the detailed analysis below will use only one reference point: the services used in response to the most severe incident.

ENCOUNTERS WITH THE POLICE

Typically, it was the abused woman (rather than a family member, friend, or neighbor) who called the police. It is also worth noting that the most severe abuse generally had occurred in the survivor's home. In a few cases, neighbors were helpful in calling the police. When the survivors were asked what the police did when they arrived at the scene of violence, their most common response was that the police removed the abuser from the premises, either by arresting him or taking him away to cool off. Sometimes, the batterer had left the scene before the police arrived. Thus, the call to the police often resulted in the batterer being, at least, temporarily removed from the premises, either voluntarily or involuntarily. Yet there were a few instances when the batterer was not removed from the site of the violence by the police; the police either questioned and released the batterer or threatened him with arrest; sometimes they did nothing.

The police also questioned the woman in many cases. However, it was only rarely that the women made any specific requests of the police. When they did make a request, it was usually to keep the batterer away from them, or to find the batterer. Only one woman specifically asked that a police report be taken down. Another asked the police not to hurt the abuser.

On balance, the survivors' encounters with the police seem to provide a temporary break in the violence. But, as we will see below, the call to the police also set in motion the criminal and family court involvement.

EXPERIENCES WITH THE CRIMINAL COURT

Thirty-seven survivors (55 percent of the sixty-seven who had called the police) who had to deal with the criminal court in connection with their most severe incident described their court experiences. Did these women understand the criminal court process? Approximately half of the women indicated that they had some understanding of the court process. About half of the most severely abused women also said that they knew that the accused abuser could be prosecuted without their agreement. Many also did know what would happen to the batterer; over a third of the women thought that the batterer would be at least arrested, including given some jail time. Victims testifying in court were not very common; only about a fifth testified in the court proceedings. Thus, more than half of the women whose cases were involved in the criminal courts were aware of the court process. But the other half (40 percent) did not understand this process.

Where were the batterers while the criminal cases were proceeding? As per the survivors, nearly half the batterers waited in jail during the court proceedings (47 percent). In a third of the cases, the batterer was released on bail or released on his own recognizance. But ultimately two-thirds of the batterers were convicted and received either jail or prison sentences, or were mandated to complete an alternative community program. Thus, the criminal court process does appear to deal with and convict the batterer. However, it seemed not to do much to protect the victims. For example, only in a third of the severe incidents were batterers given a "no-contact" order to protect the victim (but not the children or other relatives). The remaining two-thirds of the abused women were not given the "no-contact" protection.

PROBATION FOR THE BATTERER

One of the possible sentences the court can impose on a convicted batterer is probation. Out of the thirty-seven survivors whose batterers were involved in the criminal court system, there were twenty-four who were placed on probation. Below the women describe their experiences with the batterer's probation sentences.

Most batterers were given formal probation, which involves being assigned a probation officer. But only about half of the women had contact with their batterers' probation officers; the other half did not know whether, and the specifics of how, the probation sentence was carried out. Nonetheless, a majority reported that the convicted batterer was still attending the program, with another third indicating that they knew that the batterer had completed the probation program.

FAMILY COURT SERVICES

Another service available to victims of domestic violence is the family court. All the women were asked whether they had used the family court in connection with their most severe incident. Of the sixty-seven women who responded, only eight (11.9 percent; see table 6.3) had used the family court in connection with their most severe incident. But, almost always, it was the survivor who typically initiated the family court process (seven out of the eight).

The key issues involved in the family court proceedings related to custody of the children, visitation rights, and child support. These are the most common concerns that the family court is used to resolve. All, except one, also sought restraining orders against the batterer in family court. Unlike in criminal court, six, or two-thirds of the eight women, were called to testify in the family court proceedings. The proceedings most commonly resulted in (in order of frequency) granting restraining orders, child custody for the woman (victim), visitation rights for the batterer, domestic violence counseling orders, and child support arrangements. Child custody was typically given to the victim. Only in one case was custody of the children given to both the parents. In addition, the family court issued a "no-contact" order, primarily to protect the victims; only in one case were the children protected by the "no-contact" order. In another case, both the victim and her children were intended to be protected.

COURT-ORDERED BATTERER'S INTERVENTION PROGRAM

One possible outcome of the court proceedings in domestic violence cases is to have the batterer ordered to attend a year long batterer's intervention program. The purpose of this program is to teach the batterer how to stop his violent behavior. At the time of the study, some batterers entered the intervention program through diversion (discontinued in 1996, as noted in chapter 2); others were directly ordered by the courts to attend this program.

Less than 40 percent of the batterers received orders to attend a batterer's intervention program. In cases when the batterer was ordered to enroll in an intervention program, it was the criminal court that was the most likely to have ordered the batterer into an intervention program that was certified by the county. At times, enrollment in alcohol/drug programs was also ordered for some of the batterers.

BATTERED WOMEN'S AGENCY SERVICES

All respondents were asked about their experiences with battered women's agencies when they experienced their most severe incident of abuse. They were almost evenly divided between those who had contacted a battered women's agency and those who had not, when their most severe incident occurred. Forty-eight percent had contacted a BWA in the severe incident. This is consonant with the evidence in chapter 5 that the more severe the violence, the more likely the victims were to use shelter services. On the other hand, when the police are involved, the legal system often enters the picture, irrespective of the severity of the violence.

Those who contacted BWAs had done so, on average, about five times for the most severe incident, and stayed in a shelter, on average, one or two times. While at the shelter, they used individual counseling programs, support groups, legal assistance, and crisis counseling. Over 90 percent said that the services they needed were available in their primary language. At least two-thirds of the women with children, who had sought shelter services, were offered children's services. Counseling and entertainment were the most common types of children's services offered.

Women's Opinions of the Utilized Services: How Satisfied Were They?

After the survivors talked about the domestic violence services they had used, they were asked about their assessment of their experiences with different services. Once again, we will focus on the women who described their feelings about the services they used in connection with their most severe violent experience, as this is typically when the legal and community services are most urgently needed. The survivors' assessment of services may influence not only their openness to these and other new services like restorative justice, if the need might arise again in the future, but also whether they positively speak about and recommend these services to other women.

Assessment of Legal Services: Mixed Portrait

POLARIZED EXPERIENCES WITH POLICE SERVICES

The primary foci of questions assessing the services provided by the police was whether there was police follow-up and how the police dealt with the women's children when they were called after the most severe incident of violence. According to the women surveyed, police follow-up investigations were rare; only a third of the women recalled any police follow-up to their initial visit. As for the children, in many cases, at least one child was present when the police were called. However, very few women recall that the police spoke with the children or took the children into another room while the survivor or batterer was being questioned. In fact, what emerged was a polarized portrait of police dealings with children. In some women's experience, the police went beyond their strict law enforcement roles and were sensitive in their handling of the children involved. They exhibited a special way of talking to children or appearing knowledgeable about domestic violence. In contrast, the women attributed police insensitivity to rude behavior or lack of knowledge about domestic violence. Perhaps, if police are trained to go beyond their traditional portfolios of just enforcing the laws, they might become critical partners by providing critical legal backing in the restorative justice process.

FAVORABLE CRIMINAL AND FAMILY COURT EXPERIENCES

In contrast to their assessment of the police encounters, a majority of the women evaluated their criminal court experiences as either satisfactory or positive. From the earlier sections where the survivors talked about their experiences with the court system, it was clear that many of these survivors seemed quite aware of the workings of the court system, particularly the proceedings as they applied to the batterers. They were quite satisfied with the way events transpired with the batterer while waiting for the court action. The positive assessments were primarily because the judge listened, was sensitive to, and addressed the women's particular concerns about her safety and that of her children. However, for the minority of victims who found the judge to be insensitive, this was because the judge did not acknowledge their needs while dealing with the batterer. According to this small group of survivors, the courts did not do much to protect the victims and address their needs.

The overall impression of the family court was similarly positive. Most understood the proceedings to some degree. They also found the judge to be sensitive toward them, particularly when their issues were addressed. But some of the women felt otherwise, that the judge was insensitive to addressing their needs. Nonetheless, the women in the most severe incidents were at least satisfied with their family court experience. Like the police, the court system also can become critical partners in identifying harms, victim needs, and the relevant stakeholders for a restorative justice type intervention. Courts can also provide the much needed legal standing for a restorative process in a domestic violence context; such legal support is critical particularly when restraining and other no-contact orders are in play.

DIVERGENT OPINIONS OF PROBATION SERVICES AND INTERVENTION PROGRAMS

However, as with the police, the women's impressions of their experiences with the probation services were polarized. For example, the women were divided in how helpful they found the probation officer to be or whether having the batterer on probation made a positive difference. They were satisfied when the probation officer seemed to also address their needs and issues (a restorative principle). For some, probation seemed to have made the batterer aware of the consequences of future offenses. On the other hand, it was those who felt that their issues were not addressed that were less positive about probation services. This polarized portrait is depicted in the half of the women that were not at all satisfied with their experience with the probation system. The rest expressed only varying degrees of satisfaction.

In contrast, 61 percent of the women indicated that they were very satisfied or pretty satisfied with the batterers' intervention program. They had observed an adequate change in the convicted batterer's behavior during or after their participation in the program. For the women who were dissatisfied, it was due to the inadequate change in the batterer's behavior or because they wanted the batterer to serve jail time. Like the police and courts, the probation system, with a restorative orientation, can also play a role in restorative justice interventions.

POSITIVE EVALUATION OF BWAS AND OTHER COMMUNITY SERVICES

How about the nonlegal services they received from the battered women's agencies? In general, about three-fourths of the respondents who had used the services offered by the BWA during the most severe incident felt that their experience had been positive. Consequently, most would recommend the BWA services to other women. The availability and helpfulness of the shelter staff, understanding of the harms of domestic violence, of the victims' needs as well as of their overall positive experience with the services for themselves and their children provided by the battered women's agencies were perhaps the reasons why many of the women indicated that they would return, if needed, to the shelter in which they were staying.

On the other hand, a majority of the women in the survey did not know about victim witness services. Those (about a quarter of the women) who knew about the program were aware that funding for counseling and information on other services are available through victim/witness services. Under the victim/witness services provided by the National Conference on Community and Justice (NCCJ), victims of a violent crime are entitled to restitution for expenses such as medical expenses and lost wages. In addition, victim/witness centers also assist victims with emergency services (food, clothing, and shelter), follow-up counseling care, and accompany victims to court.

Concluding Comments

One overarching theme emerges out of this assessment offered by victims of intimate partner violence who have used domestic violence services in the northern California County under consideration. The more directly the services (for example, shelters and, to a lesser extent, the family court) focused on the victims and their needs, the more satisfied they were. On the other hand, cries of dissatisfaction were heard most clearly when the focus of the services was more directly on the abuser (as is the case in the criminal court or probation or batterers' intervention). In these instances, the women were not as satisfied, unless, of course, they felt that they were treated sensitively as a victim-survivor or they observed changes in the batterers' behavior as it impacted them.

More specifically, among all the services the women used, they overwhelmingly were positive about their shelter experience (80.7 percent). Next on the index of satisfaction was the batterers' intervention program, in which the convicted abuser is required to take a counseling program that has the potential to change his violent behavior. While the court systems, both criminal and family courts, and the police received overall positive ratings, many were also disapproving of their experiences with these legal and law enforcement services. They were most dissatisfied with the probation department program (50 percent).

The reasons the women gave for their varying levels of satisfaction provide additional clarification and explanations for their assessment. Shelter services that received the highest approval provided immediate safe havens for the victims from the physical abuse and had the most direct and immediate impact on the women and their children. On the other hand, the common reasons for their dissatisfaction—with, say, the courts—were perceptions that the legal systems were not addressing their unique needs and the needs of their children as victims of intimate partner violence or the lack of observable changes in the batterers' behavior. Certainly, they were appreciative when the legal system was perceived as having a positive effect. For example, those women who felt that probation

Table 6.4.   Comparative Assessment of Services

	Criminal Court (n=22)	Family Court (n=17)	Probation (n=20)	Intervention for Batterers (n=33)	Shelters (n=46)
Positive	27.3%	23.5%	25.0%	42.4%	80.7%
Satisf./OK	45.5	64.7	25.0	33.4	10.9
Negative	27.3	11.8	50.0	24.2	8.7

services made the batterer aware of his accountability for the consequences of a future intimate violence offense had a positive view of probation.

In short, how positive the survivors were about their experiences with the service system depended on three factors that reflect restorative justice principles (Van Ness and Strong 2006; Umbreit et al. 2003; Zehr 2002; 2005): how directly the services involved the women (shelters), the sensitivity of the judges and police in dealing with the battered women's unique needs in her relationship with her batterer, and perceived effectiveness of the program (as in the batterers' intervention program) in potentially changing how the batterer relates to her. Restated in Zehr's (2002) victim needs language, survivors' satisfaction with extant services depended on the extent to which their needs for clear information were met (information), they had opportunities to tell their side of the story (truth-telling), reclaim the control they lost with the violence (empowerment), and their losses are restituted, either in real terms or symbolically (restitution and vindication).

In all fairness to the legal and law enforcement service systems, part of the victims' dissatisfaction might stem from the lack of a realistic understanding of the limitations of these services; for example, what the court system can and cannot do. The legal services, such as the court system and probation, have been set up to directly focus on punishing the individual batterer, a form of retributive justice (Mills 2008; Zehr, 2002). Some of the victim's dissatisfaction might be because of unrealistic expectations that the court system, while prosecuting her batterer, will also look out for her needs.

No doubt, there is something to be said for the legal system to go beyond their traditional charges and to pay extra restorative attention to how the court and police actions might impact the victims of intimate partner violence. But the data reviewed in this monograph also raise another question. Might it not be necessary for us to think more creatively about programs that focus on the dyadic relationship between the batterer and the victim and their larger community context?

Phrased in ecological terms, the extant legal and community services are not designed to focus on the batterer-victim dyad or on their communities. To the extent that they do address the victim's needs, as when the police and court systems did, they were going beyond their traditional charges. If we value these victims' voices, it is time for us to think about restorative-type programs that focus on the micro-system as a unit (in addition to those that deal with the batterer and victim as separate entities). No doubt, there has been much discussion, both in the academic and policy arenas, about the inadvisability of forcing or mandating the batterer and his victim to come together in a service delivery context, be it for counseling or in the court system. Such concerns are particularly salient during the time the domestic violence crime is being litigated in the courts and even in the immediate aftermath of the legal process. *The victims' safety always has to be paramount.* In many cases, the new restorative dyad–focused programs might even have to wait until the victim-survivor has been helped to reclaim her inner strength and social support from her communities of care (Umbreit et al. 2003; Van Ness and Strong 2006; Zehr 2005).

In short, the new dyadic programs being recommended here are not meant to replace, but only supplement, existing legal and community services. Intimate partner violence is too serious a crime not to have the "big stick" of the legal system involved in addressing the crime. In fact, when extant services are sensitive to victims' needs and address the harms caused by the violence, they are restorative in spirit, even if not in explicit intent. Also, the existing legal and BWA services, with a restorative orientation, can be critical partners in restorative justice interventions. However, there will be a continued need for safe spaces where the victims can heal, away from the batterer and the battering environment. Yet programs using the restorative justice principles that directly and/or indirectly focus on repairing the harm and healing the battered relationships, could meet the unmet micro-system relationship needs (Zehr 2002) identified by victims in this county. What would the broad theoretical and practical contours of restorative practices for intimate partner violence look like? It is to this task that we turn in chapter 7.

Notes

1. See chapter 4 for a description of the power and control model.
2. For those interested in access to and a closer reading of the detailed tables that contain all the survey data we report on below, please contact the author at mfernandez@scu.edu.

CHAPTER 7

A Hunger for Healing and Closure

A CASE FOR RESTORATIVE JUSTICE APPROACHES IN DOMESTIC VIOLENCE SERVICES

> You know, I hated him at times, wished I wasn't with him. I, then, I'd leave him and I'd miss him when I was gone. Just terrible feeling. Yeah. 'Cuz I did love him. I still do love him. But I didn't know how to end our relationship.
>
> Survivor 26

Introduction

TWO PROBLEMATICS

Two problematics or themes have emerged out of the analysis presented thus far in which we have explored the victim-survivors' experiences with the extant domestic violence service systems. One theme is that victims of intimate partner violence do use available services to deal with their experiences with violence, even when they have encountered systematic battering. However, they are not completely satisfied with the extant services. The second is a lingering hunger for closure and healing, often palpable, in the voices of the victim-survivors. Rephrased in Zehr's victim needs terminology (2002), the analyses of victims' experiences make clear their hunger for information about the offense (why it happened and what has happened since), for telling the truth about what happened (so that healing can happen), for reclaiming the control they have lost (empowerment), and seeking restitution (either real or symbolic) of the losses as a means of vindication.

Part of the first problematic in this story is illustrated in this quote from Bill Lockyer, California attorney general in 2005, who said, "The laws already on the books should be holding batterers accountable for their violent behavior, but the criminal justice system often fails to enforce them" (California Department of

Justice 2004). Translated in terms of the experience of Victim-Survivor 2 (whose violence was "abated"),[1] who, when asked about her future plans and what she would do if she encountered violence in a future intimate relationship, responded:

> And I could still be fooled. People say, well, could you be ever be fooled by one of these men? Oh, sure. Would I stay after the first incident? No. Would I call the police? Probably not. I would very quietly leave just like every other woman that's been. Even though I had the best outcome, it was still the hardest thing I ever did. And knowing what I know now, would I report it and put myself through the system? No. And that's a hard thing for me to say because I work in the system.

Restated in restorative justice and ecological language, this victim-survivor experienced the negative effects of the legal system that, in her case, doubly victimized her and left her with few, if any, opportunities to exercise her agency on the extant service delivery system to address her needs. This double victimization is consonant with the extensive discussion of the issue in the restorative justice literature (Ptacek 2010; Umbreit et al. 2003; Van Ness and Strong 2006; Zehr 2001, 2002, 2005). To borrow a phrase coined by Mirchandani (2006), this victim-survivor felt that she was a victim of the "governance of gender" in the way the system operates rather than being able to exercise her agency as a survivor to have the systemic governance be more gendered or attuned to her needs as a victim of intimate partner violence (see also Ptacek 1999).

The second problematic is found in a hunger for healing and for closure that echoes through in the voices of the survivors whose violent experiences and service utilization patterns have been examined in earlier chapters. As was clear in chapter 6, when the survivors were dissatisfied with the services they used, it was because their needs were unmet (Zehr 2002). The services, whether provided through legal channels or through community agencies, dealt with the batterer or the victim individually and were of little assistance in helping the victims deal with their relationship with their batterers. Restoratively and ecologically speaking, what the survivors seem to be saying is that they were unable to exercise their agency in making the system work on their behalf. Whether their expectations are realistic or not, the bottom line is that even when the victims have accessed and used the legal and community services provided in the "system," there remains a hunger for healing and for closure to the traumatic relationships.

These problematics take on added significance because research (by Fleury, Sullivan, and Bybee 2000, for example, and the experiences of the interview and survey respondents covered in this monograph) has shown that terminating a violent relationship does not necessarily end the violence. The continued fear and experience of violence might sometimes be in the very violent relationship for which they sought help but remains unresolved. Or it might be in the multiple serial violent relationships some women have experienced. For yet others, violence lies in the lingering fear and weariness that women live with and approach potential new relationships.

Unmet Needs[2] and Unresolved Relationships in More Ways than One

The case that is being made in this manuscript for new supplemental domestic violence programs based on restorative principles rests to a large extent on the evidence of unmet needs and unfinished or unresolved resolution of the victim-survivors' intimate partner relationships. At this stage, it might be useful to revisit some of the evidence of unmet needs in the unresolved relationships.

"I WOULD LIKE TO TELL HIM THAT" (*TRUTH-TELLING* BY SURVIVOR 27)

As was noted in chapter 3, many of the victims in the interview and the survey samples either were divorced, separated, or had no relationship with the abuser at the time of the survey or interviews. However, more than a third of the interview sample were married or living with the batterer at the time of the interview. In some cases, the batterer had visitation rights with their children. A few were involved with the batterer of the most severe incident in a casual/dating relationship. Also, for many the battering relationship had not ended after the most severe incidence of abuse. For example, there had been another incident of violence, after the most severe incident, for two-thirds (68 percent) of the victims in the survey sample.

Several tropes that emerged in the narratives of the women from the interview sample help flesh out this numerical outline of unmet needs in unfinished relationships. We briefly turn to the victim-survivors' voices to illustrate the many ways in which these unmet needs and unresolved relationships are manifested in the lives of victim-survivors and their search for healing.

SURVIVORS SEARCHING FOR WAYS TO HEAL FROM BROKEN RELATIONSHIPS

One general theme that stood out in the victims' narratives was their search for healing and closure in their relationships with their intimate partner. Presented below are two examples.

Survivor 30, a Hispanic woman ("fragile" group),[3] explicitly mentioned the need for healing as she recalled:

> [K]new his mom before him; constant drama, with his mom, sister passively involved. And he doesn't even care. I need healing with that. I need people to talk to about that. I need some kind of support about, you know what I mean, I need to know, um, what I'm gonna do. *[Need for Information, Truth-telling, and Empowerment]*

Or as Survivor 3, a Caucasian woman whose violent experiences had occurred more than one year before the interview ("intermediate" group)[4] and whose case had been processed through the legal system, recalled:

> He pled guilty in court. So, that was nice and . . . Then we, since we've had the restraining order there hasn't really, we haven't really talked. . . . He's been very careful, because he knows. He knows I mean business now and he knows I'm just waiting. I'll call your probation officer so fast. . . . The police report was so, I mean he admitted it to the police. . . . I'm working my butt off so I can make a better life for my son and I and not have to depend on a man. And my next man that I get in my life will be there because I want him there and not because I need him there and that's not been the case in a lot of my relation—in most of my relationships. *[Need for Restitution/Vindication and Empowerment]*

EMOTIONALLY CONNECTED TO THE BATTERER IN AN UNRESOLVED RELATIONSHIP

Others spoke in ways that indicated that, despite their battering relationships, they continued to be emotionally linked to their batterers (as of the time of the interview). They have tried, often successfully, to work on their relationships and would like assistance in more effectively dealing with their troubled relationships.

Survivor 27 ("intermediate" group), a Hispanic woman who was married for three years and got a restraining order and separated from her husband, recalled her attempts to work on the relationship with her abuser husband.

> [M]y husband's into drugs and so he'd, yesterday I, I was very, very excited because he went into rehab. He's in . . . [local city] and he went into rehab, so he was getting help, and so that's, you know, something that I wanted him to do and was kind of happy with it . . . doing something for himself. Hopefully not because of me and

. . . [A little later in the interview when she was asked whether she would ever go back to her husband, she replied,] Probably not. [But then she went on to add,] No. If, if, I was, if I could see and would know that he would change, a changed man, I probably would. [Interviewer: "How would you want him to change?"] Um, I would be, I would tell because he would be more, he would have more of a, he would act more like a grown man. Like he has grown a lot and not act like a, a child. You know. That's how I would know. Acting grown, grown up. Because he would, he would say, because he would say different things, you know. And say the right things instead of the wrong things. He would say that he, he, that it was his fault and everything was his fault. And that nothing was my fault, and I'm not to blame. And that he was upset. And, and, I didn't know until later that I had the right to change my mind [she learned this at women's shelter]. I didn't know that. I thought I was, I, he said, you know what, he told me that I was crazy. I really thought I was crazy for changing my mind. I had no idea I had a right to change my mind. I had a right not to want sex with my husband if I didn't want it. I didn't know that. I thought I was supposed to do that. I thought that's what, what married people are supposed to do . . . I would like to tell him that. *[Need for Restitution, Empowerment, Truth-telling, and Information]*

Survivor 26 (part Native American, "intermediate" group) is another woman who thought she could benefit from assistance working on her relationship with her current batterer.[5] She said that she had been using the police/the system to do so. When asked to elaborate, she said:

Now, there was two questions in my mind at this time. First off, he was someone I loved. Second off, I was fearful of him going to jail. So that had to be a choice that I had to make. So, I would call them and they would come out and I would not mention that he was on, under the influence. I just would want him to leave so they would talk to him and they'd work things out between us . . . because of the program, the shelters and such want to take the women out of the home. Now that's fine but what they need is mediators. They need to develop a program that can reunite these people. If he's, has such a violence case, find the underlying problem. Get him in counseling. Get her in counseling. She needs to learn about herself. He needs to learn about his self. More to bring the family back together than to separate it. Because this is why they're unsuccessful. Because these men and women do love each other even though it is abusive. *[Need for Empowerment, Restitution, Truth-telling, and Information]*

Survivor 29 (from the "fragile" group) is a Caucasian woman who has experienced abuse in all three of her relationships. Her current boyfriend and she had a history of talking with each other, even if not successfully.

> [M]y whole history's the drinking. Yeah. With people . . . I find very abusive men. . . . And I'm just like, and I was crying, I was, I had a puffy eye, my eye was just red, I mean . . . I'd be crying and then my boyfriend knocked on the door, let me in, I want to talk to her. So I said, okay, let him in. And then he'd always want to kiss me and hug me, and I said, don't touch me. And he'd sit on the bed and we'd talk. And then I end up staying. End up staying there, and I should've left. But I didn't, at that time. When I finally left last week. . . . And I finally said, I don't want to do this anymore. And I had my daughter and, I'm sorry, you know, I just didn't want to keep doing what I was doing. *[Need for Empowerment]*

CHILDREN THAT BIND

For some, the children they have with their batterers represent the unresolved link in their battering relationships. Here are two victim-survivors' voices as they search for ways to work on their relationships, for the sake of their children.

Survivor 18 ("fragile" group), a Hispanic woman:

> When we first started going back and forth with the children, visitation, it was, it was, both of us screaming at the top of our lungs . . . my trying to defend myself and all in front of the kids. And so working with the counselors, you know, it helped me to see that even my part in it wasn't good for the kids. . . . So I had to change the way I was reacting to him, and kind of distance myself and they [counseling program] gave me a lot of tools to do that. . . . Oh, yeah. I was able to distance myself, so I wouldn't engage and totally go into that whole process where he would take me . . . I went through, from drug and alcohol counseling. And that's where I discovered that my relationship really wasn't good. And so I left him, one of the times because of the counseling I got. . . . But, when you're in a shelter, they say, okay, you need individual counseling, and you have three workshops a week. So you have to go to these workshops, you have to go to them individually. You're immersed into, okay, you're healing . . . and you're, we're gonna do our best to make sure you stay out of bad relationships. . . . But when you have kids together. *[Need for Empowerment, Restitution/Vindication, and Information]*

Similarly, when Survivor 29 ("fragile" group and has a daughter with her abuser) was asked what prompted her to make her decision to leave her abuser and whether she would consider getting back together, she recalled:

> God, I don't know. I really didn't want to. I knew I had to for my daughter. I mean there wasn't any one thing that day, it was everything. I, uh, I don't know. . . . I don't like him as a person but he loves his daughter. And she loves him. And there's some stability there, which I don't have, so I'm okay with that. And I would never keep her from him unless there was harm, you know. *[Restitution and Empowerment]*

MULTIPLE SERIAL BATTERING RELATIONSHIPS

Other survivors seemed to be searching for assistance to disrupt their histories with serial battering relationships.

Survivor 13 ("fragile" group, Hispanic):

> I had a boyfriend, you know, the boyfriend that the ex-boyfriend hated and but that wasn't real positive either. . . . And I haven't ever been really good with closures in my life so naturally we had sex the last time we saw each other. And then I found out I was pregnant. *[Truth-telling]*

CONFIDENT, BUT EVER CAUTIOUS

Yet others are confident that they would not stay in future abusive relationships, but are cautious nonetheless.

Survivor 8 ("fragile" group), a Hispanic woman:

> You know, it's like, I've had to fight for everything. And it's not just me, it's two children that I have to protect. . . . And our divorce is finalized, I filed for restraining order. . . . But I'm an adult and you know, I certainly know how to protect myself if anybody ever tried that again . . . and, now I'm just real careful about, you know, looking over my shoulder, watching my mirror, and . . . *[Need for Empowerment, Restitution/Vindication, and Truth-telling]*

Or Survivor 3, a Caucasian ("intermediate" group) woman, who said:

> So, now I'm way more cautious. I see any drinking I'm just really going to watch it very closely. And, and, I mean I'm still a hopeless

romantic. I still believe in love. Right, you know. But I gotta be cautious. *[Empowerment]*

ATTEMPTS TO LET HIM KNOW, BUT . . . (*NEED FOR TRUTH-TELLING, EMPOWERMENT, RESTITUTION*)

Some survivors' narratives indicate that they have already tried communicating with the batterer, albeit in a one-sided manner and unsuccessfully. Survivor 23 ("fragile" group), a Caucasian woman in a common-law marriage for seven years, was dissatisfied with the legal system and wanted to resolve the violent relationship with the batterer because of the children. She described how she decided to finally leave her batterer after they both met with a counselor.

> Anyway, so the main thing that got me to leave is the night prior to me leaving. I had written down a list of the things that I felt were wrong with our relationship. The communication, the respect issue, what have you, about different concerns that I had and goals and, and I sat down and I went through everything with him. I wanted to know how he felt. I wanted to know about what he had planned to do about coming to a, a conclusion as far as what we were gonna do about these specific problems. He could not come up with anything . . . not so much because he couldn't, because he just really didn't feel like putting in the brain power to do so. So, I said, well, you know what? I know what I want to do. I know what my goals are. I know what, what things I would like to accomplish in my life. And I don't see you helping me. I don't see you helping me or standing behind me or just supporting me, with words. Not money. Not and not anything else. But with your verbal support, your communication, your enthusiasm. So therefore I'm gonna ha—I'm gonna do it all myself.

Or Survivor 25 ("intermediate" group, Japanese American), who also tried to communicate with her batterer, without much success *[Need for Information, Empowerment, and Truth-telling]*:

> So that night that he had to be taken out of the home by the police, I had brought it up to him. "M, if you're using drugs, I need to know." I go, "we need to talk." And he did not want to talk. And this guy came over to pick him up and I didn't know it but that was the guy that was supplying him with the methamphetamine. And M lost control and he grabbed me, in front of my mom, in front of my children. And after all of these years, that was enough.

These quotes underscore the fact that many victim-survivors expressed a need for more resolution than what they had experienced through the extant legal and community service systems. That this is the case, regardless of how much time had elapsed since the abuse or of the type of abusive relationship from or in which the victim-survivor is seeking to find healing and closure, adds urgency to their pleas for help.

A Case for a Supplemental Domestic Violence Program Based on Restorative Justice Principles

As these narratives demonstrate, no matter what the scenario or the length of time that has passed since the abuse, there is a sense of unmet needs, unfinished business, a lack of closure, and a desire for healing from, and sometimes in, the broken intimate relationships with the victim-survivors' intimate partners. Could programs based on the restorative justice principles provide a venue where such healing might occur? Van Ness and Strong describe the praxis, and underlying theory, of restorative justice as one that "emphasizes repairing the harm caused or revealed by the criminal behavior. It is best accomplished through cooperative processes that include all stakeholders" (2006: 43). Cooperative restorative justice practices involve processes "where stakeholders affected by an injustice have an opportunity to communicate about the consequences of the injustice and what is to be done to right the wrong" (Strang and Braithwaite 2002: 4). Stated alternatively in Zehr's words, "Restorative justice is a process to involve, to the extent possible, those who have a stake in a specific offense and to collectively identify and address harms, needs, and obligations, in order to heal and put things as right as possible" (2002: 37).

With its focus on righting the damage caused in broken relationships (not necessarily reuniting the victim with her batterer), *in ways the victim-survivor chooses, with appropriate safeguards*, and with the involvement of the *community*, including the justice system, restorative justice–based programs offer victims an opportunity to exercise their agency in the healing process. Voluntary participation, informed choices, and victim safety, traditions strongly rooted in restorative justice theory and practice (see Curtis-Fawley and Daly 2005; Umbreit et al. 2003; Van Ness and Strong 2006; Zehr 2002, 2005), will have to be of paramount consideration.

We now turn to two final tasks in this last chapter: (1) to explore the theoretical linkages between the two research traditions of restorative justice and feminist theorizing of domestic violence; and (2) to identify some core principles that might guide restorative justice praxis in the domain of intimate partner violence.

Restorative Justice in Domestic Violence: A Theoretical Synthesis

Two research traditions have provided the theoretical context for the analysis of intimate partner violence presented in this manuscript—feminist and restorative justice perspectives. A summary of the theoretical linkages between these research traditions sets a valuable intellectual context for the core principles of restorative justice praxis in domestic violence services that are outlined below.

A theme that links both the feminist and restorative justice traditions of domestic violence is that they are holistic in their approaches. Feminist perspectives on domestic violence, reviewed in chapters 1 and 5, are holistic in their social analysis that broadens the theoretical and practical lenses beyond the individual victim and batterer. They emphasize the sociocultural context of the communities in which domestic violence occurs. In particular, feminists draw attention to the societal norms of male dominance and male entitlement, and the resulting inequalities in the structure of husband-wife roles, and how these structured and gendered inequalities have unfortunate theoretical and practical implications for victims of intimate partner violence. As has been noted before, ignoring the sociocultural context not only has the potential for locating the source of the problem in the individual's characteristics and prior history, but it also results in solely blaming the aggressor and the abused woman. In other words, rather than individualizing the crime and blaming the victim, feminist theorists of intimate partner violence focus on the broader structural constraints and contexts that trap women and create dependency.

Restorative justice is also holistic at many levels. It is holistic both in its understanding of the causes and processes of the crime of family violence as well as in its approaches to dealing with the crime (Zehr 2002; Van Ness and Strong 2006). RJ theory and practice focus on the harms resulting from the crime, the causes of the harms, and the resulting needs (of victims primarily, and also of the communities and offenders). No doubt, RJ is, first of all, victim-oriented in that it begins with a concern for victims of the harms. However, RJ also emphasizes the obligations and accountability of offenders and communities to understand and put right the harms. Furthermore, RJ is holistic in its collaborative and inclusive processes that involve all legitimate stakeholders (victims, offenders, their communities of care, and society) as they are encouraged to arrive at mutually agreed upon (whenever possible) rather imposed outcomes. The ultimate goal of RJ is an experience of healing and transformation that balances the concerns of all involved. In short, as Van Ness and Strong suggest, "restorative justice is a holistic approach to life and to relationships, one that has far-reaching effects beyond simply the issue of crime or rule-breaking" (2006: 41).

Thus, restorative justice theory (and Bronfenbrenner's ecological perspective) conceptually elaborates on the feminist contextual analysis by drawing out the outlines and details of the community context. To restorative justice theorists, the context includes not only the women victims but also their communities of care, the offenders, and all other relevant stakeholders (such as service providers); societal norms and resulting structural inequalities provide the backdrop against which restorative deliberations and practice are conducted.

Restorative Justice in Domestic Violence Praxis

While many anti-violence advocates are hesitant about using RJ approaches in domestic violence (for reasons outlined in chapter 1), many scholars and family violence practitioners have begun to explore restorative justice possibilities in dealing with cases of violence against women, particularly given the failures of existing legal responses to protect victim safety, autonomy, and offender accountability (for examples, see Coward 2002; Curtis-Fawley and Daly 2005; Ptacek 2010;[6] authors in Strang and Braithwite 2002; Umbreit and Coates 2000; Van Ness and Strong 2006). In fact, there are many pilot hybrid programs that combine feminist and RJ practices with the criminal justice system, primarily in indigenous communities in Australia, Canada, New Zealand, and the United States that are promising (see examples in Ptacek 2010 and Strang and Braithwaite 2002).

In acknowledgment of the veracity of the resistance in the policy, service, and victim advocate communities to introducing restorative justice in the domain of family violence, we reiterate again that the restorative justice principled programs being recommended here for victim-survivors of domestic violence are designed to strategically *supplement* and to be offered as one option, along with the existing menu of legal and community based interventions. It is worth repeating that domestic violence is too dangerous to be left without the "big stick" of the legal system. With this proposed supplemental option, the principles of retribution and rehabilitation, the foundation of the criminal justice system, are still in place. However, if the survivors, whose pleas one heard in the narratives presented in this book, are to be taken seriously, it is time for the domestic violence service and advocacy community to start exploring the potential of incorporating and integrating programs based on restorative justice principles into the extant services.

There is a clamor in the women's narratives, sometimes implicit and at other times explicit, for the opportunity to exercise their agency, by presenting/communicating to the abuser and to the service system their side of the story (Zehr's truth-telling) and having the story be acknowledged (restitution and vindication). It is fully expected that the victim-survivor will have full informed *choice* in decisions about whether, when, and how to utilize these programs (information). Thus, reinforcement of the victim-survivor's strength and determination to be stronger and more self-reliant are built into this supplement (empowerment). However, for many victim-survivors, the most effective time might be only after they have completed their involvement, with the legal and battered women's community services, to deal with their needs as individual actors in the micro-system dyad. The golden rule for the right timing will always have to be the right time as determined by the victim-survivor.

The victim-survivor should also have the *agency or choice* from among a variety of restorative justice process options. Strang and Braithwaite, as well as many of their colleagues in the 2002 edited volume, make a case for face-to-face processes between the stakeholders in realizing the full potential of restorative justice. However, face-to-face meetings between the victim and her batterer are not the only forum, and not always the safest forum, in which a victim of intimate partner violence can present her side of the story and meet her need for truth-telling. Ptacek (2010), Strang and Braithwaite (2002), Van Ness and Strong (2006), Zehr (2002), and others also offer several indirect options particularly suited for intimate partner violence situations. In addition to the indirect encounter options discussed earlier, another alternative (to face-to-face meetings) is for separate processes for the victim and the batterer, where the victim-survivor meets with her supporters (as in the Aboriginal victim circles) while the batterer meets with other offenders and supporters (offender circles). A shuttle diplomacy model where a go-between, perhaps a program coordinator, gathers information from and shares it with both sides is yet another option. A letter of apology from the batterer to the victim or victim-impact letters to the batterers are yet other options for communication, albeit limited, that might be mutually agreed upon. We fully concur with Zehr's (2002, 2005) caution against face-to-face meetings between the victim and the batterer until the batterer's patterns of domination, intimidation, and denials are certifiably broken. The ultimate goals of restoring the harm, whether it is to heal, modify, transform, or end the relationship, will have to be the choice of the victim-survivor.

OUTLINING TEN BASIC GUIDELINES FOR RESTORATIVE JUSTICE IN DOMESTIC VIOLENCE PRAXIS

The goal of this monograph is not to present a fully developed program that uses restorative justice (RJ) principles. Rather, it is to outline core principles that cannot be compromised in a restorative justice based domestic violence program. We, once again, draw on Mills (2008), Strang and Braithwaite (2002), Pranis, Stuart, and Wedge (2003), Pennell and Burford (in Strang and Braithwaite 2002), Ptacek (2010), Umbreit et al. (2003), Van Ness and Strong (2006), and Zehr (2001, 2002, 2005) as we highlight these guidelines.

1. Restorative justice programs advocated here are meant to be strategic supplements to existing legal and community programs, and are not meant to replace existing domestic violence legal and community-based programs. Domestic violence is a crime and needs to be litigated and addressed appropriately (with sentencing to jail or prisons as appropriate to the crime).
2. Safety is always first for the victim-survivor and her family and friends. The safety mechanisms available should be those that can be enforced by court sanctions.
3. Participation in the RJ program always has to be the victim-survivor's choice and at a time when she is ready.
4. The RJ program should be organized and provided through the probation department or a similar local legal entity to demonstrate to the batterer, victim, and the community that the program has the seal of approval of the legal system; this will also give the program the needed legal bite. The program facilitators will have to be certified professionals with well-developed knowledge and skills (honed through, for example, ongoing facilitator workshops or training sessions) in risk assessment and in understanding the dangers of domestic violence and in appropriately responding to power and control dynamics in intimate partner violence. The facilitator should be an advocate for the survivor, without "trashing" the batterer. If the victim-survivor starts to weaken or slip into past submissive behavior, the facilitator should be able to step in and redirect the process.
5. Local battered women's agencies will have to be critical partners in the preparation for the restorative process and follow-up to ensure the safety and well-being of victims and their supporters.
6. Victim/survivors should be provided with options and a choice of conference forums for the restorative discussions/process: indirect encounters with batterer (for example, through written and/or other mechanisms); direct face-to-face meeting with the batterer only if and when it can be ensured that

the batterer will not dominate the victim; or other encounters, such as those between victim and batterers other than her own. There should be immediate termination of the meeting if the batterer resorts to previous dominating ways.

7. If the victim-survivor chooses an encounter forum, such encounters (particularly direct encounters) will be held only if the batterer acknowledges, even if partially, his responsibility and guilt. Efforts should be made for voluntary participation by the batterer. In the event that the batterer is unwilling to participate and/or denies accountability, the victim-survivor should be given the opportunity to craft other ways of letting her voice be heard by the batterer and/or by her social network and community of care.

8. The victim-survivor and batterer choose members of their communities of care or support system (family, friends, neighbors, clergy, and other salient community members) that will be involved in the restorative process encounters. The number of supporting people included should be balanced in favor of the victim. Many of the women interviewed for this research had wide and deep networks in their communities of care that they could draw on.

9. Follow-up with victims-survivors should be provided for a reasonable period of time after the encounters.

10. The RJ program should be required to evaluate formally[7] both their processes and outcomes, and disseminate the successes and challenges of the program for at least three years. The metrics for success of how restorative the program is will be decided with full input and consultation with the victim-survivor and, if relevant, the batterer.

SOME STRATEGIC CAVEATS

Before we conclude, some caveats about strategic issues need to be reiterated. Victims' choice is a very clear and uncompromising principle that practitioners of restorative justice in the context of intimate partner violence need to keep in mind. Curtis-Fawley and Daly (2005), Umbreit et al. (2003), Van Ness and Strong (2006), and Zehr (2002, 2005) among others have detailed practical guidelines for ensuring ongoing commitment to collaborative and inclusive restorative practices that minimize coercion and maximize voluntary participation of victims, communities of care, and even offenders. Effective, inclusive restorative practice also extends to other components of the program, such as selection of parties to be involved (victim, offender, community of care members, facilitators, government representatives) and accountability for the conduct of the restorative processes and outcomes. A related issue is that of assisting victims in making informed choices. One yardstick of informed choice that Van Ness and Strong (2006) advocate is to ensure that victims and offenders perceive an advantage to taking the restorative option in addition to and/or over the criminal justice process. Offering the options in an honest, objective, and nonjudgmental manner is one way to ensure informed choices are collaboratively made, with the victims in the driver's seat.

Two other thorny questions remain to be addressed. Is restorative justice practice more suitable for situational couple violence than for systematic battering? Perhaps. But the victims interviewed for this monograph more often than not experienced systematic battering, and they also craved healing and closure. While caution is certainly needed in the restorative options offered to victims of systematic battering, it is incumbent on domestic violence practitioners and theorists to explore appropriate variations of restorative applications, in addition to the extant legal options, for systematic battering cases also. A second difficult issue is RJ's offender focus (Van Ness and Strong 2006; Umbreit et al. 2003; Zehr 2002, 2005). Holding offenders accountable for their responsibilities to victims and communities is one of the pillars of restorative justice. We concur with Zehr and others who argue that true offender accountability and reintegration cannot happen unless the offender's needs are addressed as well. That subject, however, will require data on offenders and is beyond the scope of this project.

AND FINALLY, A NOTE ABOUT POSSIBLE EXPECTED OUTCOMES

Keeping in mind that the outcomes from restorative practices should be the victim's choice and that it should be an informed choice, we outline some possible outcomes from the victims' perspective. These outcomes are certainly not exhaustive nor are they mutually exclusive. At one end of the continuum, some victims interviewed wished to legally terminate and escape their harmful relationships and sought help in doing so, while healing and seeking closure. At the other end were those who looked to reconcile with the batterer on a more equal and healthy footing (because of emotional, financial, and other relational needs around children) provided the batterer takes full responsibility for his harmful behavior and is continued to be monitored by the system. Many victim-survivors fell in between. Irrespective of where they fell on the outcome continuum, all the women sought vindication or recognition of the harm done through restitution (real or symbolic, as in an apology) (Zehr 2002). Whether the survivors were looking to "terminate and escape harmful relationships," or to "transform their broken relationships," they struggled to regain personal agency so that their future intimate relationships would be based on "equality" rather than "power and control." And ultimately they sought to be reintegrated into their care communities. Effective restorative practices, with their principles of encounters, making amends, reintegration, and inclusion, can provide constructive forums for victims of intimate partner violence.

Concluding Remarks

How needed are restorative justice approaches and community involvement in resolving intimate partner violence? Based on the empirical evidence presented in this monograph, we fully concur with domestic violence scholars such as Strang and Braithwaite (2002), Umbreit et al. (2003), Van Ness and Strong (2006), Ptacek (2010), Zehr (2002), and their author colleagues that the time is right for seriously thinking about incorporating restorative justice practices in family violence programs. At the same time, we also remain mindful of their exhortation of treading cautiously about not compromising the victim's safety.

Restorative justice principled programs broaden the notion of community in the domestic violence arena to involve the victim-survivor, her batterer, and their legal, service, social care communities, and other relevant stakeholders in addressing the crime of domestic violence. At a minimum, RJ programs give the victim-survivor a chance to tell her story to her batterer and to her community, as well as the opportunity to exercise her agency in healing her hunger for closure. These forums can also offer victim-survivors support from her social network(s) and possibly help her to (re)build a support network in her healing process. At best, they could be a forum for the victim and batterer to heal or modify, transform, or even fully terminate their relationships. RJ programs could also give the batterer a chance to reintegrate into his community. And as Pranis, Stuart, and Wedge (2003) have argued, restorative justice–based programs can provide a legitimate forum for needed community intervention in family violence and counter the bystander community effect. After all, it will take a community to heal the ravages of family violence.

The family violence movement has made enormous progress under the traditional criminal justice system. And one can never underscore enough the need to approach these new restorative initiatives with the appropriate degree of caution and skepticism. However, given the limits of the extant criminal justice and community systems, as demonstrated in the voices of the victim-survivors of intimate partner violence heard in this monograph and other evidence reviewed here, the time is ripe to explore a new partnership between the criminal law, feminist, and restorative justice processes. Such partnerships can provide more effective answers and solutions for the victim-survivors, their intimate relationships, and their community. To close in the words of Victim-Survivor 7:

[A]nd I'm frustrated with the system because we were all supposed to get counseling . . . a minimum of twelve. He did his twelve and stopped . . . well, I'm trying to get the divorce going through and I have to testify against him, you know, in the trial and that'll be kind of hard but I gotta do what I gotta do. And I'm just now trying to be proactive to see what I can do to heal from all of this. . . . It would be nice to have some help, you know.

Notes

1. "Abated" group refers to those whose domestic violence had occurred three or more years prior to the interview.

2. The four unmet needs that Zehr (2002) has identified will be referenced in *bold* in this chapter as information, truth-telling, empowerment, and restitution/vindication.

3. "Fragile" group includes women who experienced violence less than one year before the interview.

4. "Intermediate" group is where the violence occurred between one and two years prior to the interview.

5. She has had chaotic relationships in her past: she was in her third marriage at the time of the interview; the first time it was a common-law arrangement in which they had four adult children; the second time, she married a friend after a night of drinking and this lasted six months because he became too controlling of her children. After her divorce, she met her current boyfriend and had been with him for several years.

6. More specifically, see chapters by Frederick and Lizdas, Koss, Kim, Pennell and Kim, and Stubbs in the Ptacek edited volume. In the Strang and Braithwaite edited collection, see Busch, Daly, Morris, and Pennell and Burford.

7. For some program evaluation models, concepts, guidelines, and yardsticks, see Presser and Voorhis 2002; Nichols 2002; Zehr 2005.

Interview Schedule for the Qualitative Interviews
SEEKING DOMESTIC VIOLENCE INTERVENTIONS

Introduction

The purpose of this study conducted by Dr. Marilyn Fernandez of Santa Clara University is to understand better the types of services that women seek to deal with their domestic violence experiences. The findings of this project will be useful in helping domestic violence programs improve their services to better meet the needs of their clients.

During the interview you will be asked questions about your experiences with domestic violence. We will be discussing specific incidents that happened in the past as well as more recent incidents. The interview will last approximately an hour. The interview will be audiotape-recorded so that all of the information that you provide will be recorded accurately and completely. If at any time you feel uncomfortable and wish for the interview to be stopped, let the interviewer know and the interview will be terminated.

The questions you will be asked have neither right nor wrong answers. We want to know what has happened to you in your life and see what you think about the services you have received.

If you decide to participate, you will receive $25.00 when the interview session is over.

All the information that you provide will be confidential. What you tell the interviewer will not be connected to your name. No one in your community or agency that provides you services will know who said what.

Consent Form

I have read the above information. I understand that the interview will be audiotape-recorded. I understand that the information that I provide is strictly confidential. I understand that my name will not be used in connection with the information I provide. I understand that I can terminate the interview at any time. I understand that I will receive $25.00 for the completion of the interview. I understand that the interviewer will try to the best of her ability to answer any questions that I may have regarding the interview.

_____   _____

Print Name   Date

_____

Signature

Receipts for Interviewee Fees

I have received $25.00 for completing the interview for the "Seeking Domestic Violence Interventions" Project being conducted by Dr. Marilyn Fernandez.

Name or Initial   *Signature OR Initial*   *Date*
1.
2.
3.
.
.
.
35.

Interview Schedule

INTRODUCTION

Hello, my name is Marilyn Fernandez and I am an assistant professor in the anthropology and sociology department at Santa Clara University. I am conducting this research to find out the types of services that women seek to deal with their domestic violence experiences. The information that you provide will help improve the services and programs available to women who have experienced domestic violence.

I will be asking you questions about any violence that you have experienced with someone close to you. Before talking about your experiences with domestic violence, I would like to ask you some questions about your background.

I. DEMOGRAPHIC BACKGROUND

1. What city do you live in?
2. What is your date of birth?
3. With which race/ethnic group(s) do you identify yourself?
4. What is your primary language?
5. Are you currently married?
6. If yes, how long have you been married?
7. Is this your first marriage? If not, how any times have you been married? Explore marital history: age at first marriage, divorces, etc.
8. How many children do you have? How old is the oldest child? How old is the youngest child? Explore children in each marriage/relationship.

9. How many years of education have you had?
10. Do you currently work? If yes, full- or part-time? What kind of work do you do? How long have you had this job?
11. How many total years have you worked at your current and previous jobs?
12. What sources of income do you have currently?

II. DOMESTIC VIOLENCE EXPERIENCES

Now I would like for us to talk about your experiences with domestic violence. Domestic violence can include one or more of the following kinds of abuse by someone close to you:

Physical:	Pushed; shoved; slapped; restrained; grabbed; punched; kicked; choked; pulled hair; bit; burned; struck with object; used a weapon against you;
Emotional:	Putting you down; calling you names; making you think you're crazy; mind games; humiliating you; making you feel guilty;
Sexual:	Criticism of sexual performance, name calling of sexual nature; forced sexual activity; threats used if sex undesired; denial of sex; sex after beatings;
Intimidation:	Frightening you by certain looks; gestures; actions; smashing things; destroying your property or pets; displaying weapons to scare you;
Psychological:	Verbal threats; stalking; annoying telephone calls; mail threats; death or harm threats;
Isolation:	Keeps you from going places (such as work, school, seeing friends, women's groups, etc.) you choose; listens to your phone conversations; opens mail; follows you around; questions your whereabouts using jealousy to justify actions;
Minimizing:	Making light of abuse; saying it didn't happen; saying it is your fault;
Using children:	Making you feel guilty about children; using visitation to harass you; threatening to take children away; threatening to harm children;
Male privilege:	Treating you like a servant; acting like the "master of the castle"; making all the "big" decisions; defining your role/job;

Economic: Preventing you from working outside the home; making
                       you ask for money; taking your money; not letting
                       you know about family income;

Coercion and threats   Threats to take children away, to harm you or your fam-
                       ily and friends; to report you to welfare; to destroy
                       your property; to commit suicide; to leave you; to
                       force you to drop charges; to make you do something
                       illegal.

A. DOMESTIC VIOLENCE INCIDENT

1. Could we start with your most recent experience of domestic violence? Or if
   you prefer we could start with any other incident?
   • Who was the batterer?
   • When did this incident happen? Date? Time?
   • Where did the incident happen?
   • Who else was involved or present?
2. What happened during this incident?
   • How did the incident start? What were the circumstances leading up to the
     battering incident?
   • What did the batterer do? (Possible types of abuse from above)
   • How long did this incident last? Hours? Days?
3. What did you do during this incident?
   • How did you feel? (Alone, scared, angry, at fault, etc.)
   • Did you try to get help at that time? What did you do?
4. How did this incident end?
   • What did the batterer do?
   • Did you try to stop the abuse? How so?
   • Was someone else involved in stopping the incident? Describe, please.
   • How did you feel after this incident?
   • Then what happened?
5. What kind of help, if any, did you seek? (Call or visit a friend, family mem-
   ber, church, social service agency, hospital, police, crisis hotline, shelter,
   etc.)
   • Did you know what types of services were available to you? Examples?
   • If you did not seek services, why not?
   • If you did not seek help immediately after the incident, when did you start
     reaching out for help? What prompted your actions?
   • Then what happened?

6. Did the sources of help that you turned to meet your needs?
   - If yes, in what ways? How helpful were they?
   - If no, what else could they have done?
7. What was the final outcome of this incident of domestic violence?
   - Did the relationship end temporarily or permanently?
   - Was any legal action taken? What kind?

B. OTHER INCIDENTS

1. Is this the first incidence of domestic violence that you have experienced?
   - If not, when was the first incident? (Could be as early as childhood)
   - REPEAT QUESTIONS A1–A7
2. Are these the most severe incidents of domestic violence that you have experienced?
   - If not, would like for you to think about the most severe incident of domestic violence that you have experienced.
   - REPEAT QUESTIONS A1–A7

Thank you for your participation. The information you have shared is of great value and importance to this study.

Survey Instrument for the Domestic Violence Service Utilization Survey

ID Number _____

Date of Interview: _____

SURVEY OF SERVICES FOR DOMESTIC VIOLENCE VICTIMS IN SC COUNTY

May I please speak to _____?

Hello, I'm _____. I'm calling from the Domestic Violence Council of SC County. Last March, while at the Support Network for Battered Women, you agreed to participate in a telephone survey regarding your experiences with domestic violence. Is this a good time to talk with you? The survey would take at least fifteen to twenty minutes.

Yes _____ No _____

If this is not a good time, when could I call you back?

(If "yes," begin the survey)

A. *DEMOGRAPHIC BACKGROUND*

I would like to start with a few questions about your background.

A1.   What is your city of residence? _____

A2.   What is your date of birth (how old are you)? _____ _____ _____

                                                              (Mo) (Day) (Year)

A3.   With which race/ethnic group(s) do you identify yourself?

_____

A4.   What is your primary language? _____

A5a.   Are you currently married? _____ Yes _____ No.

A5b.   If "yes," how long have you been married? _____ (years) _____ (months).

A6a.   How many children do you have? _____ *(If "none," skip to Q. A7)*
A6b.   How old is the oldest child? _____
A6c.   How old is the youngest child? _____
A7.   How many years of education have you had? _____
A8a.   Do you currently work? _____ Full-time _____ Part-time ___ No. *(If "no," skip to Q. A8d)*
A8b.   What type of work do you do? _____
A8c.   How long have you worked at this job? _____
A8d.   How many total years have you worked (at your current and previous jobs)? _____

B. EXPERIENCE WITH DOMESTIC VIOLENCE
Now, I would like to ask you a few questions about possible experiences you may have had with domestic violence.

B1.   In your total experience, how many abusive relationships have you experienced? _____ abusive relationships

(Interviewer: If respondent answers "no" or "none" to Q. B1, end the interview by thanking her for her time and asking her whether she would want to hear about a list of services related to domestic violence available in Santa Clara County for future reference and/or for the reference of someone else she may know who may be experiencing domestic violence.)

B2.   When was the first time you experienced domestic violence?

____ ____ ____
(Mo) (Day) (Year)

B3.   What was your relationship with the batterer at the time of the first incident of violence? *(Circle all that apply)*

01 = Casual/dating _____ Heterosexual _____ Gay/Lesbian
02 = Live-in _____ Heterosexual _____ Gay/Lesbian
03 = Business
04 = Married
05 = Separated
06 = Divorced
07 = Through visitation with children
08 = No relationship
09 = Parent/child
10 = Relative
11 = Not currently involved
12 = Other *(specify)* _____
13 = Does not apply to me
99 = No answer

B4.   How long had you been in this relationship? _____

B5. In the first incident, what did the batterer do?

Interviewer: For each category of abuse, ask the flowing questions. As you read the different categories of abuse, please provide examples of different types.

B5a. Did he/she use:

	Yes	No
Physical abuse:	___	___
Emotional:	___	___
Sexual:	___	___
Intimidation:	___	___
Psychological:	___	___
Isolation:	___	___
Minimizing, denying, and blaming:	___	___
Using children:	___	___
Male privilege:	___	___
Economic abuse:	___	___
Coercion and threats:	___	___
Other *(specify)*:	___	___

(Interviewer: Here are some examples of the different categories of abuse.)

—Physical: Pushed; shoved; slapped; restrained; grabbed; punched; kicked; choked; pulled hair; bit; burned; struck with object; used a weapon against you;

—Emotional: Putting you down; calling you names; making you think you're crazy; mind games; humiliating you; making you feel guilty;

—Sexual: Criticism of sexual performance, name calling of sexual nature; forced sexual activity; threats used if sex undesired; denial of sex; sex after beatings;

—Intimidation: Frightening you by certain looks; gestures; actions; smashing things; destroying your property or pets; displaying weapons to scare you;

—Psychological: Verbal threats; stalking; annoying telephone calls; mail threats; death or harm threats;

—Isolation: Keeps you from going places (such as work, school, seeing friends, women's groups, etc.) you choose; listens to your phone conversations; opens mail; follows you around; questions your whereabouts using jealousy to justify actions;

—Minimizing: Making light of abuse; saying it didn't happen; saying it is your fault;

—Using children: Making you feel guilty about children; using visitation to harass you; threatening to take children away; threatening to harm children;

—Male privilege: Treating you like a servant; acting like the "master of the castle"; making all the "big" decisions; defining your role/job;

—Economic: Preventing you from working outside the home; making you ask for money; taking your money; not letting you know about family income;

—Coercion and threats: Threats to take children away, to harm you or your family and friends; to report you to welfare; to destroy your property; to commit suicide; to leave you; to force you to drop charges; to make you do something illegal.

B5b. How long did the first incident last? (i.e., an evening, a day, a couple of days, a week, etc.): _____

B6a. Did you seek help from and public or private support groups at that time?
       0 = No   *(If "no," skip to Q. B7a)*
       1 = Yes

B6b. If "yes," what support group or groups did you use? Please state which ones you used.

_____

Could you now think about your childhood?

B7a. As a child, did anyone abuse you? Yes_____ No_____

B7b. If "yes," who and how? _____

B7c. Did you know anybody in your family who was abused?
       Yes_____   No_____

B7d. If "yes,"   *Who was abused?*   *Who was the abuser?*

       _____   _____

       _____   _____

       _____   _____

C. MOST SEVERE EXPERIENCE WITH DOMESTIC VIOLENCE

I would like to ask you some questions about what you would consider the most severe incident of abuse you've experienced.

C1a. In your opinion, when did the most severe incident of violence occur?

_____ _____ _____
(Mo) (Day) (Year)   *(Write date on Q. D1)*

C1b. Where were you when this happened? _____

(Interviewer: If this incident is the same as the first incident, skip to Q. C3.)

C2. What was your relationship with the batterer at the time of the most severe incident of violence? *(Circle all that apply)*
       01 = Casual/dating _____ Heterosexual _____ Gay/Lesbian
       02 = Live in   _____ Heterosexual _____ Gay/Lesbian
       03 = Business
       04 = Married
       05 = Separated

06 = Divorced

07 = Through visitation with children

08 = No relationship

09 = Parent/child

10 = Relative

11 = Not currently involved

12 = Other *(specify)* _____

13 = Does not apply to me

99 = No answer

C3. What is your present relationship with the batterer? *(Circle all that apply)*

01 = Casual/dating _____ Heterosexual _____ Gay/Lesbian

02 = Live-in _____ Heterosexual _____ Gay/Lesbian

03 = Business

04 = Married

05 = Separated

06 = Divorced

07 = Through visitation with children

08 = No relationship

09 = Parent/child

10 = Relative

11 = Not currently involved

12 = Other *(specify)* _____

13 = Does not apply to me

99 = No answer

C4. How long have (had) you been in this relationship? _____
(Years, Months, or Days)

C5. What are the factors keeping (kept) you in the relationship with the batterer of the most severe incident? *(Please circle all that apply)*

01 = Fear of the batterer

02 = Children

03 = Financial

04 = Religion

05 = Pressure from extended family

06 = Security

07 = Married status

08 = Self-pressure

09 = Other *(specify)* _____

10 = Other *(specify)* _____

11 = Other *(specify)* _____

99 = Does not apply to me/not in relationship right now

(Interviewer: If most severe incident is the same as the first one, skip to Q. C8a.)
C6a.   In the most severe incident, what did the batterer do?
(Interviewer: For each category of abuse, ask the flowing questions. As you read the different categories of abuse, please provide examples of different types.)
Did he/she use:

	Yes	No
Physical abuse:	___	___
Emotional:	___	___
Sexual:	___	___
Intimidation:	___	___
Psychological:	___	___
Isolation:	___	___
Minimizing, denying, and blaming:	___	___
Using children:	___	___
Male privilege:	___	___
Economic abuse:	___	___
Coercion and threats:	___	___
Other *(specify)*	___	___

C6b.   How long did this most severe incident last? _____
C7a.   Is the abuser in this most severe incident the same person from the very first abuse experience?
         0 = No *(If "no," skip to Q. C8a)*
         1 = Yes
         9 = No answer
C7b.   If "yes," has the relationship changed now? (e.g., from marriage to divorce, separation, remains the same) _____

C8a.   During the most severe incident, did the batterer threaten to harm you or anyone less?
         0 = No   *(Skip to Q. C9)*
         1 = Yes
         8 = Does not apply to me   *(Skip to Q. C9)*
         9 = No answer
C8b.   If "yes," did you believe the treat when it was made?
         0 = No
         1 = Yes
         8 = Does not apply to me
         9 = No answer
C9.   Were you afraid that the batterer would kill you?
         0 = No
         1 = Yes

2 = Not sure

8 = Does not apply to me

9 = No answer

C10. Are you currently afraid that the batter might kill you?

0 = No

1 = Yes

2 = Yes and No

8 = Does not apply to me

9 = No answer

C11a. Was the most severe incident the most recent incident of abuse you have experienced?

0 = No

1 = Yes

9 = No answer

C11b. Please describe why you answered "yes"/"no" _____

(Interviewer: Probe for what happened and how long ago. Please try and get the exact date: _____ Month, _____ Day, _____ Year.)

D. POLICE INVOLVEMENT IN THE MOST SEVERE INCIDENT

Now let's focus on the most severe incident, though there may be other incidents on your mind.

D1. When the most severe incident occur: _____ (month), _____ (day), _____ (yr) (to be filled by the interviewer from C1a)

Were the police called? _____ Yes _____ No

Interviewer: If "yes" (i.e., police were involved in the most severe incident), skip to Q. D2 below. If "no," ask Q. D1a.

D1a. Was there another incident in which police were called?

_____ Yes _____ No

Interviewer: If "yes," ask the remaining questions on the survey, beginning with Q. D1b, pertaining to the most recent incident in which the police were called. If "no," skip to Q. E1.

D1b. When did this incident (the most recent incident with police involvement) occur? _____ (month), _____ (day), _____ (yr).

D1c. What happened during this incident? _____

_____

D1d. Where were you when this happened? _____

_____

D2. Who called the police? _____

_____

D3a. What did the police do with the batterer when they arrived? _____

_____

D3b.   What did the police do with you when they arrived? _____
_____

D3c.   What did the police do with the child(ren) when they arrived? *(If there are no children, skip to Q. D4a.)* _____
_____

D4a.   Did you make any specific requests to the police? _____ Yes _____ No
D4b.   If "yes," what was (were) the request(s)? _____
_____

D5.   Was there a follow-up investigation by the police in the most severe incident?
       0 = No
       1 = Yes
       8 = Does not apply to me
       9 = No answer

D6.   Did you know then that criminal charges could be brought against the batterer without your agreement?
       0 = No
       1 = Yes
       8 = Does not apply to me
       9 = No answer

Interviewer: If a child or children were interviewed by a police officer for this domestic violence battering incident, ask Q. D7 and Q. D8. (If not, skip to Q. E1.)

D7.   Was the child interviewed in a sensitive manner (meaning that the police officer was gentle and sympathetic in his/her handling of the child, showed concern for the child, seemed to understand that the child may be afraid, has been traumatized, etc.)?
       0 = No
       1 = Yes
       8 = Does not apply to me *(Skip to Q. E1)*
       9 = No answer *(Skip to Q. E1)*

D8.   Why did you think the police officers were (or were not) sensitive to the children? _____

E. *CRIMINAL COURT INVOLVEMENT*
    E1.   In the most severe incident of abuse against you *(or the most recent incident in which the police were called)* what types of court involvement were there?
    Interviewer: Check whether the following questions are based on:
           a) Severe incident _____
           b) Recent incident with police involvement _____

Interviewer: Circle all that apply.

    0 = No criminal court involvement *(Skip to Q. H1a)*
    1 = Criminal court *(Skip to Q. E2)*
    2 = No court trial, just diversion *(Skip to Q. G1)*
    8 = Does not apply to me *(Skip to Q. H1a)*
    9 = No answer *(Skip to Q. H1a)*

E2.   Did you understand the court process in the most severe incident?
    0 = No
    1 = Somewhat/kind of/a little bit
    2 = Yes
    8 = Does not apply to me
    9 = No answer

E3.   Did you understand the charges against the batterer?
    0 = No
    1 = Somewhat/kind of/a little bit
    2 = Yes
    8 = Does not apply to me
    9 = No answer

E4.   Did you know what would happen to the batterer?
    0 = No
    1 = Somewhat/kind of/a little bit
    2 = Yes
    8 = Does not apply to me
    9 = No answer

E5.   What did you think would happen to the batterer? _____
_____

E6.   Did you testify?
    0 = No
    1 = Yes, against the abuser
    2 = Yes, for the abuser
    8 = Does not apply to me
    9 = No answer

E7.   While waiting court action, where was the batterer?
    1 = In jail
    2 = Out on bail
    3 = Released on OR (own recognizance)
    4 = Released under supervision by court personnel
    5 = Other *(specify)* _____

E8.   On a scale of 0 to 5 (lowest to highest), rate your satisfaction with what happened to him, while waiting for court action related to the most severe incident (or the most recent with police involvement):

0 = Not at all satisfied
1 =
2 =
3 =
4 =
5 = Very satisfied
8 = Don't know what happened
9 = No answer

E9. Do you believe that the judge was sensitive toward you?
0 = No
1 = Somewhat/kind of/a little bit
2 = Yes
8 = Does not apply to me
9 = No answer

E10. What did the judge do (or not do) to make you feel that the judge was sensitive/insensitive toward you? _____
_____

Outcomes of Criminal Court Involvement

Now, let's talk about what happened in criminal court in connection with the most severe incident (or the most recent incident in which the police were called).

E11. During the criminal court involvement for the most severe incident (or the most recent incident in which the police were called), was the batterer convicted?
1 = No *(Skip to Q. G1)*
2 = Yes
8 = Does not apply to me *(Skip to Q. G1)*
9 = No answer

E12. During the criminal court involvement, if the batterer was convicted, what type(s) of sentencing did the batterer receive? *(Interviewer: Circle all that apply.)*
1 = A jail sentence imposed *(Interviewer: Jail is local; write the name of the place)* _____
2 = Prison sentence imposed *(Interviewer: Prison is in the state system; write the name of the place of incarceration.)* _____
3 = Electronic monitoring
4 = Work furlough
5 = Community alternative program
6 = Other *(specify)*
8 = Does not apply to me *(Skip to Q. G1)*

E13. How long were the sentences? _____

E14a. Was a "no-contact" order made by the criminal court? *(Circle all that apply)*
0 = No *(Skip to Q. E15 below)*
1 = Yes
2 = Don't know
9 = No answer

E14b. If "yes," whom did the "no-contact" order protect?
1 = Yes, a "no-contact" with me
2 = Yes, a "no-contact" with the child(ren)
3 = Yes, a "no-contact" with other relatives/friends
4 = Don't know

E15. Overall, was your criminal court involvement in the most severe incident (or the most recent incident with police involvement):
0 = Negative
1 = Satisfactory/"OK"
2 = Positive
9 = Does not apply to me

E16. Why do you think that? _____

_____

F. PROBATION

F1. During the criminal court involvement for the most severe incident (or the most recent incident in which police were called), if the batterer was convicted, was the batterer placed on probation?
0 = No *(Skip to Q. F8)*
1 = Yes
2 = Other *(specify)*
3 = Don't know
8 = Does not apply to me
9 = No answer

F2. What type of probation did the batterer receive?
1 = Formal probation (Probation officer involved)
2 = Court probation (court in charge of probation with no supervision)
3 = Other *(specify)* _____
8 = Does not apply to me
9 = No answer

F3. Did you have contact with the probation officer?
0 = No
1 = Yes

2 = Other *(specify)* _____

8 = Does not apply to me

9 = No answer

F4.   On a scale from 0 to 5 (lowest to highest), how helpful was the probation officer?

0 = Not at all helpful

1 =

2 =

3 =

4 =

5 = Very helpful

F5.   Please explain your response to the previous question. _____
_____

F6.   Did having the batterer on probation make a difference?

0 = No

1 = Yes

2 = Other *(specify)* _____

8 = Does not apply to me

9 = No answer

F7.   Please explain your response to the previous question. _____
_____

F8.   Is there any type of assistance that you feel you needed, but were unable to obtain?

0 = No (Skip to Q. F10)

1 = Yes

8 = Does not apply to me *(Skip to Q. F10)*

9 = No answer *(Skip to Q. F10)*

F9.   If "yes," what type of assistance did you need that you were unable to get? _____

F10. On a scale of 0 to 5 (lowest to highest), how do you feel about your experience(s) with the probation system when you dealt with it for the most severe incident (or the most recent incident with police involvement)?

0 = Not at all satisfied

1 =

2 =

3 =

4 =

5 = Very satisfied

F11. Please explain your response to the previous question. _____
_____

G. DIVERSION

G1.   Was the batterer granted diversion (court-ordered batterer's treatment program) in the most severe incident (or the most recent incident in which the police were called)?

0 = No *(Skip to Section H1a)*
1 = Yes *(Skip to Q. G2)*
2 = Do not know *(Skip to Section H1a)*
8 = Does not apply to me *(Skip to Section H1a)*
9 = No answer *(Skip to Section H1a)*

G2.   If "yes," what type of treatment programs were ordered? _____
_____

G3.   Did the batterer complete the treatment program(s)?

0 = No
1 = Yes *(Skip to Q. G5)*
2 = Other *(explain)* _____
      (Skip to Q. G5)
8 = Don't know *(Skip to Q. G5)*
9 = No answer *(Skip to Q. G5)*

G4.   How come the batterer did not complete the counseling program?
_____

G5.   On a scale of 0 to 5 (lowest to highest), rate your satisfaction with this outcome—that is, of the batterer being granted diversion?

0 = Not at all satisfied
1 =
2 =
3 =
4 =
5 = Very satisfied
9 = No answer

G6.   Why do you feel so (either satisfied or dissatisfied)? _____
_____

H. FAMILY COURT

H1a.   Was there family court involvement in any of the following:
_____in most severe incident or in the most recent incident in which police were called *(Interviewer: Skip to Q. H1e)*
_____in another recent incident *(Interviewer: Begin with Q. H1b)*
_____if no family court involvement at all *(Interviewer: Skip to Q. I1a)*

H1b.   When did this incident in which family court were involved occur?
_____ (Month), _____ (Day), _____ (Yr).

H1c. What happened during this incident? _____
_____

H1d. Where were you when this incident happened? _____
_____

H1e. Now I would like to ask you a few questions about family court involvement.
Interviewer: Check whether questions refer to:
_____ *Most severe incident*
_____ *Most recent incident with police involvement*
_____ *Most recent incident with family court involvement*

H1f. Did you understand the family court process?
0 = No
1 = Somewhat/kind of/a little bit
2 = Yes
8 = Does not apply to me
9 = No answer

H2. Which of the following issues were involved in your family court proceedings? *(Interviewer: Check all those that apply.)*
_____ Custody
_____ Visitation rights
_____ Child support
_____ Restraining order
_____ Separation
_____ Divorce
_____ Other *(specify)* _____

H3. Who initiated the family court proceedings in the most severe incident (or the most recent incident with police involvement or with the recent incident with family court involvement)?
_____ You
_____ The batterer
_____ Other *(specify)* _____

H4. What were the results of these family court procedures? *(Check all those that apply, and add details, when possible.)*
_____ Custody for you _____
_____ Custody for the batterer _____
_____ Custody for both _____
_____ Visitation _____
_____ Child support _____
_____ Restraining order _____
_____ Domestic violence counseling _____

_____ Parenting education _____

_____ Separation

_____ Divorce

_____ Other *(specify)* _____

H5. Did you testify at the family court proceedings?

0 = No

1 = Yes

8 = Does not apply to me

9 = No answer

H6. Do you believe that the judge was sensitive toward you?

0 = No

1 = Yes

8 = Does not apply to me

9 = No answer

H7. What did the judge do (or not do) to make you feel that the judge was sensitive/not sensitive toward you? _____

_____

H8a. Was a "no-contact" order made by the family court in the most severe incident (or most recent incident with the police involvement or the most recent incident with the family court involvement)?

0 = No *(Skip to Q. H9 below)*

1 = Yes

2 = Don't know

9 = No answer

H8b. If "yes," whom did the "no-contact" order protect? *(Circle all that apply.)*

1 = Yes, a "no-contact" with me

2 = Yes, a "no-contact" with the child(ren)

3 = Yes, a "no-contact" with other relatives/friends

4 = Don't know

H9. Overall, was your family court involvement regarding the most severe incident (or most recent incident with the police involvement or the most recent incident with the family court involvement):

0 = Negative

1 = Satisfactory/"OK"

2 = Positive

8 = Does not apply to me

9 = No answer

H10. Why do you think so? _____

_____

I.   COUNSELING

I1a.   Did the batterer receive a counseling order in the most severe incident?
       0 = No *(Skip to Q. I1.b)*
       1 = Yes *(Skip to Q. I2)*
       2 = Don't know *(Skip to Q. I1.b)*
       8 = Does not apply to me *(Skip to Q. I1.b)*
       9 = No answer *(Skip to Q. I1.b)*

I1b.   Did the batterer receive a counseling order in the most recent incident with police involvement?
       0 = No *(Skip to Q. I1.c)*
       1 = Yes *(Skip to Q. I2)*
       2 = Don't know *(Skip to Q. I1.c)*
       8 = Does not apply to me *(Skip to Q. I1.c)*
       9 = No answer *(Skip to Q. I1.c)*

I1c.   Did the batterer receive a counseling order in any other recent incident?
       0 = No *(Skip to Q. J1a)*
       1 = Yes *(Skip to Q. I1d)*
       2 = Don't know *(Skip to Q. J1a)*
       8 = Does not apply to me *(Skip to Q. J1a)*
       9 = No answer *(Skip to Q. J1a)*

I1d.   When did this incident occur? _____ (Month), _____ (Day), _____ (Yr).

I1e.   What happened during this incident? _____
       _____

I1f.   Where were you when incident happened? _____
       _____

I2.   Who ordered the counseling? *(circle all that apply)*
       00 = Criminal judge
       01 = Family court
       02 = Self-initiated
       03 = Other *(explain)* _____

I3.   If "yes," what type of counseling was ordered for the batterer? *(Please circle all answers that apply.)*
       1 = Group (certified group counseling program thirty-two weeks and one year)
       2 = Other group counseling
       3 = Individual
       4 = Alcohol/drug
       5 = Parenting

6 = Other *(specify)* _____

8 = Does not apply to me

9 = No answer

14. Did the batterer complete the counseling program?

0 = No

1 = Yes *(Skip to Q. 16)*

2 = Other *(explain)* _____

8 = Don't know *(Skip to Q. 16)*

9 = No answer *(Skip to Q. 16)*

15. How come the batterer did not complete the counseling program?

_____

16. On a scale of 0 to 5 (lowest to highest), how satisfied were you with the counseling order that the batterer received for the most severe incident (or the most recent incident with police involvement or the incident for which the batterer received counseling)?

0 = Not at all satisfied

1 =

2 =

3 =

4 =

5 = Very satisfied

17. Why did you feel so (either satisfied or dissatisfied with the counseling order)? _____

_____

OTHER SERVICES: BATTERED WOMEN'S AGENCIES, VICTIM WITNESS SERVICES, AND BATTERED WOMEN'S SHELTER

Now I'd like to ask you some questions about the services you may have used.

J. BATTERED WOMEN'S AGENCIES

J1a. In connection with the most severe incident of violence against you, did you contact a battered women's agency and/or shelter services?

0 = No *(Skip to Q. J1b)*

1 = Yes *(Skip to Q. J2)*

8 = Does not apply to me *(Skip to Q. J1b)*

9 = No answer *(Skip to Q. J1b)*

J1b. In connection with the most recent incident with police involvement, did you contact a battered women's agency and/or shelter services?

0 = No *(Skip to Q. J1c)*

1 = Yes *(Skip to Q. J2)*

8 = Does not apply to me *(Skip to Q. J1c)*
9 = No answer

J1c. In connection with any other recent incident, did you contact a battered women's agency and/or shelter services?
0 = No *(Skip to Q. K1)*
1 = Yes *(Skip to Q. J1d)*
2 = Do not know *(Skip to Q. K1)*
8 = Does not apply to me *(Skip to Q. K1)*
9 = No answer *(Skip to Q. K1)*

J1d. When did this incident occur? _____ (Month), _____ (Day), _____ (Yr).

J1e. What happened during this incident? _____
_____

J1f. Where were you when this incident happened? _____
_____

J2. What services did you use? *(Circle all that apply.)*
0 = Shelter
1 = Legal assistance
2 = Support group
3 = Individual counseling
4 = Hotline
5 = Crisis counseling
6 = Other *(specify)* _____
7 = Does not apply to me
8 = No answer

J3. Of the above-mentioned services, which one did you use most in the most severe incident (or the most recent incident with police involvement of one incident mentioned in Q. J1c)? *(Circle only one.)*
1 = Shelter
2 = Legal assistance
3 = Support group
4 = Individual counseling
5 = Hotline
6 = Crisis counseling
7 = Other *(specify)* _____
8 = Does not apply to me
9 = No answer

J4. Were these services available in your primary language?
0 = No
1 = Only some
2 = Yes

8 = Does not apply to me

9 = No answer

J5. What services did you need, but were not available in connection with the most severe incident (or the most recent incident with police involvement or the incident mentioned in Q. J1c)? _____

_____

J6. Would you recommend these services to other battered women?

0 = No

1 = Yes

8 = Does not apply to me

9 = No answer

J7. Why do you say so? _____

J8. What was your overall experience with these services for battered women that you used in the most severe incident (or the most recent incident with police involvement, or the one incident mentioned in Q. J1c)?

0 = Negative

1 = Adequate/"OK"/All right

2 = Positive

3 = Other (explain) _____

9 = No answer

J9. How many times have you contacted battered women's agencies?

_____

SERVICE SHELTERS

Now we are going to ask some specific questions about your experiences with shelter services, if/when you used them.

(Interviewer: Check Q. J2 to see if a shelter was used. If "yes," go to Q. J11. If "no" service shelter used, skip to Q. K1.)

J11. After the most severe incident (or the most recent incident with police involvement or the one incident mentioned in Q. J1c), how long did you stay in the shelter? (Or if currently staying in the shelter, how long have you been at the shelter?) _____

_____

J12. If currently in the shelter, how much longer do you think you will stay at the shelter? _____

J13. On a scale from 0 to 5 (lowest to highest), how helpful was the staff at the shelter, when you were there for the most severe incident (or the most recent incident with police involvement or the one incident mentioned in Q. J1c)?

0 = Not at all helpful
1 =
2 =
3 =
4 =
5 = Very helpful

J14.   Why did you feel so (about the helpfulness of the staff)? _____
_____

J15.   If you experience abuse again, would you return to the shelter?
0 = No
1 = Yes
8 = Does not apply to me
9 = No answer

(Interviewer: If no children involved, skip to Q. J21.)

J16.   Did this shelter offer services for children?
0 = No *(Skip to Q. J21)*
2 = Yes
8 = Does not apply to me *(Skip to Q. J21)*
9 = No answer

J17.   What type of services did the shelter offer for children? _____
_____

J18.   How helpful were the services that were offered to your children when you were there after the most severe incident (or the most recent incident with police involvement of the incident mentioned in Q. J1c)?
0 = Not at all helpful
1 =
2 =
3 =
4 =
5 = Very helpful

J19.   Why did you think the services offered to your children were ____?
_____

J20.   What services were needed by the children but were not available at the shelter? _____

J21.   Overall, how many times have you stayed at a shelter? _____

K. *MISCELLANEOUS*

K1.   Do you know about victim witness services?
0 =No
1 = Yes

8 = Does not apply to me

9 = No answer

K2.   If you do, could you tell me what you know about it? _____

_____

_____

L. CONCLUSION

In closing, I would like to ask you a few questions about your future.

L1.   How are things going for you right now? _____

_____

L2.   Do you think you will be battered again?

0 = No

1 = Yes

2 = Don't know

8 = Does not apply to me

9 = No answer

L3.   Why do you think, you will/will not/do not know whether you will be battered again? Please explain. _____

_____

L4.   If you are ever battered again, what will you do? *(Interviewer: Do not read the list. Please circle all that are mentioned.)*

0 = Nothing

1 = Do not know

2 = Call or report to police

3 = Request prosecution

4 = Seek counseling

5 = Go to a shelter

6 = Seek help from a family member

7 = Get out of the situation

8 = Will see to it that I am never battered again

9 = Other *(specify)* _____

10 = Does not apply to me

L5.   Could you explain why you would choose this/these alternatives?

_____

_____

Interviewer: End the interview with the following "thank you" statement:

Thank you for sharing your experiences with us. I realize it may have been difficult for you. But your opinions and experiences will really help the Domestic Violence Council. They are looking at existing programs to see how to improve the services for battered people. And what you have shared with us will be extremely helpful.

There are many services available today in Santa Clara County to help people who experience domestic violence. Would you like any of the "hotline" numbers? ____ Yes ____ No

Would you like to get a copy of the service list with their telephone numbers? ___ Yes ___ No

If "yes," to what address would you want us to send this list to? Let me reassure you that this address will be kept in the strictest confidence. _____

_____

(Interviewer: Assure the respondent that the address will be kept separately from her survey, so that their anonymity will always be ensured.)

NOTE: Source of subject's name (please check relevant one):
_____ Probation files
_____ Shelter contacts
_____ District attorney's office
_____ Other *(specify)*

References

American Bar Association, Commission on Domestic Violence. 2005. Retrieved June 27, 2005. www.abanet.org/domviol/stats.html.

Bachman, Ronet, and Dianne Cyr Carmody. 1994. "Fighting Fire with Fire: The Effects of Victim Resistance in Intimate Versus Stranger Perpetrated Assaults Against Females." *Journal of Family Violence* 9(4): 317–31.

Bandura, Albert. 2003. *Self-efficacy: The Exercise of Control* (sixth edition). New York: Freeman.

Benson, Michael L., John Wooldredge, Amy B. Thistlewaite, and Greer Litton Fox. 2004. "The Correlation between Race and Domestic Violence Is Confounded with Community Context." *Social Problems* 51(3): 326–42.

Braithwaite, John. 2002. *Restorative Justice and Responsive Regulation*. New York: Oxford University Press.

Bronfenbrenner, Urie. 1979. *The Ecology of Human Development: Experiments by Nature and Design*. Cambridge, MA: Harvard University Press.

Browne, Angela. 1987. *When Battered Women Kill*. New York: Free Press.

Browning, Christopher. 2002. "The Span of Collective Efficacy: Extending Social Disorganization Theory to Partner Violence." *Journal of Marriage and the Family* 64: 833–50.

Burke, Jessica G., Andrea Carlson Gielen, Karen A. McDonnell, Patricia O'Campo, and Suzanne Maman. 2001. "The Process of Ending Abuse in Intimate Relationships: A Qualitative Exploration of the Transtheoretical Model." *Violence Against Women* 7(10): 1144–63.

Busch, Ruth. 2000. "Innovative Approaches to Child Custody and Domestic Violence in New Zealand: The Effects of Law Reform on the Discourses of Battering," in *Children Exposed to Domestic Violence: Current Issues in Research, Intervention, Prevention, and Policy Development*, Robert Geffner, Peter G. Jaffe, and Marlies Sudermann (eds.). New York: The Haworth Press.

———. 2002. "Domestic Violence and Restorative Justice Initiatives: Who Pays If We Get It Wrong?" in *Restorative Justice and Family Violence*, Heather Strang and John Braithwaite (eds.), 223–48. New York: Cambridge University Press.

Byrne, Michelle. 2001, February. "Sampling for Qualitative Research." *AORN Journal* 73(2). Retrieved December 24, 2008.

California Department of Justice, Office of the Attorney General. 2004. "Domestic Violence Task Force Report, News Release." July 2005. www.ag.ca.gov.

California Partnership to End Domestic Violence. 2007. "Statewide Press Release." September 2007. www.cpedv.org/docs_2007/DVAM_2007_STATEWIDE_PRESS_RELEASE.pdf.

Cameron, Angela. 2005. "Restorative Justice: A Literature Review." *The British Columbia Institute Against Family Violence*. Vancouver, Canada, BC. Retrieved June 29, 2005. www.bcifv.org/pubs/Restorative_Justice_Lit_Review.pdf.

Campbell, Jacquelyn C., Linda Rose, Joan Kub, and Daphne Nedd. 1998. "Voices of Strength and Resistance: A Contextual and Longitudinal Analysis of Women's Responses to Battering." *Journal of Interpersonal Violence* 13(6): 743–62.

Cherlin, Andrew J., Linda M. Burton, Tera R. Hurt, and Diane M. Purvin. 2004. "The Influence of Physical and Sexual Abuse on Marriage and Cohabitation." *American Sociological Review* 69(6): 768–89.

Coker, Donna. 1999. "Enhancing Autonomy for Battered Women: Lessons from Navajo Peacemaking." *UCLA Law Review* 47(1): 1–111.

———. 2002. "Transformative Justice: Anti-Subordination Processes in Cases of Domestic Violence," in *Restorative Justice and Family Violence*, Heather Strang and John Braithwaite (eds.), 128–52. New York: Cambridge University Press.

Curtis-Fawley, Sarah, and Kathleen Daly. 2005. "Gendered Violence and Restorative Justice: The Views of Victim Advocates." *Violence Against Women* 11(5): 603–38.

Coward, Stephanie. 2002. "Restorative Justice in Cases of Domestic and Sexual Violence: Healing Justice." *Abuse Info and Resources*. Retrieved June 29, 2005. www.hotpeachpages.net/canada/air/rj_domestic_violence.html.

Dobash, R. Emerson, and Russell P. Dobash. 1979. *Violence Against Wives: A Case Against Patriarchy*. New York: Free Press.

———. 1992. *Women, Violence, and Social Change*. New York: Routledge

Dobash, Russell P., Russell Emerson Dobash, Margo Wilson, and Martin Daly. 1992. "The Myth of Sexual Symmetry in Marital Violence." *Social Problems* 39(1): 71–91.

Dutton, Mary Ann. 1992. *Empowering and Healing the Battered Woman: A Model for Assessment and Intervention*. New York: Springer Publishing Company.

———. 1996. "Battered Women's Strategic Response to Violence: The Role of Context," in *Future Interventions with Battered Women and Their Families*, Jeffrey L. Edleson and Zvi C. Eisikovits (eds.), 105–24. Newbury Park, CA: Sage Publications.

Dutton, Mary Ann, and Lisa A. Goodman. 2005. "Coercion in Intimate Partner Violence: Toward a New Conceptualization." *Sex Roles* 52(11/12): 743–57.

Edleson, Jeffrey L., and Zvi C. Eisikovits (eds.). 1996. *Future Interventions with Battered Women and Their Families*. Thousand Oaks, CA: Sage.

Feldman, Clyde M., and Carl A. Ridley. 2000. "The Role of Conflict-Based Communication Responses and Outcomes in Male Domestic Violence toward Female Partners." *Journal of Social and Personal Relationships* 17(4–5): 552–73.

Fernandez, Marilyn, Kichiro Iwamoto, and Bernadette Muscat. 1997. "Dependency and Severity of Abuse: Impact on Women's Persistence in Utilizing the Court System as Protection Against Domestic Violence." *Women and Criminal Justice* 9(1): 39–63.

Ferraro, Kathleen J. 1993. "Cops, Courts, and Woman Battering," in *Violence Against Women*, P. B. Bart and E.G. Moran (eds.), 165–76. Newbury Park, CA: Sage.

———. 1997. "Battered Women: Strategies for Survival," in *Violence between Intimate Partners: Patterns, Causes, and Effects*, Albert P. Carderelli (ed.), 124–40. New York: Allyn and Bacon.

Fine, Michelle. 1989. "The Politics of Research and Activism: Violence Against Women." *Gender & Society* 3(4): 549–58.

Finkelhor, David. 1983. "Common Features of Family Abuse," in *The Dark Side of Families: Current Family Violence Research*, D. Finkelhor, R. Gelles, G. Hotaling, and M. Straus (eds.), 17–28. Beverly Hills, CA: Sage.

Fleury, Ruth E., Cris M. Sullivan, and Deborah I. Bybee. 2000. "When Ending the Relationship Does Not End the Violence: Women's Experiences of Violence by Former Partners." *Violence Against Women* 6(12): 1363–83.

Fox, Greer Litton, and Michael L. Benson (eds.). 2000. *Families, Crime, and Criminal Justice*. New York: Elsevier Science, Inc.

Gelles, Richard J. 1974. *The Violent Home: A Study of Physical Aggression Between Husbands and Wives*. Beverly Hills, CA: Sage.

———. 1976. "Abused Wives: Why Do They Stay?" *Journal of Marriage and the Family* 38: 659–68.

———. 1980. "Violence in the Family: A Review of Research in the Seventies." *Journal of Marriage and the Family* 42(4): 873–85.

———. 1989. *Intimate Violence: The Causes and Consequences of Abuse in the American Family*. New York: Simon and Schuster.

Gondolf, Edward W., and Ellen R. Fisher. 1988. *Battered Women As Survivors: An Alternative to Treating Learned Helplessness*. Lexington, MA: Lexington Books.

Grau, Janice, Jeffrey Fagan, and Sandra Wexler. 1983. "Restraining Orders for Battered Women: Issues of Access and Efficacy," in *Criminal Justice Politics and Women: The Aftermath of Legally Mandated Change*, Claudine SchWeber and Clarice Feinman (eds.), 13–28. New York: The Haworth Press.

Hart, Barbara J. 1993. "Battered Women and the Criminal Justice System." *American Behavioral Scientist* 36(5): 624–38.

Herbert, Tracy B., Roxane C. Silver, and John H. Ellard. 1991. "Coping with an Abusive Relationship: How and Why Do Women Stay?" *Journal of Marriage and the Family* 53: 311–25.

Holtz, Howard, and Kathleen Furniss. 1993. "The Health Care Provider's Role in Domestic Violence." *Trends in Health Care and the Law* 8: 43–49.

Holtzworth-Munroe, Amy, and Gregory L. Stuart. 1994. "Typologies of Male Batterers: Three Subtypes and the Differences among Them." *Psychological Bulletin* 116(3): 476–97.

Holtzworth-Munroe, Amy, Jeffrey C. Meehan, Katherine Herron, Uzma Rehman, and Gregory L. Stuart. 2003. "Do Subtypes of Maritally Violent Men Continue to Differ over Time?" *Journal of Consulting and Clinical Psychology* 71(4): 728–40.

Hotaling, Gerald T., and David B. Sugarman. 1986. "An Analysis of Risk Markers in Husband to Wife Violence: The Current State of Knowledge." *Violence and Victims* 1: 101–24.

Johnson, Michael P. 2006. "Conflict and Control: Symmetry and Asymmetry in Domestic Violence." *Violence against Women* 12(11): 1003–18.

———. 2008. *A Typology of Domestic Violence: Intimate Terrorism, Violent Resistance, and Situational Couple Violence.* Boston: Northeastern University Press.

Johnson, Michael P., and Kathleen Ferraro. 2000. "Research on Domestic Violence in the 1990s: Making Distinctions." *Journal of Marriage and Family* 62(4): 948–63.

Johnson, Michael P., and Janet M. Leone. 2005. "The Differential Effects of Intimate Terrorism and Situational Couple Violence: Findings from the National Violence against Women Survey." *Journal of Family Issues* 26(3): 322–49.

Kantor, Glenda Kaufman, and Jana L. Jasinski. 1998. "Dynamics and Risk Factors in Partner Violence," in *Partner Violence: A Comprehensive Review of 20 Years of Research*, Jana L. Jasinski and Linda M. Williams (eds.), 1–43. Thousand Oaks, CA: Sage.

Kantor, Glenda, and Murray A. Straus. 1989. "The 'Drunken Bum' Theory of Wife Beating," in *Physical Violence in American Families: Risk Factors and Adaptation to Violence in 8,145 Families*, Murray A. Straus and Richard J. Gelles (eds.), 203–24. New Brunswick, NJ: Transaction Press.

Kirkwood, Catherine. 1993. *Leaving Abusive Partners: From the Scars of Survival to the Wisdom for Change.* Newbury Park, CA: Sage.

Leone, Janet M., Michael P. Johnson, and Catherine M. Cohan. 2007. "Victim Help-Seeking: Differences between Intimate Terrorism and Situation Couple Violence." *Family Relations* 56(5): 427–39.

Leone, Janet M., Michael P. Johnson, Catherine M. Cohan, and Susan Lloyd. 2004. "Consequences of Male Partner Violence for Low-income, Ethnic Women." *Journal of Marriage and Family* 66(2): 471–89.

Lloyd, Susan, and Nina Taluc. 1999. "The Effects of Male Violence on Female Employment." *Violence Against Women* 5(4): 370–92.

McCloskey, Deirdre. 1998. *The Rhetoric of Economics* (second edition). Madison: University of Wisconsin Press.

McCloskey, Donald. 1985. "The Loss Function Has Been Mislaid: The Rhetoric of Significance Tests." *American Economic Review* 75(2): 201–5.

Macmillan, Ross, and Rosemary Gartner. 1999. "When She Brings Home the Bacon: Labor-Force Participation and the Risk of Spousal Violence against Women." *Journal of Marriage and the Family* 61(4): 947–58.

McNeely, R. L., and Coramae R. Mann. 1990. "Domestic Violence Is a Human Issue." *Journal of Interpersonal Violence* 5: 129–32.

Miller, Susan L. 2005. *Victims as Offenders: The Paradox of Women's Violence in Relationships*. New Brunswick, NJ: Rutgers.

Mills, Linda G. 2008. *Violent Partners: A Breakthrough Plan for Ending the Cycle of Abuse*. New York: Basic Books.

Mirchandani, Rekha. 2006. "'Hitting Is Not Manly': Domestic Violence Court and the Re-Imagination of the Patriarchal State." *Gender & Society* 20(6): 781–804.

Murphy, Susan. 1992. "Assisting the Jury in Understanding Victimization: Expert Psychological Testimony on Battered Woman Syndrome and Rape Trauma Syndrome." *Columbia Journal of Law and Social Problems* 25: 277–312.

New York Victims Service Agency. 1987. "Report on the Costs of Domestic Violence." New York: Victims Service Agency.

Nichols, Laura. 2002. "Participatory Program Planning: Including Program Participants and Evaluators." *Journal of Evaluation and Program Planning* 25(1): 1–14.

Pagelow, Mildred Daley. 1981. *Woman-Battering: Victims and Their Experiences*. Newbury Park, CA: Sage.

———. 1992. "Adult Victims of Domestic Violence: Battered Women." *Journal of Interpersonal Violence* 7: 87–120.

Pence, Ellen, and Michael Paymar. 1993. *Education Groups for Men Who Batter: The Duluth Model*. New York: Springer.

Pennell, Joan, and Gale Burford. 2002. "Feminist Praxis: Making Family Group Conferencing Work," in *Restorative Justice and Family Violence*, Heather Strang and John Braithwaite (eds.), 108–27. New York: Cambridge University Press.

Pranis, Kay, Barry Stuart, and Mark Wedge. 2003. *Peacemaking Circles: From Crime to Community*. St. Paul, MN: Living Justice.

Presser, Lois, and Patricia Van Voorhis. 2002. "Values and Evaluation: Assessing Processes and Outcomes of Restorative Justice Programs." *Crime and Delinquency* 48(1): 162–88.

Ptacek, James. 1999. *Battered Women in the Courtroom: The Power of Judicial Responses*. Boston: Northeastern University Press.

——— (ed.). 2010. *Restorative Justice and Violence Against Women*. New York: Oxford University Press.

Riger, Stephanie, Courtney Ahrens, and Amy Blinkenstaff. 2001. "Measuring Interference with Employment and Education Reported by Women with Abusive Partners: Preliminary Data," in *Psychological Abuse in Violent Domestic Relations*, Daniel K. O'Leary and Roland D. Maiuro (eds.), 119–33. New York: Spring Pub. Co.

Roberts, Albert R. (ed.). 1996. *Helping Battered Women: New Perspectives and Remedies*. New York: Oxford University Press.

——— (ed.). 2002. *Handbook of Domestic Violence Intervention Strategies: Policies, Programs, and Legal Remedies*. New York: Oxford University Press.

Rosenbaum, Alan, and K. Daniel O'Leary. 1981. "Children: The Unintended Victims of Marital Violence." *American Journal of Orthopsychiatry* 5: 689–99.

Santa Clara County Probation Department. n.d. *From This Day Forward: Domestic Violence Information and Referral Handbook*. San Jose, CA.

Schechter, Susan. 1982. *Women and Male Violence: The Visions and Struggles of the Battered Women's Movement*. Boston: South End Press.

Shepard, Melanie F., and Ellen Pence (eds.). 1999. *Coordinating Community Responses to Domestic Violence: Lessons from Duluth and Beyond.* Thousand Oaks, CA: Sage.

Shupe, Anson, William A. Stacey, and Lonnie R. Hazelwood. 1987. *Violent Men, Violent Couples: The Dynamics of Domestic Violence.* Lexington, MA: Lexington Books.

Stark, Evan. 2007. *Coercive Control: The Entrapment of Women in Personal Life.* New York: Oxford University Press.

Steinmetz, Suzanne K. 1977/1978. "The Battered Husband Syndrome." *Victimology* 2: 499–509.

Stets, Jan E., and Murray A. Straus. 1989. "The Marriage License as a Hitting License: A Comparison of Assaults in Dating, Cohabiting, and Married Couples." *Journal of Family Violence* 4(2): 161–80.

Stith, Sandra M., Karen H. Hosen, Kimberly A. Middleton, Amy L. Busch, Krsten Lundeberg, and Russell P. Carlton. 2000. "The Intergenerational Transmission of Spouse Abuse: A Meta-Analysis." *Journal of Marriage and the Family* 62(3): 640–54.

Strang, Heather, and John Braithwaite (eds.). 2002. *Restorative Justice and Family Violence.* New York: Cambridge University Press.

Straus, Murray A. 1973. "A General Systems Theory Approach to a Theory of Violence between Family Members." *Social Science Information* 12(3): 105–25.

———. 1980. "A Sociological Perspective on the Causes of Family Violence." In *Violence and the Family*, M. R. Green (ed.), 7–31. Boulder, CO: Westview Press.

Straus, Murray A., Richard J. Gelles, and Suzanne K. Steinmetz. 1980. *Behind Closed Doors: Violence in the American Family.* New York: Doubleday/Anchor.

Stubbs, Julie. 1995. "Communitarian Conferencing and Violence Against Women: A Cautionary Note," in *Wife Assault and the Canadian Criminal Justice System*, Mariana Valverde, Linda MacLeod, and Kirsten Johnson (eds.). Toronto: Centre of Criminology, University of Toronto.

———. 2002. "Domestic Violence and Women's Safety: Feminist Challenges to Restorative Justice," in *Restorative Justice and Family Violence*, Heather Strang and John Braithwaite (eds.), 42–61. New York: Cambridge University Press.

Sullivan, Cris M., and Deborah I. Bybee. 1999. "Reducing Violence Using Community-Based Advocacy for Women with Abusive Partners." *Journal of Consulting & Clinical Psychology* 67(1): 43–53.

Sutherland, Cheryl A., Deborah I. Bybee, and Cris M. Sullivan. 2002. "Beyond Bruises and Broken Bones: The Joint Effects of Stress and Injuries on Battered Women's Health." *American Journal of Community Psychology* 30(5): 609–36.

Tjaden, Patricia, and Nancy Thoennes. 2000. U.S. Dep't of Justice, NCJ 183781, *Full Report of the Prevalence, Incidence, and Consequences of Intimate Partner Violence Against Women: Findings from the National Violence Against Women Survey* (2000). Retrieved on September 5, 2008. www.ojp.usdoj.gov/nij/pubs-sum/183781.htm.

Umbreit, Mark S., and Robert B. Coates. 2000. "Multicultural Implications of Restorative Justice: Potential Pitfalls and Dangers." Center for Restorative Justice and Peacemaking. Retrieved June 29, 2005. www.ojp.gov/ovc/publications/infores/restorative_justice/restorative_justice-ascii_pdf/ncj176348.pdf.

Umbreit, Mark, S., Betty Vos, Robert B. Coates, and Katherine A. Brown. 2003. *Facing Violence: The Path of Restorative Justice and Dialogue*. Monsey, NY: Criminal Justice Press.

U.S. Census Bureau. 2000. American FactFinder. factfinder.census.gov/home/saff/main.html?_lang=en.

U.S. Department of Justice, Bureau of Justice Statistics. 2005. "Family Violence Statistics," June 2005.

U.S. Senate Judiciary Committee. 1992. *Violence Against Women*. Washington, D.C.: Government Printing Office.

Van Ness, Daniel W., and Karen Heetderks Strong. 2006. *Restoring Justice: An Introduction to Restorative Justice* (third edition). www.lexisnexis.com/anderson/criminaljustice.

Walker, Leonore. 1979. *The Battered Woman*. New York: Harper and Row.

———. 1984. *The Battered Woman Syndrome*. New York: Springer Publishing Co.

Warshaw, Carole. 1989. "Limitations of the Medical Model in the Care of Battered Women." *Gender & Society* 3(4): 506–17.

Wodarski, John S. 1987. "An Examination of Spouse Abuse: Practice Issues for the Professions." *Clinical Social Work Journal* 15: 172–87.

Yllo, Kersti, and Michele Bograd (eds.). 1988. *Feminist Perspectives on Wife Abuse*. Newbury Park, CA: Sage.

Zehr, Howard. 2001. *Transcending: Reflections of Crime Victims: Portraits and Interviews*. Intercourse, PA: Good Books.

———. 2002. *The Little Book of Restorative Justice*. Intercourse, PA: Good Books.

———. 2005. *Changing Lenses: A New Focus for Crime and Justice* (third edition). Scottsdale, PA: Herald Press.

Index